This book is a critical and historical study of the theory of criminal law which examines, in particular, the relationship between legal tradition and national identity, while developing a radically new approach to questions of responsibility and subjectivity. Previous studies have focused either on the philosophical bases of the criminal law or on the sociology and social history of crime, but there has been little exchange between the two. Lindsay Farmer's is one of the first extended attempts to draw on both fields in order to analyse the body of theorising about the criminal law as a whole. It displays a rare knowledge of the legal, institutional and historical contexts in which criminal law is practised, in combination with an informed understanding of the law itself. Dr Farmer uses contemporary social theory to develop an account of the relationship between legal practice and national culture in Scotland, analysing the belief in the distinctive spirit or 'genius' of Scots law. An exploration of the boundary between national limits and the universal aspirations of criminal law theory reveals the specifically modern characteristics of the criminal law and exposes how contemporary criminal law theory fundamentally misrepresents the character of modern criminal justice.

Criminal law, tradition and legal order

Criminal law, tradition and legal order

Crime and the genius of Scots law,
1747 to the present

Lindsay Farmer

Birkbeck College, University of London

CAMBRIDGE
UNIVERSITY PRESS

Published by the Press Syndicate of the University of Cambridge
The Pitt Building, Trumpington Street, Cambridge CB2 1RP
40 West 20th Street, New York, NY 10011-4211, USA
10 Stamford Road, Oakleigh, Melbourne 3166, Australia

First published 1997

Printed in Great Britain at the University Press, Cambridge

A catalogue record for this book is available from the British Library

Library of Congress cataloguing in publication data

Farmer, Lindsay, 1963–
Criminal law, tradition and legal order: crime and the genius of
Scots law, 1747 to the present / Lindsay Farmer.
    p.   cm.
Includes bibliographical references.
ISBN 0 521 55320 2 (hb)
1. Criminal law – Scotland – History.   2. Criminal justice,
Administration of – Scotland – History.   3. Crime – Scotland – History.
I. Title.
KDC910.F37   1997   345.411 – dc20   [344.1105]   96-15170   CIP

ISBN 0 521 55320 2 hardback

To my family

'The genius of our law rests on a principle diametrically opposite to that of England; the Courts of criminal jurisdiction being authorised to punish crimes without any positive enactment'.

Lord Justice-Clerk Hope in *Rachel Wright* (1809) in Burnett 1811, app. VII, p. xxix.

'And having only designed to establish solidly the Principles of the Criminal Law, I wanted room for treating learnedly each particular case, or even for hinting at all such cases as may be necessary; And without wearying my Readers with Citations, (which was very easie) I have furnished the Book with as much reason as is ordinarily to be found in legal treatises'.   Mackenzie 1678 (The Design).

Contents

Acknowledgements

In the all too lengthy process of writing and re-writing I have incurred an enormous number of debts, intellectual, emotional and (more often than I would have wished) financial. I cannot easily repay these, but by their acknowledgement I can formally record my gratitude to some of the people who have responded to my many requests for assistance.

The book is based on work done in three institutions, and owes much to the enduring influence of a fourth. It has its specific origins in my initial attempts at teaching criminal law at Strathclyde University. Knowing very little indeed about the criminal law, I none the less took great liberties in the teaching of it. That anything survived from this at all is due to the forbearance of both students and colleagues. While it is difficult to single out particular people, Joe Thomson and Kenny Miller are owed special thanks for their confidence in me and their encouragement, and both contributed substantially to my enjoyment of my time at Strathclyde. I was then extremely fortunate to be given the opportunity to work on the Scottish criminal law in the unlikely setting of the European University Institute in Florence. My supervisor there, Gunther Teubner, must frequently have wondered what he had let himself in for as I presented him with another chapter on the arcaneries of nineteenth-century Scottish criminal procedure! I owe much to him for allowing me to define the project in my own way while also contributing through pushing me to tackle unfamiliar ideas. Catherine Barnard, John Donaldson, Klaus Eder, Paul McAleavey, Sally Sheldon, Steven Simblett and Arpad Szakolczai, amongst others, contributed in different ways at various times.

The last stages of research and rewriting have been carried out at Birkbeck College. Peter Goodrich has been an excellent Head of Department, as well as being extraordinarily generous in reading and commenting on different versions of the manuscript. Matthew Weait has been a good colleague and friend throughout a difficult period, to say nothing of his invaluable knowledge of the criminal law. It also gives me great pleasure to thank Nicola Lacey, now a colleague, whose assistance has gone well beyond the elucidation and defence of the different types of reductivism. Valerie Hoare, Anton Schütz and Costas Douzinas have all helped in different ways.

Finally, I would like to record a long-standing debt to the Centre for Criminology and the Philosophical and Sociological Study of Law at the University of Edinburgh. My interest in research was first stimulated while an undergraduate there, and members of the Centre and the Law Faculty encouraged me to continue to study and eventually to undertake this research. Their willingness to read and comment on pieces of work, often at very short notice, and more generally to discuss historical and theoretical ideas has continually exceeded what I would have been entitled to expect. I would particularly like to thank John Cairns for sharing his unparalleled knowledge of early Scots law. To mention Beverley Brown's contribution in reading and commenting on the manuscript in various forms alone would not begin to do justice to the generosity and encouragement she has shown towards me for many years. Peter Young has been encouraging and generous over a long period of time. His advice on research and writing greatly simplified the process. He was co-supervisor of the original thesis and helped enormously in the project at all stages from the original proposal through to the final versions of the manuscript. He was trusting in allowing me to define the project in my own way, and encouraging at the times when I was stuck. More recently he has helped with invaluable advice on publication. I would never have reached this point without him.

There are two other people who deserve special mention. Sean Smith has been a good friend for a number of years, and many of the ideas in the book have their origins in conversations with him. I would thank him for his interest and his friendship. Paula Cardoso made the book in many other ways. She suffered with me, and because of me, throughout the process of writing. She taught me the meaning of *saudades*. I thank her now for everything that she gave.

I would like to record my gratitude to the Trustees of the National Library of Scotland for their permission to use the print of James McKean at the Bar on the cover of the book.

1 The boundaries of the criminal law: criminal law, legal theory and history

> You will permit me however very briefly to describe, rather what I conceive an academical expounder of the laws should do, than what I have ever known to be done . . . He should consider his course as a general map of the law, marking out the shape of the country, its connexions and boundaries, it's greater divisions and principal cities: it is not his business to describe minutely the subordinate limits, or to fix the longitude and latitude of every inconsiderable hamlet. His attention should be engaged . . . 'in tracing out the originals and as it were the elements of the law'.[1]

The need to talk about and establish boundaries is perhaps stronger in relation to the criminal law than any other area of law. The field of criminal law marks itself out by its history of preoccupation with limits – of the law, of the sanction, of criminalisation. These images of space and landscape continue with descriptions of the contours of liability, the field of punishment, the frontiers of criminality, or the territory of the law. It is thus appropriate that we should begin with a passage from Blackstone's *Commentaries* that recognises, in a particularly elegant manner, the significance of boundaries and divisions. It is rarely referred to now, but Blackstone's exposition of the common law of crime has been of enduring importance to modern ideas about the law.[2] Equally, it is far from inappropriate that a study which takes the Scottish criminal law – law from over the border – as its subject should begin with the writings of a man conventionally regarded as a founder of the English common law and perhaps its greatest 'academical expounder'. Scots lawyers have consistently underestimated the influence of English law in this area, in

---

[1] Blackstone 1765 I, p. 35; cf. Kames 1792: 'Law, like geography, is taught as if it were a collection of facts merely: the memory is employed to the full rarely the judgement'. Cf. also Austin 1885, p. 1082.

[2] 'Since the publication of Blackstone's *Commentaries* hardly any work has been published in England upon the Criminal Law which aims at being more than a book of practice . . . simply compilations of extracts from text-writers, and reports arranged with greater or less skill – usually with almost none – but representing the aggregate result of a great deal of laborious drudgery' Stephen 1883 II, pp. 218–19.

preference for the more reassuring belief that Scots criminal law is a purely native product. There will be much to say about this in due course, but the immediate interest lies in the suggestive use of the metaphor of the map, rather than in questions of the origins of substantive law, for it points to two issues which lie at the heart of the argument of this book.

The first of these is the connection that is drawn between the law and physical space. The power of law is a territorial question. This is an obvious point but its significance should not be underestimated. Geographical boundaries are never only natural; they are the point at which nations, and national legal competences, begin and end.[3] The law draws physical boundaries in geographical space, shaping and giving identity to that space. It is thus that the territory of the law is formed: its jurisdiction. It is co-extensive with that geographical space, while sharing none of its physical features. Jurisdiction is divided into political and administrative units, drawing further boundaries between the competences of different regions and areas of law. Although recent writings have tended to treat these as subordinate questions, legal sovereignty means nothing without these physical aspects of space and organisation.[4] The study of the law, then, is not something that can be abstracted from the history of the drawing of these boundaries, or indeed the law's connection with a particular physical space. To study the law is to raise continually the question of how legal structures are built, how lines of communication are drawn, how powers and competences are spatially distributed. In short, it is to ask how the force of the law is maintained. And the answers to these questions are connected to, and reveal, the changing contours of authority and shifting landscapes of power. The law, it must be remembered, is always also the law of the land.

It follows from this, as Blackstone points out, that the process of expounding the law is a process of mapping.[5] This is to acknowledge, as he was clearly aware, that the law is always also a process of representation – it can never lose its metaphorical character. Just as maps recreate space by the use of imaginary or scientific devices, the law, in the form of doctrine or academic treatises, must be capable of representing itself. Legal doctrine is a guide, not to the geographical territory, but to the territory of the law, to the imaginary space that the law occupies. From their earliest

[3] This, of course, is to recall Pascal 'A funny justice that ends at a river! Truth on this side of the Pyrenees, error on that', quoted in Teubner 1989a, p. 414 where this is discussed as a problem of 'interlegality'.
[4] On the absence of the element of 'territoriality' from legal and political theory, see Baldwin 1992 at pp. 207–14.
[5] For a more detailed exploration of cartography and mapping in relation to the law, see Goodrich 1990 passim; Sousa Santos 1987. Generally on the relationship between law and geography, see Blomley 1994.

days law students are taught that to venture into this territory without a map is foolhardy. It is vast and ancient, full of unseen dangers. It is possessed of a strange and wonderful beauty that cannot be perceived by the untrained eye. The law as it is taught and written is always an attempt to impose an order on this unruly country by marking out the 'greater divisions and principal cities'. It is always the result of a process of selection, and the symbolic order that is constructed mirrors, or more precisely refracts, the legal ordering of space. These guides show us cities of elegant buildings neatly dissected by wide avenues. Or perhaps, in the case of the common law, the sleepy quarters of faded towns where rambling old buildings, rebuilt and extended time after time, reveal worn charms.[6] But what lies in the shaded areas of the map, in the slums and rookeries? What network of pipes and passages lies under our feet? Which spaces are enclosed and which set free? The map requires us to ask the question of what is being represented and why. Further, it demands that we question the measures and divisions that are used, the terms of the legal order that is being imposed. We can never be sure that we are being shown the most important features of the legal landscape, for a map is really only an accurate guide to itself. Understood in this sense, we can see that the law is always a distortion – although this is not to imply that it is necessarily inaccurate or untruthful.[7] As with all maps, choices of scale and projection affect our perception. Certain features are placed at the centre of the map or given greater prominence in relation to others. The mechanisms of distortion are not chaotic but determinate, they have developed over time in response to changes in that landscape itself, and the symbols by which the law is represented carry their own history and significance. So, in order to understand the law, it is necessary to have some understanding of how the map is made. As the process of representation, or the imagination of the law, becomes our object of study we are once again brought up against the boundaries and divisions of the law.

Crime and the criminal law exercise a boundless fascination for contemporary society – a fascination which has itself been boundlessly documented. There have been many explanations offered for this, certain of which stand out to the lawyer or sociologist, for whom the study of crime and the criminal law is understood to offer a passage to the core values and preoccupations of any society. The crime rate has for a long

---

[6] See e.g. Blackstone 1765 III, ch. 17; cf. Walter Scott on Baron Hume quoted in Stein 1988, p. 379, 'the fabric of the law . . . resembles some ancient castle, partly entire, partly ruinous, partly dilapidated, patched and altered during the succession of ages by a thousand additions and combinations' and so on.   [7] Sousa Santos 1987, p. 282.

time been taken to be not only a matter of considerable political and social concern, but also a barometer of the health or pathology of a particular society. The way that a particular society punishes wrongdoers is regarded as indicating its level of civilisation. Restitutive is compared favourably with repressive punishment. The increase in humanity in the trial and punishment of crime has been almost everywhere treated as a mark of social progress. It is notable that this understanding has been underpinned by a fundamental and, until recently, unbreakable link between the criminal law and modernity. The modern criminal law has been associated with the founding of the modern nation state and the emergence from the period of absolutism and arbitrariness. It is one of the most potent symbols of the move towards humanitarianism and rationalism in government, and its failures are correspondingly hard felt. The measurement and control of crime by means of the criminal law were linked with the emergence of social statistics and the discipline of sociology. The crime rate was taken, along with indicators of suicide and mortality, to be an index of social solidarity, and the criminal law became an instrument in the fight against crime.

However, even as these two modes of thought have dominated thinking about crime and the law in the modern period, there have been challenges to the beliefs that linked modernity with the measured humanity of the law or that saw the control of crime as a sign of progress. Governments have shown an increased willingness to accept a high crime rate as an inevitable and irremediable fact of social life, and there has been a turn towards harsher punishments which are not justified in terms of whether or not they are effective or deter crime, but in terms of an increased punitiveness for its own sake. The fascination with crime remains undiminished, but it is increasingly regarded as the symbol of failure, loss of control and the malaise of government. It is against this background – the loss of faith in the ability of the law to solve the problem of crime – that this book is written. It examines critically the nature of the relationship between the criminal law and modernity by means of a historical reconstruction of the origins of some of the fundamental concepts and institutions of the modern law. It does not join the chorus of advocates of a return to the so-called philosophical or conceptual basics of the law. Rather it pursues the more radical argument that, through their attachment to those supposed basics, criminal lawyers have systematically misunderstood and misrepresented the nature of the modern law, and that this misunderstanding is an important and unacknowledged feature of the crisis of ideas currently afflicting criminal justice. It is thus an attempt to loosen the conceptual straitjacket that has bound the law, developing a critical account of the emergence of the modern criminal law in order to restore a means of analysing the criminal law as a historical practice.

There has been remarkable revival of interest in theories of the criminal law and punishment in recent years. There is an ever-growing body of work that has sought to broaden the narrow technical concerns of criminal lawyers, and that also reflects the sense that all is not well in criminal justice. The starting point for most of these texts, whether conventional or critical, is that there is special relationship, or 'natural affinity' between criminal law and moral philosophy. Thus, Fletcher's analysis of the criminal law begins in the following way:

> Criminal law is a species of moral and political philosophy. Its central question is justifying the use of the state's coercive power against free and autonomous persons. The link with moral philosophy derives from one answer to the problem of justifying the use of state power. If the rationale or limiting condition of criminal punishment is personal desert, then legal theory invariably interweaves with philosophical claims about wrongdoing, culpability, justifying circumstances and excuses.[8]

First, the limits of state power must be specified, according to the standard of the autonomy of the individual; then the criminal law, using the same standard, can attempt to specify the exact conditions under which individuals may be held responsible by the law for their actions. It has followed from this that the sphere of the responsibility of the criminal law is reasonably well defined. It is to be regarded as a relatively neutral, conceptual exercise that must define in turn the grounds of individual liability, the actions that are prescribed by law and the socially important values (such as bodily autonomy and property) that must be protected by the law.

This same relationship – viewed in a rather different light – has been accepted as fundamental even in the avowedly critical analyses of Norrie.[9] The claim that criminal law is a species of moral philosophy is accepted at face value in order that the law can be depicted as formal and abstract. From this point of view the 'juridical form' (the free and autonomous individual) is seen as the product in the legal system of specific economic and social conditions. The critique is then driven by an examination of the contradictions in the economic base of society. The juridical form can be criticised from a sociological point of view for being reductive of the complex social conditions and pressures that in fact determine human actions. The significant point is that in both cases it is taken for granted that moral philosophy and criminal law are different levels of the same discourse. The law is thus regarded as no more and no less than the elaboration of the fundamental philosophical or normative concepts which are the terms in which the relationship between state and the free

---

[8] Fletcher 1978, p. xix. See Nelken 1987a, p. 142 for the natural affinity.
[9] Norrie 1991, ch. 1; 1993 chs. 1 and 2. For an extended criticism of this position, see Farmer 1995.

individual is to be worked out. It is assumed that the route to a better
theoretical understanding of the criminal law follows from the clarification, or critique, of those same concepts. But is this necessarily the case?
Why should we begin with this conceptual structure? The problem with
taking this as a starting point is simply that it is too narrow, leaving too
many questions unasked. There may be an affinity, but surely understanding of the criminal justice system would be improved by also asking
why this should be the case. Where does this affinity come from?

It is clear that it is not 'natural'. The relationship between liberal moral
and political philosophy and the criminal law would seem to be a product
of the struggle against absolutism in the eighteenth century. Repressive
and violent laws and institutions were attacked by reform-minded
philosophers and lawyers. In Europe this led to the drawing up of the great
penal codes of the Enlightenment according to new measures of restraint,
certainty and humanity in punishment.[10] Legal limits were imposed on
the exercise of power in the same period as the boundaries of the modern
nation state were drawn, establishing a range of both internal and external
constraints on sovereignty. The demand that the criminal law respect the
principle of legality, that the criminal process be subjected to rules and
constraints, and that punishment be administered only in measured and
determinate amounts, set the terms of the compact that was established
between the criminal law and modernity.[11] This very history, if we accept
it, suggests that this is far from being a 'necessary' relationship – only that
it has been perceived as fundamental to a certain characterisation of the
modern state. Even if we go so far as to accept that the relationship is
desirable, this tells us nothing about how the practices of criminal law are
related to philosophising about state power and punishment. Indeed,
much of the available evidence suggests that they have little to do with
each other. Philosophers have pointed out that the doctrine of the criminal
law frequently fails to meet the criteria of philosophical adequacy,[12] and
theoretically minded criminal lawyers complain that judges and other
criminal justice professionals show little enthusiasm for conceptual
clarification or philosophical rigour.[13] And if we look to the sociological
literature, we find many studies which demonstrate that the 'justice' in the

[10] See von Bar 1916, chs. 9–15.
[11] See Foucault 1977, pp. 74–5. Foucault's work dramatises the dubious connection
between modern systems of punishment and civilisation. We should note that, in the same
period, 'moral' behaviour came to be conceived of as the following of rules rather than the
pursuit of the good. This suggests another basis for the natural affinity. See Macintyre
1985, pp. 118–9.   [12] Duff 1987.
[13] Willock 1981 points out that Scottish judges have failed to respond to Sheriff G. H.
Gordon's conceptually sophisticated account of the Scottish criminal law (1967 and
1978). Lacey 1985 argues that the judicial reception in England of elaborate conceptual
analyses of the law suggests that academic lawyers overestimate its importance.

criminal justice system is a product of bureaucratic pressures rather than normative or philosophical ideals.[14] Obviously, this must lead to a questioning of the relevance of academic debate over the philosophical foundations of the criminal law.[15] In spite of the continuing conflict between judges and academics over, say, the subjective or objective character of *mens rea* or the permanently unresolved state of the debate on the punishability of impossible attempts, there remains a limited sense in which the criminal justice system continues to work rather effectively – at least if the sheer number of people that are prosecuted each year is taken as a measure. Criminal law theory is caught in a position where it neither reflects the state of criminal justice nor is able to engage with the contemporary sense of crisis. To be sure, moral philosophy may be important to the law as it is currently conceived, but it may not represent the only, or even the best, route to an understanding of that law.

This suggests that there are serious limitations inherent in a study that takes the criminal law conceived of as a philosophical system as the central object of study. However, even as these arguments undermine an understanding of the criminal law as a form of moral philosophy, they reveal how the territory of the law, and the types of questions that fall to be addressed by criminal law theory, has already been marked out in a way that establishes moral philosophy as the only legitimate mode of analysis. Important boundaries are established from the outset between theory and practice and between criminal law and criminal justice. Barriers have been erected to prevent other types of philosophical or theoretical understanding being brought to bear on the criminal law. Most contemporary writing on the issue of crime and the criminal law respects these boundaries, drawn by criminal lawyers, that establish the autonomy of the law.[16] Yet this autonomy is difficult to sustain. In the modern nation state the criminal law is expected to be both an instrument of modern government and a barrier between state and citizen. The theoretical understanding of criminal lawyers is only achieved by the blurring of the distinction between these two functions or, more commonly, by ignoring the distinction altogether.

For example, where the connection between the incidence of crime and particular instances of criminal policy is addressed, the criminal law is regarded both instrumentally, as the means by which policy can be implemented and, more neutrally, as something that escapes reduction to

[14] There are numerous studies in this area. See, for example, Carlen 1976; McBarnet 1981; McConville *et al.* 1991. Much of this literature is reviewed in Nelken 1987a.
[15] Or at least there is a problem with the particularly impoverished notion of philosophy that is adopted, where analytical clarity often seems to be confused with philosophical analysis. For an example of this, see Shute *et al.* 1993.
[16] This has been mapped out at some length in Nelken 1987a and b.

the simple terms of policy. In this way it manages to be both less and more than particular instances of its application, conceived of either as a conduit through which criminal policy must necessarily pass, or as part of a framework of normative rules. From neither perspective does it appear that the criminal law is regarded as part of the problem of crime. The limits of the law are only seen either in practices which can be regarded as marginal to or outside the law (such as the existence of discretion or social inequality) that are said to undermine it, or in the terms of the normative philosophical question which asks which types of action are harmful or blameworthy. This allows the law to be seen as an autonomous philo-sophical system rather than as something that has its origins in particular practices or policies or systems of enforcement. When policies fail they, and not the criminal law, are to blame. To the criminal lawyer, the question of enforcement is seen as something beyond the law, to be carried out by the agencies and institutions of criminal justice.[17] The law stands above and beyond the sphere of public debate and policy. This, moreover, reinforces the ambitions of criminal lawyers for whom the criminal law must be more than just an instrument or tool of government.

Paradoxically, when criminal lawyers acknowledge the importance of criminal justice this is in order to support the belief that the law is completely autonomous. The modern criminal law is presumed to pursue certain ends, whether these be deterrence, retribution or rehabilitation, or some combination of the three, no matter how incompatible they appear to be.[18] In these terms it would then appear that the important question that the law would have to answer would be that of whether or not it achieved these ends, or as it is more conventionally put, whether or not it worked. However, while it is normal for these ends to be recognised by criminal lawyers – in an acknowledgement of the social functions of the modern law – it is extremely difficult to trace their exact status in criminal law doctrine. There is a crucial slippage by which they disappear from the discussion. After an initial appearance they are not subsequently regarded as relevant to the question of guilt or responsibility, but only to sentencing or punishment – which are not conventionally treated as part of criminal law doctrine.[19] Difficulties or inconsistencies can be deferred to the sentencing stage in order to preserve the theoretical purity of the law, and the blame for the failures of criminal justice can be placed elsewhere. The impression is reinforced that these failures – in prosecution, in enforce-

[17] Where the question of enforcement arises at all, it is in terms of the enforcement of morality. For the classical expression of this, see Devlin 1965.

[18] See e.g. Smith and Hogan 1992, p. 3; Ashworth 1995, pp. 14–17 although he moves to an emphasis on the importance of the values that the law should enforce. On incompatibility, see White 1985, pp. 194–203.   [19] See esp. Norrie 1993, ch. 10.

ment, in the courts, in punishment – are a failure of institutions, policy, procedure.[20] Law becomes an issue in criminal justice only in relation to questions of procedural justice – the legality of police action, of detention, the admissibility of evidence. Amidst the wringing of hands and pointing of fingers, the criminal law is rarely, if ever, implicated. This is a remarkable state of affairs: the institutions that enforce the criminal law are guilty; criminal procedure has taken a wrong turning; sentencing policy requires reform and rehabilitation. But the criminal law, it would appear, has little or nothing to do with criminal justice.

It may, of course, be the case that the criminal law is perfectly conceived and ideally adapted to the social demands that are placed on it. This seems unlikely, however, and at the very least worthy of demonstration. In addition, as I suggested above, there are signs that criminal lawyers are themselves unhappy with this structure of institutional purposes and want the criminal law to be rather more, in order to preserve something of its perceived social significance. This extra factor has been sought either in the values that the criminal law is said to protect or reinforce, or in some socially significant practice, such as 'blaming', that is said to represent the core of the expressive function of the law.[21] However, there is little evidence of the consensus that must lie at the heart of what criminal lawyers say about values, or indeed of any agreement over the core values that the law is said to protect. It is rather as if thinking about the law is carried out within such extraordinarily narrow confines in order to protect the illusion of consensus. Equally, it is hard not to be sceptical about attempts to get back to basics in criminal law, for in the modern criminal law such expressive functions must always be performed by and through institutions. If we blind ourselves to the operation or practices of these institutions it is unlikely that anything of the experience or meaning of the modern criminal law will ever be captured. In view of this, it is even more strange that we should be bound by rigid theoretical distinctions between the different parts of the criminal justice system, so that the way in which justice is discussed in the texts of the criminal law is far removed from the day-to-day operation of the system.

This raises a number of important questions for the future of the criminal law, questions which criminal lawyers do not or will not face,

[20] Interestingly, this is no less true of historical work. A recent history, Wiener 1990, tells the story of the move from 'moralism' to 'causalism' in Victorian penal thought, and in particular the emergence of penal policy in the modern sense. Although it is argued that the penal law is transformed – through, for example, the creation of new categories of offenders and offences as the result of changes in criminal policy – the end result seems simply to be the tracing of the emergence of the category of policy as something separate from law. The question of transformation in the criminal law is left largely unexplored.

[21] On values, see the summary in Ashworth 1995, ch. 2; on the expressive function, see White 1985.

preferring to relegate them to the realms of policy or process, so better to preserve the theoretical purity of the law. Foremost amongst these is the question of why there is a split between the criminal law and policy, or between criminal law and criminal justice. This leads on to the question of how can we conceive of justice in the criminal law.

There have been attempts to bridge this gap, to make contextual or interdisciplinary studies of the criminal law. Indeed, it has been argued that the criminal law offers an unparalleled prospect to those interested in interdisciplinary study because of its unique combination of the technical, institutional arrangements, procedural and evidential rules, and normative theory.[22] But, if it is reasonably straightforward to point to the complexity and diversity of modern criminal justice systems, it has proved rather more difficult to produce a genuinely interdisciplinary theory of law that does justice to that complexity. It is clear that the promise of inter-disciplinary or contextual study remains unfulfilled. While reference to the need for interdisciplinary or contextual study has practically become a fetish – who today dares to deny the importance of 'context'? – the issue of each new text containing an expanding set of references to philosophical, criminological, psychological and historical works, is accompanied by a growing confusion about how it is all supposed to fit together. It is as if there is the hope that, by bringing along an ever greater part of the context, understanding must magically follow. The danger of according too great a status to context may simply be that of ending up with increasingly diffuse accounts of social control. As the context is brought in, the law is inexorably reduced to that context.[23] Yet this leaves us with something of a conundrum. Sociological approaches to the law in terms of a process of 'criminalisation' are said to miss something of the normative qualities of the law,[24] while those same normative qualities are understood not to be susceptible to study except in terms of precisely the moral philosophy that established them in the first place![25] The divide between criminal law and justice is reproduced at the level of theoretical understanding, as the studies of context reinforce the idea that there is a core understanding of law. Once again we find that boundaries have been drawn in advance by the philosophical conception of the criminal law.

[22] See generally Tur 1986, pp. 195–9.
[23] See Cohen 1989. Cf. the reductive approach of Lacey et al. 1990, pp. 7–12, where the multitude of practices of social control that are 'analogous' to the criminal law are listed.
[24] e.g. Lacey 1995 on the process of criminalisation. Why should the sociological category of criminalisation be accorded an a priori status? See also Farmer 1996, pp. 59–62.
[25] See also Nelken 1987a, pp. 140–3; 1987b, pp. 107–9. This reinforces an important point about the nature of context, for to study context is also implicitly to reinforce the idea that there is a core, that contextual study can be used to prop up the sense of the discipline. This idea of the core and the margin is something that also returns in relation to the core values that the law is said to protect.

Yet even in the face of these limitations it would surely be going too far to jettison the interest in theoretical or philosophical explanation entirely, treating it as so much ideological baggage. The criminal law may ultimately be a mode of social control, but a recognition of this does not free us from the obligation to examine the logic of the law. A study of the criminal law cannot begin by denying those specific features that mark out legal forms of regulation. If nothing else, the fact of the continuing strength of the belief in the philosophical foundations of the criminal law must draw our attention. Its distinctive relationship with the liberal principles of autonomy and responsibility must historically have played a part in the formation of a certain complex of relations between political, legal and penal institutions. But to state the problem in this way is already to diminish philosophy's claim to foundational status. It can no longer be assumed that philosophical concepts are straightforwardly reproduced in criminal law or that the relationship between moral philosophy and law is its defining characteristic. This points towards something else, namely the recognition that the criminal law is, above all, a practice that has its own history.

But what does it mean to argue that the criminal law has its own history? The most immediate consequence is that we must begin to look at the criminal law as a practice that is independent from the practice of philosophy. Rather than regarding law and philosophical reason as concepts that stand above criminal justice and outside history, we must look at legal practices and the types of rationality that develop in and through these practices. Reflections on the nature of law do not occur in a historical void, but are attempts to order and make sense of the changing forms of legal practice. They are the means by which a particular field of legal practices is organised. Thus the history that interests us is the history of changes in the ways of thinking about, or reflecting on the law. This points to the second consequence. This, to paraphrase Macintyre, is that the philosophy of the criminal law is always dependent on the history of the criminal law.[26] In the terms in which we have been discussing it, the problem for the philosophy of law is to explain the reasons for which, at a particular moment in time, legal practices come to be defined in a certain way.[27] A critical theory, a theory of 'critical positivism', must therefore begin from the analysis of this complex of practices, to look at how the

---

[26] Macintyre 1985, p. 268 'The philosophy of physical science is dependent on the history of physical science. But the case is no different with morality'. See also Ewald 1985, p. 133 'The philosopher must conceive of himself as himself belonging to the history of law, and history itself becomes the only manner of thinking of the law. And, correspondingly, the law does not exist as an object exterior to the philosophy that defines it' (my translation).

[27] Ewald 1986c, p. 138.

object of the criminal law is defined and the theoretical boundaries of the field maintained. If we accept that there is no transcendent reason, then there can be no retreat from historicism.

The study of the doctrine of the criminal law must therefore begin by shifting attention onto the relationship between legal practices and moral philosophy itself. It should look at its origins, the ways that this has been invested with significance, and its actual significance to the operation of the criminal justice system. This entails looking at it as one practice within a complex of practices – the philosophising of the criminal law in the field of the administration of the criminal law and criminal justice – where the relationship is not given, once and for all, but must always be in the process of re-establishing itself.[28] The true significance of each of these practices in a specific period must be traced and weighed against the others. The organising concepts of the criminal law do not have an *a priori* existence, springing fully formed from the head of some god-like philosopher. They emerge from institutional practices and their study must begin by looking at their uses in this system of practices.[29] In these terms the question of 'responsibility', for example, can no longer be understood simply as the moral philosophical question of specifying the conditions under which an autonomous individual may be held culpable for certain acts, and is therefore a justifiable object of state punishment. The question of who is subject to the law and under what conditions has also to be seen as a question that is subject to the constraints of organisation, power and culture. The language of legal responsibility has to be seen as one way in which the relations between legal and political organisation are mediated,[30] and as one, but only one, of the organising concepts of the criminal justice system. To avoid the reproduction of an artificial barrier between law and context, this must be formulated as part of the relationship between the law (narrowly conceived as legal doctrine) and legal practices. By systematically attempting to specify the relationships between different areas of practice, it is possible to begin to develop a critical understanding of the conditions that shape the modern criminal law. The study of the practices of the criminal law and criminal justice opens a different perspective on the narrow theoretical formulations that have been taken for granted for too long.[31]

If we take legal practices as our starting point, the concept of law is not bound to any one type and we cannot assume the existence of any core

---

[28] Deleuze 1988, pp. 32–44.   [29] Nietzsche 1969, p. 77.

[30] 'Penal law concerns those aspects of criminal material that can be articulated: it is a system of language that classifies and translates offences and calculates sentences; a family of statements that is also a threshold' Deleuze 1988, p. 32.

[31] See Foucault 1991c, p. 75; Ewald 1985, p. 133; Pasquino 1991, pp. 247–8; on beginning from practices, see also Teubner 1989a and 1989b.

rules or values. The idea of historical change, in definitions, institutions
and so on, is built into our account. There are many different types of legal
order or jurisdiction, each of which is articulated around a particular legal
rationality. Each system of law thus includes, 'not only a certain normative
content, a set of special rules depending on the criterion of legality
peculiar to the system considered, a way of practising legal judgement . . .
but also a body of doctrine through which the whole set of these practices
are reflected and regulated . . .'[32] The study of the law thus requires a
recognition and tracing of the positivity of the modern law, the particular
content of the criminal law and the terms according to which legal rules
are recognised as being valid.[33] But there is a further question involved,
taking this question of rationality beyond the normal terms of legal
positivism,[34] to ask a series of 'second order' questions about the law and
legal authority. This 'rule of judgement', as it has been termed, is thus
something that is wider than the simple idea of legal validity or even legal
principle:

Statute, doctrine, and case law derive from it and express it; but it can never be
reduced to these. It is a sort of necessary ideal on the basis of which legal practices
reflect the constraint that binds them, their unity and their systemacity. Constant-
ly reformulated, it never ceases to depart from itself through the judgements that
express it.[35]

The legal institution defines the boundaries of its jurisdiction and renders
intelligible the practices within that system, but it is at the same time itself
defined and constrained by its capacity to do so.[36] It is in this continual
departure from itself that the rationality of law is marked out as something
that has a history and that produces history. It cannot be reduced to
positive law or doctrinal formulations of, say, the determination of the
validity of legal rules or the competence of certain legal actors. Equally, it
cannot be abstracted from the legal and social practices that shape it. It
opens up a more complex relationship with context, for we are not
concerned solely with the question of the identification of the rule of
judgement, but also with the conditions and relations that make successive rules of judgement possible. In more conventional terms, it can be

[32] Ewald 1988, pp. 43–4.
[33] e.g. 'The only sound proposition is to cleave persistently to the single-minded goal of
elucidating the existing penal law, asking only – which theory will maximise our
understanding of that law?' Hall 1960, p. 2; cf. Tur 1993.
[34] e.g. Hart 1983; Williams 1955.
[35] Ewald 1988, p. 38; see also 1985; 1986b Introduction; 1986c; 1987. Cf. Foucault 1991b,
p. 54 where he discusses criteria of formation, transformation and correlation for
discourses.
[36] Cf. Pasquino 1991, p. 247: 'an intelligibility which at once traverses and is incorporated in
these practices'.

argued that the formulation of the 'rule of judgement' in these terms entails the recognition of the historical nature of legal practices. The concern with the identity and the conditions of possibility of particular rules of judgement allows the occupation of a position that neither wholly adopts the law's point of view, nor wholly collapses it into the social.

If the task of legal history and philosophy is thus the tracing of the way that these abstractions are made, viewing them as reflexive and authoritative accounts of the legal system at a particular point in time, then, schematically, the 'context' of legal theory is to be sought in the responses to three different questions about the nature of legal order. The first is the question of what is produced by legal order. This raises the question of legal theory's relation to its past. Looking at the practice of theorising about the law, it is necessary to be sensitive to the way in which certain questions are formulated. There must be an awareness of shifts in emphasis and focus that are often concealed by conceptual vocabularies which stress continuity and authority or which claim a fundamental relationship between criminal law and moral philosophy. Second, there is the question of the conditions of legal order. This requires study of the relationship between legal theory and the practices of the legal system: the correspondences that are established, the practices that are given priority, the terms in which they are represented and so on. But the point that the intelligibility of practices need not depend on their conformity to reason must be underlined. The 'rationality' of law may be partial or incomplete, in the sense of not treating all legal practices equally, or drawing on non-'legal' or non-'rational' sources.[37] The decisive consideration is that they be regarded as having the force of 'truth' for that legal system. The notion of the rule of judgement, 'juris-diction', must be seen as referring to legal culture, or, as it will be referred to throughout this book, legal tradition. Third, it is necessary to look at the broader significance of the rule of judgement. This is the means by which the law responds to the process of social change. The functions of the criminal law may change, or legal institutions may be re-ordered in response to the perception of new social problems. Although the law may be co-extensive with social field, the institutions of the law are not always distributed with equal force or impact over that field. The social field, in turn, is composed of a network of rationalities, intersections and interferences which may produce a subtle impact within the rationality of the law.[38] This demands an

---

[37] A perfect example of this can be found in the idea of the common law tradition. There is a developing critical literature on this. See notably Goodrich 1986 ch. 5 and 1992, p. 8: 'It will be argued here, however, that history is the reality (the trauma) of legal practice and tradition the narrative logic of its development'; Cotterrell 1989, ch. 2; Murphy 1991; Lobban 1991; Postema 1986.

[38] Foucault 1977. See also the discussion in Murphy 1991, pp. 185–94 on the adjudicative episteme of the common law. Cf. Rose 1995 arguing for a stronger political sociology.

examination of how the legal system manages its relations with other social institutions and maintains its own autonomy. It is, in short, about the order of law.

It should by now be clear that in concentrating on the issue of boundaries in the criminal law, we have been returning to and developing the idea of a legal cartography introduced by the quotation from Blackstone. Our concern is the mapping of a particular legal field and the shifting relations between the forces that comprise and define that field.[39] In mapping these various relations the aim is to introduce the dual critical elements of displacement and replacement. Displacement comes from the concentration on practices, shifting the normal starting point, altering the perspective or the terms of representation. The purpose of displacement is to search out inconsistencies and incompleteness in the law: that which is not explained and why, or the assumptions that structure legal argument. In the terms of one of the more conventional formulations of critical legal studies this may be expressed as the recovery of the repressed in the history of law. The theorist must seek out the histories that have not been told, and discover sites from which it is possible to criticise the law. This comes through the multiplying of the representations of the law.[40] And a crucial, often overlooked, element of this process of displacement is that of searching for continuities where we have been taught to see rupture and vice versa. The field of the law must be mapped out, to explore the tensions within and between the different fields, and through a series of such displacements to develop our understanding of the nature and the boundaries of the legal order. The second element of this 'critical positivism'[41] is that of replacement, reintroducing the displaced into a reflexive engagement with the rule of judgement. It is never sufficient just to develop alternative understandings. The law as an institution does not change freely, and its authority is founded on the policing and control of meaning. The task of critical positivism is to question the operation of these 'truth-games' in a given system, to understand the limits of the rationality of law and uncover the spaces where there is room for argumentation or resistance. Only then does it begin to be effective to confront the law with alternative and 'better', in the sense of more complete, accounts of legal rationality, by playing on the gaps, flexibilities and weaknesses of the law.

This can be illustrated by a brief consideration of the famous passage in

[39] Deleuze 1988, pp. 34–5 describing the *diagram* as a series of relations between discursive and non-discursive formations, and the social theorist as the cartographer mapping the relations between them.

[40] Cf. R. W. Gordon 1984 and Goodrich 1990 ch. 2 offer different versions of the telling of alternative or suppressed histories. See also Macintyre 1977, pp. 453–72.

[41] Cf. Ewald 1986c, describing critical positivism in rather vague terms as the question that law (judgement) must ask of legality (validity).

his *Historical Law Tracts* where the philosopher–judge, Lord Kames, drew a comparison between the study of the law and the course of the river Nile:

When we enter upon the municipal law of any country in its present state, we resemble a traveller, who, crossing the Delta, loses his way among the numberless branches of the Egyptian river. But when we begin at the source and follow the current of the law, it is in that course no less easy than agreeable; and all its relations and dependencies are traced with no greater difficulty, than are the many streams into which that magnificent river is divided before it is lost in the sea.[42]

This poses the relation between the land, history and the law in a particular way. The legal historian was the traveller swept down to the sea, understanding of the present coming only as a result of the cultivation of a historical perspective. For Kames the purpose of history was to unify understanding, as the passage through time revealed the conceptual coherence or unity of the law. Just as in the old philosophical conundrum the river is never the same river, the common law can both change and be the same, linked by the experience of its historical journey. Goodrich has argued for displacement, that this projection maps only one experience, excluding the possibility or validity either of alternative experiences or alternative forms of mapping.[43] However, although there may be alternative ways of traversing this landscape, or of mapping it, the river remains the central, defining feature, and we should neither ignore this nor stray too far from it. The displacement, in this sense, must continually be brought back to the map that it challenges. But there is a second important sense in which Kames might be understood. As a metaphor for history, the river passes through the legal landscape, transforming it as a river may erode a rock. This process of change and transformation must be described. The space of criminal jurisdiction emerges from the relationship between the river and the landscape.

The criminal law is, in a very real sense, the 'law of the land'. Our conduct is ordered by its precepts, our transgressions punished. The guilty cannot run from the 'long arm of the law'. These are questions of criminal jurisdiction at a given place and time. They concern the substantive content of the criminal law: the types of behaviour that are censured, the types of punishment and the relationship that is constructed between the two. No matter how abstract the formulation of the law, it can never be completely disembedded from social space. These, then, are also questions of the application of the law – who is subject to and of the law and under what circumstances – questions that are obviously also

---

[42] Kames 1792, pp. vii-viii. Cf. Maitland 1911, p. 493.
[43] Goodrich 1990, p. 17: 'The pattern of such development, of the common law as a tradition, is most usually presented as one of linear emergence: the law is a route, a path across time and across experience'.

dependent on the existence of an apparatus that is capable of enforcing and adjudicating on the law. These questions of jurisdiction relate to the policing of the boundaries of the permissible, and are also questions of the boundaries and internal ordering of the legal system. This draws a strong parallel with the first sense of Blackstone's metaphor. We must attempt to map or describe the physical apparatus of the criminal law as it is inscribed on a particular physical space. We must look at the way in which power is actually exercised and the way that this changes over time. We are concerned with the changing physical organisation of the law in territorial space.

Yet this alone would never be sufficient. Alongside these 'physical' questions, we are concerned with what might be termed the 'metaphysical'.[44] Criminal jurisdiction also concerns the various criteria according to which the conceptual structure of the law is organised. This is the question of legal rationality, the legal order's reflexive account of itself, the way that it renders intelligible the diverse practices of the system. The concern is not simply with where boundaries are drawn but how they are drawn, and the relationship between this and the internal distribution of forces within the legal system. Boundaries are related to the legal landscape that they seek to contain. As in the case of maps, this is not only a question of interpretation of the landscape, but also raises the issue of the power to speak the law, and the means by which the process of definition is controlled. The law establishes the official representation of that landscape, the one that is considered to be the true representation. This is the question of legal authority, both in the narrow sense of the building of a system of precedent, and in the broader one of the establishing of an authoritative account of the origins and operation of the legal system. This 'metaphysical' sense also involves questions of the application of law in space and time. The map of the law creates an imaginary space within which it operates. This is none other than law's empire: the space within which law is seen as the fundamental social institution, within the bounds of which its truth holds sway over those of economy, politics, science. It is also typically the nation. More than just geographical space, it is a way of imagining a shared way of life, common values and community. This space is what marks out the law, or a particular legal tradition, as not only being distinct from its neighbours, but very probably also superior to them.[45] Existing in the continual present of legal practice, its imaginary time is a history that tells the story of aging, of shared development, of triumph over adversity. This map of the law is complex. The task to be

---

[44] Goodrich 1995, ch. 1 '[T]he law depends upon a geography of mental spaces, which cannot be reduced to its physical presences, its texts, or its apparent rules' at pp. 8–9.

[45] B. Anderson 1983; Goodrich 1992, pp. 9–10.

faced is, thus, the complex one of trying to build a critical understanding of the boundaries of the criminal law, the interaction of the physical and the metaphysical, through a form of historical jurisprudence.

It is clear that, in challenging the terms of the representation of the law, we are ourselves involved in the process of representation. We face a question that was already familiar to Blackstone. How is the 'academical expounder' of the law to approach the subject? The crucial argument is that in reconceiving the question of the boundaries of the law, we must restore the sense in which this is a question of the means by which the criminal law organises and protects its territory over time. And if we do not vindicate the established representations of the spaces, structures and boundaries of the law, then we are at least bound to study the process by which they have been drawn. We must remain truthful to the features of the landscape of the law, though our choice of map will, of course, depend on what we wish to conceal or reveal. We may, and indeed we must, distort reality but we should beware distorting the truth.

This, then, is an essay about the criminal law, written with the aim of establishing foundations on which a radical critique of the existing conceptual structure of the law can be built. It is not possible to begin from those concepts and attempt to reshape,[46] rethink,[47] or reconstruct them.[48] Such attempts, it seems, lead to repetition rather than resurrection. The approach taken here is partial. This is not only because it is critical of the existing order and explicitly sets out to challenge the easy assumption that this or any other area of the law is exclusively technical in character, but also because it does not pretend to deal with every area of the criminal law as this is conventionally understood. It is selective and argumentative. Examples are chosen, and, by the same token, topics are omitted, for what they can contribute to the argument or reveal about the whole, rather than to follow tired conventions of organisation and exposition. But the greatest change is in the treatment. This deliberately cuts across the categories that normally structure thought about the criminal law, to provide a more detailed historical account of the development of legal concepts and methods. It does not, and indeed cannot, touch up some of the more glaring inconsistencies of case law or doctrine. It can produce no recommendations for legal reform. Rather, it seeks to challenge the very value and validity of this as a worthwhile academic activity. Nor, it should be stated, is this an attempt to produce a critical criminal law – whatever that means – although the aims are no less critical for that. There can be no single critical version of the law, and I have no desire to foster such an

[46] Glazebrook 1978.   [47] Fletcher 1978.   [48] Lacey *et al.* 1990.

illusion. The aim is thus more limited – and more demanding. It is to develop a reading of the modern criminal law as a system of criminal justice.

This is approached through two different claims. The first is that it is possible to reinstate the centrality of the question of the criminal law by broadening our understanding of the meaning of law and legality – to disrupt the boundaries that criminal lawyers have drawn around their subject. Just as studies devoted to the examination of the philosophical basis of the criminal law rarely consider the legal, institutional or historical context in which criminal law is practised, so the literature on the sociology and social history of crime and punishment is rarely informed by a legal understanding. This book seeks to bridge this gap and so challenge the boundaries of the criminal law. This is done initially through the argument that legality, and consequently the perception of the criminal law, can only be understood within particular legal traditions. It then presents a detailed reconstruction of the characteristics of the modern criminal law, by tracing the practices that have developed within the Scottish legal tradition. While this sets a limit to the rationalism of law, it is argued that it opens up the historical analysis of legal practices in a new and critical manner.

The second claim is that the interpretation and the application of the law cannot be viewed in isolation from the emergence and operation of certain modern institutions of criminal justice. A central argument of the book is that there is a fundamental shift in the jurisdiction and organisation of the criminal law in the course of the nineteenth century, exemplified by the rise of procedure. This is in turn reflected in a complex manner in the definition and structure of the criminal law. Particular conceptions of the subject and legal order are examined to show how contemporary criminal law theory misrepresents the character of modern criminal justice through its attachment to certain fundamental assumptions about the foundations and nature of law. The task for criminal law theory is to replace the vague assumptions of legal tradition with a broader understanding of legal culture, thus incorporating a historical understanding of the law and the contemporary criminal justice system.

Finally, though this should not be necessary, something can be said about the choice of Scotland as the case study. While this certainly requires no apology, it might help if there were a word of introduction. As will be explained at greater length in the following chapter, the Scottish criminal law is a system of common law – even more so than the English criminal law. To this extent, then, as a common law system that has developed with a distinctive character on the margins of Anglo-American criminal law, it offers both the opportunity to study the development of a particular system, and a unique vantage point from which to reappraise criminal law theory. The development of Scots criminal law is thus of particular significance, and has been unjustly neglected by lawyers and historians alike. But this is not a conventional comparative study. The primary concern is to establish the importance of tradition to the interpretation and understanding of the modern law. In the case of Scotland, where there has long been a preoccupation with the preservation of national identity in the face of the encroachments of alien ideas and institutions, a particularly strong sense of national legal culture and tradition has been constructed. This can be of central importance to an understanding of the Anglo-American tradition of criminal law which has sheltered behind what are supposedly more universal and abstract ideas. The attraction, in part, is that it offers an inversion of the normal pattern which asserts the identity of the Scots system solely in terms of difference from England – thereby denying the appropriateness of comparison. The Scottish genius and character are said to have developed a singular criminal law. However, although many of the institutions are different, and may be unfamiliar, the patterns of development are broadly similar and both have been subjected to many of the same influences and pressures. The masking of these similarities is itself worthy of remark, and draws our attention to those other factors that are at work in the process of the interpretation and exposition of the law. Finally, it remains only to note that the detailed study of a particular national legal culture allows issues of much wider relevance to law and legal theory to be raised, not least because it poses the question of the boundaries of the law in a particularly stark and revealing manner.

2 The genius of our law: legality and the Scottish legal tradition

Introduction

A condition of the Treaty of Union between Scotland and England in 1707 was that the Scottish legal system, together with the education system and the church, should remain separate administrative entities. The British state was thereby created.[1] The study of Scots law is impossible without some awareness of this fact. This is not only because of the curious institutional arrangement to which the Union gave rise: the Scottish legal system exists without its own legislative body and the British Parliament passes laws that may be administered differently within the same country. It is essential because an awareness of this difference pervades every area and every aspect of writing, speaking and thinking about the law in Scotland. It has been central to the development of Scottish legal culture and, to a lesser extent, a Scottish national identity. Whatever our feelings about nationalism in general, and Scottish nationalism in particular, this circumstance cannot be ignored. Consequently any discussion of criminal jurisdiction, although apparently technical in character, begins at and continually returns to this point.

The Scottish criminal law has been shaped by its determination to remain independent from its English neighbour. In other areas of the law the practical consequences of the separate systems diminished under the weight of economic and administrative pressures, and as legislation revised or replaced much of the common law. Not so with the criminal law. The more serious offences are still to be found in common law, not statute. There has been stubborn resistance to the idea of codifying the substantive law. The system has its own courts, rules of procedure and evidence, and even penal system. Perhaps most significantly of all, it is, unlike the civil law, completely self-contained, there being no appeal outside Scotland to the House of Lords on criminal questions. This independence has not occurred by chance but is the result of deliberate and hard-fought resistance on the part of Scottish lawyers, and writing

[1] On the negotiations that preceded the Treaty on this point, see Levack 1987, chs. 1, 3.

about the criminal law accordingly carries a special burden of hopes and fears. Though frequently hidden behind a façade of technicality, much of the writing on Scots criminal law either assumes or celebrates this difference. It may be expressed in the crude belief that Scottish law is better than English law, or, more usually, in an unreflective separatism that assumes that being Scottish, and a subject of the Scottish legal system, confers certain benefits and that this should not be tampered with or criticised for fear of endangering a hard-won independence. Either way, this cannot be treated as irrelevant to our concerns.

It is the argument of this chapter that there is a distinctive tradition in Scottish criminal law. The bulk of writing and speaking about the law – in judgements, comments and academic texts – is conducted from within this tradition and on the basis of assumptions that are rarely questioned because they are unseen and beyond argument. Initially, at least, the term 'tradition' is not being used in any technical sense, but has simply been borrowed from the title of an influential pamphlet written by Lord Cooper and first published in 1949. This sought to provide a general introduction to the distinctive features of the legal system. He regarded the 'tradition' as a distinctive body of legal principles and institutions linked to the history of the Scottish nation and the national character.[2] It is this loose idea of a tradition, between history and conceptual reasoning, that I wish to borrow. By allowing us to give due weight to legal doctrine without needlessly confining the terms of the analysis, it proves useful as both a descriptive and an analytic category. This is, in an important sense, the type of inversion of the normal process of analysing the law that was argued for in the last chapter. Rather than beginning by specifying a certain form of rationality and attempting to analyse the law in its terms, we begin from an analysis of the distinctive practices of the tradition to go on to examine the assumptions on which the tradition is based, and the way that authority is constituted and certain conceptual and theoretical boundaries drawn. It will become increasingly clear that the understandings of this legal tradition are central to our misunderstanding of the modern law.[3] To approach our subject in this way is to address the question of the criteria of legality of the system – the rule of judgement. This is initially a question of the sources of law and the rules of validity, and so a natural starting point is the narrower question of the 'principle of legality', or the rule of law. In Scotland this has been discussed in the

---

[2] In Cooper 1957, p. 172: 'Scots law is in a special sense the mirror of Scotland's history and traditions and a typical product of the national character . . .'; reprinted 1991 with re-assessments by M. C. Meston and W. D. H. Sellar.

[3] This is not to fall back on the antinomy between tradition and modernity discussed in Krygier 1986, but to argue that acknowledgement of the existence of tradition does not free us from the requirement of analysing their relationship with modernity.

context of the debate over the so-called 'declaratory power' of the High Court.

The inherent powers of the Scottish criminal law

The genius of our law rests on a principle diametrically opposite to that of England; the Courts of criminal jurisdiction being authorised to punish crimes without any positive enactment.[4]

The principle of legality is declared to be fundamental to the modern law. It affirms the protection of individual autonomy by placing limitations on the power of the state. No judge or state official can be above the law. They can only apply pre-existing and properly formulated laws. The judge can be no more than the 'mouth of the law'.[5] This has a special application in the criminal law, summarised by the Latin maxim *nullum crimen sine lege* – no crimes without laws.[6] While there is some dispute as to the origins of this term, there can be no doubt that it came to prominence in the eighteenth century as part of that movement that sought to restrict arbitrary royal power, and defend the absolute value of law.[7] It is thus inextricably bound up with views of the modernity of law, and it has subsequently been considered a fundamental principle of Western systems of penal law that legal punishment can only be inflicted when the act in question has been clearly defined in advance as a crime.[8]

For almost 200 years there has been debate over the application and scope of the principle of legality in the Scottish criminal law. This has focused on the question of whether the High Court either does, or should have, the power to 'create crimes' by declaring that behaviour of an obviously 'wrong', 'wicked', 'grossly immoral and mischievous' or 'criminal nature' that does not fall under the existing heads of the law should be

---

[4] Lord Justice-Clerk Hope in *Rachel Wright* (1809) in Burnett 1811, app. VII, p. xxix. Cf. for England, 'All offences of a public nature, that is, all such acts or attempts as tend to the prejudice of the community, are indictable' (Lawrence J. in *R v. Higgins* (1801) 2 East at p. 21). This is discussed below.

[5] The expression comes from Montesquieu (1949, p. 159) '[T]he national judges are no more than the mouth that pronounces the words of the law, mere passive beings, incapable of moderating either its force or rigour'; Hall 1960, ch. 2, p. 28: 'The essence of this principle of legality is limitation on penalization by the State's officials, effected by the prescription and application of specific rules.'

[6] Hall 1960, p. 27: 'it qualifies and is presupposed by everything else in penal theory'.

[7] For discussion and history, see Pasquino 1991, p. 237; Hall 1960; Glaser 1942. See also Cooper 1957, pp. 199–200.

[8] See e.g. European Convention on Human Rights Art. 7(1): 'No one shall be held guilty of any criminal offence on account of any act or omission which did not constitute a criminal offence under national or international law at the time it was committed. Nor shall a heavier penalty be imposed than the one that was applicable at the time the criminal offence was committed.' See also US Constitution Art. 1.

regarded as punishable.[9] This power has consistently been regarded as the fundamentally controversial aspect of the system. This question is appropriate for our study because it runs parallel to the debate over the boundary between law and morality, the limits of law and the powers of the English courts, that has so preoccupied jurists in recent years.[10] The debates are remarkable for the fact that they have very quickly settled into standard patterns. Most contributions do little more than repeat the basic terms of the argument, only updating the subject matter to include the latest controversy. The features of the Scottish debate are roughly as follows.

The authoritative statement of the law, as in most other matters criminal, is to be found in Baron Hume's *Commentaries on the Law of Scotland Respecting Crimes*. He refers to an 'inherent power' resting with the court 'to punish (with the exception of life and limb) every act which is obviously of a criminal nature'.[11] The leading case, and indeed the only modern case in which the court acknowledged that it was exercising the power, is the case of *Bernard Greenhuff*.[12] There is a string of more recent cases in which three broad types of judicial behaviour can be identified. In some there has been an implicit criminalisation of behaviour coupled with an explicit denial that the court is using the power.[13] Alternatively the court has affirmed that they consider that the power definitely exists, whilst declining to use it in the specific instance.[14] The third possibility, which is perhaps also the most common, is that the court gives absolutely no clue at all to the logic that is guiding its actions, although giving rise to a strong presumption that it is using the power.[15] There have been disapproving commentaries by a series of distinguished legal figures which

---

[9] These terms are all taken from the judgements in the case of *Bernard Greenhuff* (1838) 2 Swin. 128 and 236. The most complete account of the debate can be found in G. H. Gordon 1978, pp. 23–43.

[10] This is summarised in Ashworth 1995, ch. 3; A. T. H. Smith 1984.

[11] Hume 4th edn 1844 I, pp. 12–13. See also I, p. 496; II, pp. 168–9 and Bell's Notes II, pp. 173–5. Unless otherwise stated references are to the fourth edition. For a contrary view on the permissible extent of punishment, see the case of *Wright* 1809 (above, n. 4) where a capital sentence was upheld.

[12] Above, n. 9. Although the case of *Chas. Sweenie* (1858) 3 Irv. 109 is sometimes regarded as having created the offence of 'clandestine injury to women'. See also the cases on workmen's combinations referred to by the judges in *Greenhuff* and by Hume 1844 I, ch. 24.

[13] *HM Adv. v. Martin* 1956 J.C. 1; For a recent example see *R. v. HM Adv.* 1988 S.C.C.R. 255.   [14] e.g. *Grant v. Allan* 1987 S.C.C.R. 402.

[15] e.g. *Strathern v. Seaforth* 1926 J.C. 100; *McLaughlan v. Boyd* 1934 J.C.19; *Kerr v. Hill* 1936 J.C. 71; to these may now be added *Stallard v. HM Adv.* 1989 S.L.T. 469; 1989 S.C.C.R. 248 in which the court held that marital rape could be considered a crime under the law of Scotland.

take their cue from the dissent of Lord Cockburn in the *Greenhuff* case.[16] The current academic orthodoxy can be summed up in the following way. It is argued that the power runs contrary to the principle of legality – that there should be no crimes without laws – and that penal laws should be promulgated in advance by the legislature. It is further suggested that the power is anachronistic, having ceased to exist by reason of desuetude, a feature which is also taken to demonstrate that it is ill-suited to a developed, modern system of law. Finally it is pointed out that the common law system allows plenty of scope for development within existing principles. This flexibility, or 'native genius', is normally depicted as the distinctively Scottish characteristic of our system – and it is not regarded as something that conflicts with that all important principle of legality. The discussion will commonly conclude with either a plea for moderation on the part of the judiciary or a demand that they formally eschew the use of the power, or, in especially controversial cases, both.

It is not my intention to join this debate. I do not want to take sides between the relative values of legality and flexibility, or between academic commentators and the judiciary. Rather I want to argue that this standardised and repetitive debate is not worth joining because the two sides should not be regarded as offering real alternatives. The debate should instead be seen as a 'red herring' – that is to say, it is something that is put in the plot of a story about crime to distract the reader's attention from the really important clues. This, of course, does not mean that it is of no interest. Its principal value, as I have already suggested, is as an introduction to the values of the Scottish legal tradition. The debate constructs a false dichotomy between the ability of the law to create, in terms of the declaratory power, and the principle of legality. In other words, there is an implicit claim that the principle of legality is part of the system and should be the yardstick by which individual parts are measured. Either practices conform with this standard or they are considered to be 'outside' the law. The declaratory power is identified as being obviously in breach of this and therefore abnormal and so is safely separated from other 'normal' practices. However, this reference to an abstract standard has meant that attention is directed away from the actual practices of the system, and thus from the meaning of legality within the system. The implication is that once the aberration represented

---

[16] For nineteenth-century examples, see Alison 1825 and 1832, ch. 39 on innominate offences; Lord Ardmillan (James Crawfurd) 1846, pp. 313–46; for more contemporary accounts; see Elliott 1956; J. Walker 1958; G. H. Gordon 1978; Willock 1981 and 1989; Jones 1990. Styles 1993 is a rare voice in defence of the power, but the arguments are depressingly formulaic and unconvincing.

by the power has been contained, either by not using it or by its abolition, the legalistic rationality of the system will be complete. By not looking too closely at the practices, the protagonists of the debate are essentially in agreement over the nature of the law. As an alternative, I propose that rather than regarding the declaratory power as an anachronistic and isolated feature of the law, we should allow ourselves to look at the continuities, the features that are shared in common between the 'normal' and the 'abnormal' practices. The power should be regarded as no more than an extension of the standard practices, throwing these into sharper relief.

This can be illustrated in a straightforward manner, by looking at how the supposedly alien feature of 'creation', associated with the declaratory power, actually pervades the criminal law. The law is shot through with a belief in the value of flexibility.[17] In addition to the declaratory power we can point to the apparent acceptability of what has been termed its *de facto* use.[18] There is also the manipulation of the terms of existing, apparently fixed, definitions,[19] or the open expansion of the existing heads of crime to cover new situations.[20] Judicial interpretation of certain crimes, such as breach of the peace, is so wide as to catch almost any type of behaviour.[21] This is a feature of the law that is actively encouraged by criminal procedure. The form of the indictment need not specify which crime is charged but merely relate facts which constitute 'an indictable crime', and certain terms relating to knowledge or intention need not be specified but are implied in all indictments.[22] And finally, right at the centre of the law we find that such key standards as 'recklessness', 'intention' and causation are governed by an ill-defined and inconsistently applied notion of 'reasonableness'.[23]

We can thus see that the main characteristic of the criminal law is its refusal of 'precise and exact categorisation',[24] in favour of loose definitions and procedures that allow adaptation to the exigencies of particular

[17] For a more detailed discussion of the following, see Willock 1981; Farmer 1989a; Jones 1990.
[18] See especially *Watt v. Annan* 1978 J.C. 443 and subsequent cases on shameless indecency in Gane and Stoddart 1988. See also *Stallard v. HM Adv.* above, n. 15.
[19] e.g. *HM Adv. v. Wilson* 1983 S.C.C.R. 420.   [20] e.g. *Milne v. Tudhope* 1981 J.C. 53.
[21] Christie 1990, ch. 2.
[22] See Criminal Procedure (Scotland) Act 1975 ss. 44–8, 312 consolidating the Criminal Procedure (Scotland) Act 1887 ss. 5–8, 58, 59. For an example of this, see *Lord Advocate's Reference (No. 1 of 1994)* 1995 S.L.T. 248; 1995 S.C.C.R. 177 where the charge specified neither the crime that was being charged nor the mental state of the accused.
[23] See e.g. *HM Adv. v. Khaliq* 1984 S.C.C.R. 483. For comment, see Farmer *et al.* 1987. See now also the cases of *Ulhaq v. HM Adv.* 1990 S.C.C.R. 593 and *Lord Advocate's Reference (no. 1 of 1994)* 1995 S.L.T. 248; 1995 S.C.C.R. 177.
[24] Lord Justice-General Clyde in *McLaughlan v. Boyd* above, n. 15.

situations. It might indeed be said that creation is inherent in the law.[25] At this point, we run into some difficulties with the 'principle of legality' for although it is clearly not respected to the letter in the Scottish system, some writers obviously regard it as a value to which the law should aspire. And while one could hardly dispute the general terms of the argument in favour of the rule of law, an abstract and general standard such as this, that diverges markedly from the practice, cannot tell us very much about the actual criminal law. What is surely more interesting is the fact that the orthodox view holds that 'flexibility' and creativity are in some way consistent with the principle of legality. This does not mean that the law is completely indeterminate, but it does open up the possibility that while the principle of legality may not be fundamental to the modern law there is none the less a sense in which the claim of legality is not completely meaningless. The principle of legality clearly takes on a specific meaning in relation to the practices of the Scottish system. To put this slightly differently, there is no reason to believe that the system does not make sense in its own terms. If this coherence cannot be seen to derive directly from the abstract principle of legality, then our next step must be to try and understand the way in which the Scottish criminal law can be understood as a related set of practices. The debate on the declaratory power clearly alludes to the relationship between doctrine, procedure and institutional powers and it is in this network of relationships, rather than in abstract or universal terms, that we must look to understand the Scottish legal tradition.

This tradition has been constituted by the manipulation of certain key themes, but before discussing these I want to answer two possible objections. The first would be that the sheer lack of size of the Scottish system has constrained the development of criminal jurisprudence by allowing for the management of the system along more practical and informal lines. The objection would be, therefore, that I am attempting to make a mountain out of a molehill. My reply to this would be that, regardless of whether or not this is the case, (and I think that it is not), what is significant is that there is a continuing claim to represent a system of criminal jurisprudence. It is this claim that I am proposing to investigate. Thus when Professor Walker claims that Hume systematised and arranged in rational order the propositions of the criminal law,[26] we must ask along what lines and by what standards this, and subsequent, rationalisations were made. The second objection would be that it is rather obvious to point to the influence of Hume in the formation of the

---

[25] As, of course, it is inherent in all law to some extent. See generally Goodrich 1986, chs. 5 and 6.   [26] Introduction to the 1986 reissue of Hume's *Commentaries* (1844).

Scottish criminal law tradition. The *Commentaries* are a major work of reference and have long been accorded 'institutional' status.[27] Subsequent writers are therefore bound to draw heavily on them. This is undoubtedly the case and much of what follows will be a restatement of certain well-known characteristics of the Scottish system. But the aim of this chapter is precisely that of taking these as objects of study. Only by subjecting them to critical examination, and understanding the historical circumstances in which they emerged, can we hope to arrive at an understanding of the actual working of the law.

Native principles and native methods: the dominant tradition

It is contrary to the tradition and genius of our criminal law to deal with its basic conceptions *in vacuo* . . . By the application of our native methods to our native principles it has proved possible . . . to keep the law sufficiently flexible and elastic to enable a just discrimination to be applied to the ascertained facts of each case, and sufficiently rigid to prevent proved guilt from escaping the just consequences on any mere technicality.[28]

It is possible to identify four central and interlocking themes. These are the maturity of the system, independence and national identity, the centrality and nature of the common law, and the existence of shared or community attitudes towards wrong.

In the following discussion I will attempt to show not only how these themes are central to the practice of law, but also the ways in which the tradition has constructed certain understandings of criminal law and justice.

Maturity

The Scottish criminal law did not reach maturity until the late eighteenth century. The Romanistic approach of Mackenzie's time had been followed by a period of selective borrowing from the English practice, until by the time of Hume an articulate synthesis had been achieved.[29]

The declaratory power as described by Hume is, we are told, anachronistic:

Two opinions are represented in Scotland, but for over a hundred years few, if any, responsible judges or advocates would have been prepared to urge that Hume's statement represents the modern attitude.[30]

[27] See D. M. Walker 1985, pp. 329–33; H. Cockburn 1846, pp. 196–223; For a contrary view of the meaning of an 'institutional' work, see Cairns 1983.
[28] Lord Cooper 1950, p. 428 para. 4.
[29] T. B. Smith 1961, p. 95; see also Hume 1844 I, p. 4.   [30] *Ibid*, p. 100.

The two opinions collapse, then, into one modern attitude. We can gain a clue as to the content of this modern attitude from a much-cited article by Elliott:

In earlier times when the purposes of government and the amount of parliamentary legislation were limited, there was more excuse for deliberate judicial law-making.[31]

A clear line is thus drawn between the pre-modern and the modern period on the basis of the principle of legality. In the words of a near contemporary of Baron Hume, while the power was once 'freely exercised and boldly defended' now, 'we believe it to be ridiculous in negation and tyrannous in exercise, and indicative not of health or energy, but of the feverishness and weakness and disorder of the judicial system'.[32] The 'modern attitude' then rests on the belief that the law matured in the late eighteenth century, taking the form of liberal and flexible principles, set out clearly for the first time by Hume. The consequence of this maturity was that the scope for judicial law-making was circumscribed. It should not be done, but it should not be necessary because all conceivable crimes were, in principle, already recognised by the law. We have already seen that this is not an accurate picture of the law – which might tempt us to speculate as to the legitimatory or ideological functions of the repetition of the debate. The rule of law is perhaps less a pillar of the defence of freedom in the modern state, than an elaborate façade concealing the repressive operation of the law.[33] However, if it is hard to define maturity or modernity – the terms are used interchangeably – simply on the basis of the acceptance or non-acceptance of the principle of legality, this does not exhaust its significance for the tradition.

The most immediate characteristic of the use of the term is its vagueness. This is not confined to a vagueness about the actual features of the law, but extends also to the historical process that it presumes to represent. This can be seen in a certain ambiguity towards the status of Hume, who is regarded by modern lawyers as the founder of the modern law. He is is said to have systematised and rationalised the law – achieving the 'articulate synthesis' between native custom and Roman and English influences. He catalogued and defined the graver crimes[34] and described institutions and procedure in a form recognisable to a modern audience. However, Hume himself claimed only to be describing the contemporary practice, consequently regarding the 'inherent power' of the High Court

---

[31] Elliott 1956, p. 27.   [32] Ardmillan 1846, pp. 313–14.
[33] McBarnet 1981, chs. 7, 8; Norrie 1993, chs. 1, 2.   [34] T. B. Smith 1961, p. 99.

as quite unremarkable.[35] Even the most cursory study of the *Commentaries* suggests the existence of a vast gulf between that and contemporary experience. There would thus seem to be a lack of fit between Hume's contemporary reputation and his actual achievements. If, as will be argued, Hume does no more than he claims to do, then this must lead us to ask for a more discerning account of the development of the law. If maturity is to be read as a synonym for modernity, as seems to be the practice, then we need to understand better what is meant by modernisation within the tradition. Attempts to supply this deficiency normally claim that Hume's efforts in describing the law and the high authority with which his text was treated actually had the effect of reducing the scope of discretion that was available to judges. In the splendidly evocative description of one writer, his work acted as 'a sedative to the bench',[36] curbing their wilder creative impulses. He therefore made progress possible.[37] This has the beginnings of a more plausible account, but at the same time it threatens Hume's traditional authority.[38] More importantly, it still leaves us some distance from understanding the nature of the modernising transformation. In part this is because it does not offer a plausible account of what was significant about Hume's text, other than its completeness, but it is also because the narrowness of the focus means that institutional and social changes are only considered in a very limited way.

This idea of 'maturity' also carries with it a certain, distinctively 'Whig' view of history.[39] The present is justified by the invocation of the 'dark ages' of the past. A typical history of the law of crime will divide the subject matter between the institutions and the substantive law. The account of the development of each will then be organised around certain key dates which are the milestones on the road towards the modern system. There is the establishing of the office of Lord Advocate (1587), the foundation of the Court of Justiciary (1672), the abolition of heritable jurisdictions (1747) and the publication of the first edition of

[35] 'Neither have I any intention of turning censor on our practice; and suggesting changes and reformations, which might fit it to some higher perfection than our forefathers had in view' (Hume 1844 I, p. 14).
[36] Ardmillan 1846, p. 317. Although given well-recorded drinking habits of Scottish judges of the period it may be thought surprising that any sedative was necessary!
[37] See especially Cairns 1993, p. 174 'for the first time lawyers had access to a comprehensive and fully argued account of crimes, defining them, explaining their nature, and discussing them on the basis of the records of the Justiciary Court'.
[38] In fact, as I shall argue below, judicial reasoning has been able to exploit this to escape Hume's authority when it suits. See text at pp. 39–40.
[39] The relationship between 'Whig' historiography and Scottish national identity is the subject of a valuable recent study, see Kidd 1993. See also Fry 1992 esp. at pp. 75–6.

Hume's *Commentaries* (1797). The history describes how certain defects – which mirror the assumed qualities of the modern system – have gradually been remedied. In the pre-modern period there was no organised police force, the courts sat irregularly, jurisdictions overlapped, judges were corrupt, the royal prerogative was abused and, to cap everything, sentencing was harsh and arbitrary.[40] The history of our law is told as a movement towards central organisation and rationality – the qualities of maturity – and we readily assign the labels of barbarism and irrationality to the law of the period preceding Hume. The history of the law becomes a self-fulfilling prophecy.

Recent studies have challenged these 'Whig' histories,[41] for they have fostered a cavalier attitude towards the understanding of the pre-modern system. Our relatively clear-cut distinctions between institutions and types of law are not necessarily helpful when analysing the practice of law in an earlier period. It is far from clear that those things that we would consider as defects were regarded as such by contemporaries, nor that they prevented the effective operation of the system. In the pre-modern courts there was no clear distinction between civil and criminal law, or private and public wrongs. The corollary of this is that we find it difficult to distinguish between the function of punishment and the practice of remission or composition for crimes.[42] Prosecution might have been in the name of the crown, or initiated by the aggrieved person or their relatives – or indeed even some combination of the two – and a legal settlement would probably be the last rather than the first resort.[43] The wholesale importation of modern categories into the past has hitherto obscured complications such as these, and we are increasingly aware that this method of doing history imposes serious limitations on our understanding of both the operation of pre-modern systems and the process of historical development.

The process of revision has been slower in Scotland than in England, but recent accounts are beginning to tell a story that sets the transformation of systems of criminal law and punishment within the context of broader European developments. Three general lines of development

[40] See Cameron 1988, para. 854 entitled 'The Deficiencies of the Justiciar's court'. These histories mirror the conventional story of the reform of the criminal law in England. The classic account is Radzinowicz 1948. See also Hostettler 1992.

[41] For critical surveys of the relationships between law and history, see the papers by R. W. Gordon 1981 and 1984; Hay 1984; Sugarman and Rubin 1984.

[42] Young forthcoming, ch. 3; Wormald 1980.

[43] The literature on bloodfeud in Scotland has made this very clear. See Wormald 1980 and 1981, which also shifts our perspective on the pattern of legal development. For example, K. M. Brown 1986, p. 240 plays down the significance of the creation of the office of Lord Advocate in 1587 by showing how it was part of a struggle over bloodfeud.

have been identified.[44] First, there is the emergence of the centralised state. In Scotland this process has been complicated by the relationship between British and Scottish administrative systems, and the fact that there has been a high degree of autonomy in the localities.[45] Second, it has been argued that changes in beliefs about crime and punishment are clearly related to Protestant beliefs about sin, obedience to authority and the effectiveness of the moral discipline enforced by the Kirk Session. Third, accounts of the development of legal institutions have begun to look in a different way at the differentiation between the law of crimes and the law of personal injury, the operation of courts, the role of institutional writings and so on. Most importantly for the present argument, these histories, by their close attention to legal practice, force us to develop a much more specific sense of the meaning of modernity – separating it from the vague sense of maturity which obscures our understanding of the present.

This view of maturity has had another, even more curious, consequence. This is that history 'stops' in the early nineteenth century when the institutions that are regarded as important to us are recognisably in place. Lord Cooper, writing about the Scottish legal tradition in 1949, made this explicit: 'In law the last one hundred and twenty years belong to the dynamic present rather than the historic past'.[46] After a certain point the sources of the law are regarded as more settled, the administration less political and so on. All that has subsequently occurred has been a fine-tuning of these rules – a matter more suitable for legal than historical analysis. History is thus redundant.

The point is best made by the use of illustrations and these can be provided by the essays on the criminal courts, law and procedure in the Stair Society's *Introduction to Legal History*.[47] An essay on the 'Justiciary Court' deals with the nineteenth century in just two paragraphs, mentioning the formalisation of the linkages between the Justiciary Court and the Court of Session, the establishment of an appeals procedure and the regulation of court circuits. Smith and Macdonald in their essay on the criminal law show a greater awareness that the law is a process of continual change. They point to the fact that the recent creation of statutory

---

[44] For a full account of these developments in Scotland, and with a particular emphasis on the role of monetary sanctions see Young forthcoming, ch. 3; see also K. M. Brown 1986, chs. 9 and Conclusion; Larner 1981 discusses the influence of religious beliefs. Cairns 1983, 1984, 1988, and 1993 on the changing status of legal writings; Lenman and Parker 1980a and 1980b remain the most complete overviews of European trends.

[45] Whetstone 1981; for a more general account, see Paterson 1994, chs. 3 and 4.

[46] Cooper 1957, p. 179.

[47] See Dickinson 1958; J. I. Smith 1958; Smith and Macdonald 1958; see also Black 1975 on assythment, and D. M. Walker 1952 on the growth of the law of reparation.

offences has been undermining the 'fundamental common law concepts of a crime',[48] and they recognise the importance of 'the growth of the modern state'[49] in this process. Yet rather than consider the implications of statements such as these they prefer to concentrate on the development of the common law concepts of crime up to the time of Hume. The limited discussion of nineteenth- and twentieth-century developments is confined to such standard topics as the rise of diminished responsibility and the position of the Scottish courts in relation to the McNaghten rules on criminal insanity. We learn very little indeed about the nineteenth century from these essays.

The difficulties raised by such an approach are obvious. The emphasis on institutions such as the Justiciary Court and the serious common law crimes assumes rather than demonstrates their centrality. This in turn leads legal historians to ignore other developments which might be regarded as having undermined or altered the significance of the traditional core. It is surely wrong to exclude consideration of the growth of local, inferior courts, or of statutory law and the administrative powers of the state. This view of maturity has led us to place ourselves in a position where we consistently misread the significant elements of our contemporary criminal justice system. There is more than this, however. Not only is history being written, and the map of the law drawn, so as to privilege the common law, but in the 'dynamic present' of the law the dynamic is something that is wholly internal to the legal discourse. The demands of practice are paramount and all-consuming. History serves the law which, as Lord Cooper unwittingly makes clear, exists in a continual and timeless present. The demand is not for historical accuracy but for authority through an imaginative recounting of the past. The use of history, and the dehistoricising of legal practice, is sustained and circumscribed by the limits of the legal imagination.[50] The problem is less that of historical inaccuracy than the paucity of the legal imagination. This, incidentally, coincides with Hume's own view on the relationship between law and history. Even had he not addressed the topic specifically, it would be clear from the wealth of historical detail in the text of the *Commentaries* that he valued the importance of history. However, this was for the conservative purpose of justifying contemporary practice and authority, rather than an attempt to project this onto the wider and more speculative plane of historical understanding developed by the lawyer–philosophers of the Scottish Enlightenment.[51] This, however, points to the specific and more

---

[48] Smith and Macdonald 1958, p. 282.   [49] *Ibid.*, p. 293.
[50] Goodrich 1986, ch. 5 and 1992.
[51] Hume 1939, p. 8; cf. Stein 1988 esp. at pp. 378–80; Cairns 1988. See also the discussion in Kidd 1993, pp. 107–29.

controversial sense in which this is a Whig history. As will be argued at greater length in the following sections, the sense of historical development and maturity of the Scottish legal tradition is one that raises specific questions of identity, for modernisation has been tied into the process of integration into the British state. In the next section, then, we must begin to examine the specific form of Scottish identity that has been produced by the tradition.

Independence and national identity

In the Introduction to the *Commentaries*, Hume explains that he has been motivated to write by, 'the desire of rescuing the law of my native country from that state of declension in the esteem of some part of the public, into which, of late years, it seems to have been falling'.[52] The cause of this falling esteem is clearly identified as 'those multiplied references to the criminal law of England'.[53] He proceeds to devote some pages to an enumeration of the advantages of the Scottish system although, as a firm supporter of political union, he points out that this is not intended to disparage the English system but merely dispel 'superstitious admiration' of the English law.[54] In making these claims Hume was carrying out a careful balancing act. On the one hand, he declares provocatively that he regards the English system as 'liberal and enlightened' due to the 'much greater number of dissolute and profligate people' and 'the greater progress . . . of every sort of corruption'.[55] The English courts, in other words, get more practice! But on the other hand, as Cairns has pointed out, Hume made 'multiple references' to the law of England, and this was regarded as a legitimate way of filling the gaps in Scots law and permitted under Scottish criminal procedure.[56] It would thus appear that the more

---

[52] Hume 1844, pp. 3–4. Later reviewers have also commented on Hume's 'sturdy nationalism'; Gillon 1936, p. 371.

[53] Hume 1844, p. 4. Henry Cockburn, who never quite forgave Hume for his 'High Tory' sentiments, suggests in his review of the fourth edition of the *Commentaries* that the cause of the falling esteem was the highly controversial series of sedition trials undertaken against Scottish radicals in the wake of the French Revolution. One response to this would be – 'Well he would, wouldn't he!', since Cockburn remained the Tory administration's strongest critic on this point, eventually producing a critical account of the trials. See H. Cockburn 1846 and 1888. Since Cockburn also makes the rather extravagant claim that Hume undertook the work solely to vindicate government actions during the trials, we should beware such a narrow explanation. The Introduction treats several areas of controversy (including committal for trial, juries, public prosecution and sentencing) and it is probably better to take a broader view of the causes of falling esteem. The Introduction is retained in a largely unchanged form throughout the four editions, during which time controversy over the sedition trials died down while comparisons with England continued unabated.   [54] Hume 1844, pp. 3–13.   [55] *Ibid.*, p. 4.

[56] Cairns 1993, pp. 139, 177–8. Hume 1844 I, p. 4: 'it is entitled to deference and may with propriety be quoted in those matters which our own custom or statutes have not settled'.

forthright statements suggest a desire to assert the distinct identity of the
Scots law. Even if it were to draw on English sources, it was doing this for
reasons that were derived from the Scottish experience. It is an important
characteristic of the *Commentaries* that Hume was able to defend the
autonomy of Scots law in terms that drew on, and did not threaten, the
prevailing political orthodoxy.

It is in this introductory part of the text, and not in the main body, that
Hume makes reference to the inherent powers of the High Court. This is
the statement that has subsequently come to be regarded as the authoritative general definition of the power – although it is clear from the context
that this was not being offered as a definition.[57] The statement should
instead be read in the context of an assertion of the value of a system based
on 'the testimony of experience' against one based on 'the fallacious con-
jectures of human wisdom before the event'.[58] This must be read in several ways. It clearly refers to a general debate about the relative values of
common law and statute law. There was a great deal of criticism being
directed at the overall quality of the legislation that was being produced by
the eighteenth-century Parliament, and in particular the harsh penal legislation. Hume does not shrink from making a series of barbed comments
about this,[59] in order to assert the value of a system that developed in
accordance with the manners and experience of the people. This must also
be read within the specific Scottish context. There was a longstanding
belief that the new British Parliament was not providing adequately for
Scottish needs. However, Scottish lawyers were not making a plea for
more attention, but were asserting their own self-sufficiency. Legislation
would not be necessary because the Scottish common law was capable of
responding with the necessary 'native vigour'.[60]

It seems reasonably clear that there was a certain judicial antipathy to
the use of national statutes. This is pointed out by Gray who has argued
that an ambiguity in the Combination Acts of 1799 and 1800 over the
question of whether or not they applied to Scotland, was exploited by
Scottish lawyers who preferred to rely on the common law.[61] Later, in an

---

[57] There are passing references in Hume 1844 to the 'native vigour' of the High Court in the
main text, but these are exclusively in the context of specific crimes (e.g. workmen's
combinations, p. 496, threatening letters, p. 441 and sedition, p. 555). The powers are
also referred to in the context of the form of the libel against the accused *ibid.*, II, pp.
168–9. See below, ch. 4 on the 'well governed realm'.   [58] *Ibid.*, p. 13.

[59] e.g. *ibid*; 'knowing the wisdom of their Legislature, I will presume that it is necessary, in
their state of wealth, society and manners'. See generally Lieberman 1989 Introduction
and, chs. 9 and 10; Postema 1986, pp. 15–19.

[60] Hume specifically refers to the 'Black Acts' in these terms 1844 II, pp. 440–1. See also
Hay *et al.* 1975; E. P. Thompson 1975.

[61] Gray 1928, pp. 332–50. This is set in a broader context in Fraser 1988a, ch. 5. See also
Straka 1985.

important case of culpable homicide, which arose from the setting of spring-guns to protect private property, the Scottish bench firmly refused to apply the special laws that had been introduced by statute in England.[62] For another illustration of this general point we can turn to the leading case on the declaratory power.[63] Here it is often overlooked that the initial question that the court had to address was whether two English statutes prohibiting gaming applied in Scotland. The court concluded that they did not – a decision that was at least partly founded on the fact that, in the words of Lord Justice-Clerk Boyle, 'no mention is made of them either by Baron Hume or Mr Burnett, both of whom paid so much attention to every branch of our criminal law'.[64] He goes on to suggest that the conduct libelled would undoubtedly be indictable at common law – as it later was. A similar rejection is evident in the controversy over whether the House of Lords had the power to review decisions from the Scottish criminal courts. MacLean has argued that, although the question is not normally regarded as having been settled until the case of *Mackintosh v. Lord Advocate* in 1876,[65] the issue was effectively settled in the late eighteenth century. The established right of appeal was rejected by Scots lawyers largely on the grounds that it would be damaging to the administration of criminal justice in Scotland, but also because it was argued that it would be inconsistent with the Articles of Union.[66] Hume's assertion, in the face of the available evidence, that there had never been a right of appeal subsequently provided the basis for the decision of the House of Lords in the case of *Mackintosh*.[67]

Rather than being an embryonic Romantic political nationalism – the non-appearance of which in Scotland has so frustrated nationalist political theorists[68] – these statements are representative of the 'safe' nationalism that developed following the Union. The legal system may have preserved some sense of national identity, but it did so in a conservative and politically neutral way, subsuming Scottish identity within a larger Anglo-British identity.[69] Scots law had begun to take on a distinct national identity following the gradual rejection of the civilian tradition in the

---

[62] *Jas. Craw* 1827 Syme 188 and 210. See esp. the judgements of Lords Mackenzie and Alloway.   [63] *Greenhuff* above, n. 9.   [64] *Ibid* at p. 147.   [65] (1876) 3R (H.L.) 34.
[66] MacLean 1985, pp. 192–226. On appeals from Scotland to the House of Lords in general, see Gibb 1950.   [67] Hume 1844 II, pp. 504–8.
[68] See e.g. Harvie 1987; Nairn 1981, ch. 3; Stein 1980, ch. 3 on the German Romantics. Cf. Kidd 1993, p. 144: 'One of the unsubstantiated legends of Scottish history is that, following the loss of parliamentary autonomy in 1707, the distinctiveness of Scots law provided a compensatory basis for national identity.'
[69] For this argument I am greatly indebted to Kidd 1993 esp., chs. 6, 7, 9 and 11. This thesis is also associated with the work of Phillipson 1969, 1981 and 1989. Cf. Ash 1980 arguing that the turn to antiquarianism represented a failure of nerve on the part of Scottish historians.

seventeenth and eighteenth centuries.[70] Although Scotland had, not altogether unwillingly, been shorn of its political identity, the autonomy of the legal system had been preserved by the Treaty of Union. Power passed into the hands of a small oligarchic elite of lawyers who 'managed' what remained of the Scottish political system for their masters at Westminster until well into the middle of the nineteenth century.[71] This political power, coupled with the relative neglect by Westminster, encouraged resistance to the assimilation of Scots law and the seeking of 'native' solutions to problems as they arose. But this assertion of identity was of a limited political significance. The Scottish Whig historiography that had celebrated native political liberties had been undermined – its myths of origin discredited, associated with tyranny, and blamed for the economic backwardness of the country. The advancement of liberty and economic progress were tied to the British state and the English constitution. For Hume, indeed, this gave another justification for unacknowledged borrowing from the English law for 'the form of our Government, and the general spirit of our jurisprudence, are the same with those of England'.[72] The study of Scots law turned inwards and backwards, denuded of ideological significance. The assertion of Scottish identity, then, was carried out with the aim of perfecting rather than undermining the Union. It is tempting also to conclude that, in protecting the few indigenous institutions that had survived the Union, the legal profession were essentially protecting their own self-interest. Legal antiquities were studied, but as a nostalgic celebration of a past and always with an eye to a share of the very tangible economic benefits of the Union. The imaginary space that was created for the assertion of difference and natural evolution was recognisably Scottish, but its force has always been muted by its place within the story of Anglo-British progress.[73]

A conservative and romantic nationalism remains a dominant characteristic of the tradition. This story of early development and decline is built within the tradition of 'safe' nationalism. In the modern revival of the 'Scottish legal tradition', led by Lord Cooper and Professor T. B. Smith, we find a turn towards a mythical past in order to define and defend the origin and characteristics of the law. The virtues of the Scottish people both define the character of the law and represent the source of its redemption.[74] The law of Scotland, like its people, was considered to have

---

[70] See Cairns 1983.   [71] See Lenman 1981; Murdoch 1980.
[72] Hume 1844 I, p. 13. The actual extent of borrowing from the English remains unclear, and though the argument refers to several instances of this, it would need to be the subject of a separate study.
[73] This is the mythical space of Ukania, discussed at length by Nairn 1988, esp. at pp. 88–98.
[74] See Cooper 1950 and 1957; T. B. Smith 1961 (esp. ch. 5) contains the best summary of his views. See also 1962, 1970 and 1982. For a critical discussion, see Willock 1976.

had a free and democratic past. This democratic spirit was reflected in the law itself which had always remained cosmopolitan and open to European influences. It had its classical, or 'golden' age in the eighteenth century – or more precisely the period stretching from the publication of Stair's *Institutions* (1681) to the publication of Bell's *Commentaries* (1804) – in which period it was thought to have achieved a rational and distinctive synthesis of these diverse influences. It became, in the words of T. B. Smith, 'a finished philosophical system in advance of its time'.[75] Decline followed inevitably from exposure to English law, which at the time was 'subinsular and intolerant'.[76] Since 1800 the smaller Scottish system has struggled to resist the assimilating influence of the English, whose Parliament and lawyers have failed to respect the letter of the Treaty of Union. For these writers it is in some sense true, then, that Scottish legal history stopped in 1800, providing us with another explanation for the neglect of modern history. Criminal law alone, it is said, has resisted this intrusion. This was the result of institutional separation, but also because the 'native genius' of the Scots gave rise to a system of sufficient flexibility to make legislative intervention unnecessary in the face of social change.[77] It thereby avoided the harshness and confusion that was the hallmark of the English criminal law in the early nineteenth century. As the High Court developed a system of criminal jurisprudence, the English system has, in fact, benefited by the statutory adoption of concepts originally developed in Scotland. The standard examples given are those of 'diminished responsibility' – existent in the Scottish law since 1867 and adopted in England by the Homicide Act 1957 – and 'automatism', where a nineteenth-century Scottish case appears to have had some influence on the development of the English law.[78] The liberal principles extend also to the field of procedure where Smith suggests that 'it may be a legitimate criticism of the Scottish procedure that too many guilty persons escape trial'.[79]

The contemporary implications of all this start to become clear when we set this thesis beside the familiar concern of common lawyers, shared by Cooper and Smith, that the profusion of statute law threatens to

[75] T. B. Smith 1961, p. 18. See generally, chs. 1 and 3. Stein 1988, p. 363 suggests comparison with Roman law.   [76] T. B. Smith 1970, p. 35.

[77] Ironically, it would appear that the early schemes for union of the laws were only concerned with criminal and public laws. See Levack 1987, ch. 3.

[78] On diminished responsibility, see *Alex. Dingwall* (1867) 5 Irv. 466 (see below, ch. 5). On automatism *Simon Fraser* (1859) 3 Irv.467. It is ironic to note that in both these areas the High Court has been reluctant to accept the implications of these changes.

[79] T. B. Smith 1961, p. 123. See also Macdonald 1891, p. 1: 'Very early in Scottish history the innate love of liberty and justice which characterises the Scottish Anglo-Saxon prevailed to plant in this country a system of criminal law procedure fitted to secure justice against offenders.'

undermine the common law. The threat does not only lie in the fact that it is statute law, but that it is United Kingdom statute law.[80] What is being threatened is an idea of Scotland and Scottish identity – the genius of our law – because 'the law is a reflection of the spirit of a people, and so long as the Scots are conscious that they are a people, they must preserve their law'.[81] The power to create would be destroyed, the spirit of the law suppressed. A soulless, alien legality would smother the creative Scottish genius. This apocalyptic vision has restricted our capacity to think about the criminal law, filling the limited imaginary space of the Scots criminal law, blocking the growth of alternative visions. In mythologising the happy and free days of the past, it does not stand in opposition to the present system as it likes to suggest, but is an integral part of it. Its vision of the future is the continual return to the simple pieties of a past that probably never existed. Generally, it raises the more fundamental question of whether the principles of the law, developed by Hume and sustained by the tradition, are adequate to allow us to understand the modern Scottish system. In the following two sections, we will examine this question by looking at the way in which the idea of separate development is embedded in the traditional reasoning of the law.

The common law

Whether the declaratory power is praised, because it is considered to allow for the proper evolution of the law, or condemned, because the system is flexible enough to respond on the basis of existing principles, within the Scottish criminal law tradition there is a shared understanding of the nature of the common law and the collective wisdom that informs its development. The central feature of this view is the belief that the law is a mixture between the principles that were laid down by Hume and a system of precedent akin to the English jurisprudence of the common law, which accepts that the law both can and should develop on a case by case basis.[82] In practice this produces a fundamental ambiguity around the question of authority. This, which derives from the status of Hume as an 'institutional' writer, is central to the operation of the law, and is 'managed' by the judiciary in the following ways. If a line of precedent is leading away from the position the court desires to take, it may be able to disregard it by the

---

[80] Cooper 1957 in particular acknowledges that much of the common law is founded on statutes of the pre-Union Scottish Parliament, p. 283; for an early expression of this fear, see Alison 1833, Introduction. Paterson 1994, ch. 2 makes a similar argument about significance of the autonomy of Scottish institutions.

[81] Cooper 1957, p. 199, continuing 'this would involve the swift annihilation of what is left of Scotland's independent life and culture'.

[82] See Simpson 1973; Postema 1986, ch. 1.

invocation of Hume's statement of the 'true position' of the law. If, on the other hand, Hume does not appear to offer the desired solution then he can safely be regarded as a representative of an earlier age and a more 'up-to-date' solution preferred. Equally, it is frequently argued that in expounding the common law Hume would not have intended to lay down an absolute rule, while, as Sheriff Gordon has pointed out, the High Court has recently shown a disturbing tendency to treat statements by Hume as if they had legislative effect.[83] The ritual invocation of Hume ensures that his authority survives intact, although given this inconsistency there is no absolute standard by which that authority can be judged. The issue here is clearly that of legal validity, but the important point is that the rejection of fixed rules or standards of interpretation does not necessarily entail either indeterminacy or inconsistency – except historically. Nor does it entail the rejection of the principle of legality. It is merely the rejection of the type of conceptual thinking that would regard these positions as inconsistent. We can now begin to see that in the place of indeterminacy there is a practical reason that lends the tradition a measure of internal cohesion.

This is achieved by the emphasis on the practice and experience of the law.[84] Conceptual difficulties are regarded as things that are to be avoided and which can be over-ridden by the requirements of legal practice. This is summed up perfectly by Lord Cooper in his evidence to the Royal Commission on Capital Punishment:

The Scottish law of crime never approaches a problem like this in the abstract. The approach is always from the other end and any attempt to imprison such conceptions within the framework of a definition would be, in my judgement, inevitably disastrous, and would gravely embarrass, even cripple, the administration of law for an indefinite period.[85]

The wisdom of the law lies with the practitioner rather than the legislator or the academic. Legal practice is given priority over abstract theory – after all, who needs theory if you've got native genius!

Once again this can be traced back to Hume. He eschews any discussion of the philosophical basis of either crimes or punishments. This may be

[83] For examples of these positions see: *Brennan v. HM Adv.* 1977 SLT 151 overturning *HM Adv. v Campbell* 1921 JC 1; *Stallard* above, n. 15; *Thomson v. HM Adv.* 1983 SCCR 368 (Lord Justice-General Wheatley). On the uses of Hume generally, see D. M. Walker's introduction to the 1986 reprint of Hume 1844, and Sheriff Gordon's commentary to *HM Adv. v. Wilson* 1983 SCCR 420. The interpretation of Hume on the declaratory power is a prime example of his legislative effect.
[84] 'Decisions and practice make the great body of our criminal law', Lord Deas in *Clendinnen v. Rodger* (1875) 3 Coup 171 at p. 180.
[85] Cooper 1950, p. 432 qn 5398. This sentiment was echoed by the normally more sober Scottish Law Commission: 'We do not believe that there is any need to burden our courts with repeated philosophical analyses of the mental element . . . and we doubt whether our courts as presently constituted could cope with the extra work that would be involved' (1983 para. 2.36).

'amusing and interesting' and provide employment for 'an ingenious mind' but is not relevant to his project which is described as 'the investigation of one peculiar system'.[86] He intends rather 'to initiate the young lawyer in the Elements of our Criminal Practice'.[87] He accordingly rejected the suggestion that there might be a philosophical basis to the ordering of crimes and declares that they should be treated in order of their practical importance.[88] This attitude was to be shared by later treatise writers, principally Alison and Macdonald, who mainly produced simplified and updated versions of Hume for either the student or the practitioner. Archibald Alison, the sheriff of Lanarkshire and historian, published two volumes, on the principles and the practice of the criminal law respectively.[89] The title of the first volume, *The Principles of the Criminal Law in Scotland,* can be misleading, though, for both books are little more than manuals, updating the case law and offering advice to the practitioner on how best to plead and proceed. The principles of the law are sought through attention to the details of practice.[90] This was to reach its most attenuated form in Macdonald's *A Practical Treatise on the Criminal Law of Scotland* which went through five editions between 1867 and 1948 and treated both substantive law and practice in a single volume. Most remarkably of all, given the acknowledged growth in the scale of state regulation between these dates, the fifth edition is shorter than the preceding ones! It was also Macdonald who, as Lord Advocate, introduced the rules that entrenched this approach in Scottish criminal procedure by reducing the strictness of procedural requirements in the interests of speed and economy.[91] It is further indicative of the practical concerns of Scots criminal lawyers that Macdonald records in his memoirs that the bill was prepared on his own initiative while Lord Advocate, without formal

---

[86] Hume 1844, I, p. 14. See also Hume 1797 I, p. 2. Hume's remarks appear to be directed particularly against Lord Kames, 1792 and see Lieberman 1983. See also Hume 1939, p. 5; 'He runs a great risk of becoming ingenious rather than sound as a lawyer, and in his public appearances may oftener do honour to his own acuteness than good to his client's cause.' Also at pp. 6–7.

[87] Hume 1844 I, p. 13. See also Inglis 1863, p. 8: 'There is something in the national character . . . that tends to induce an unphilosophical mode of approaching professional studies.'

[88] Hume 1844 I, pp. 18–19. In large part this meant following Blackstone – this point is treated at length in Cairns 1988; see also below, ch. 4. It is also interesting to note that Hume's views on practice shared something with the English orthodoxy of the time. See Lobban 1991, ch. 3.

[89] Alison 1832 and 1833. Reprinted with introduction by J. Irvine Smith in 1989. An obituary in the leading Scottish law journal described him as 'a manufacturer of incumbrances for bookshelves'! (Anon 1867).

[90] Alison 1883, p. 299: 'Practice had sufficiently shown me that there was principle in every part of the law, and that it was the power of reaching and applying that principle which constituted the great characteristic of a profound lawyer.'

[91] Criminal Procedure (S.) Act 1887 (50 and 51 Vict. c. 35). See Macdonald 1891, pp. 23–31; the fifth edition of Macdonald's *Practical Treatise* was also reissued recently.

consultation and passed without discussion (and almost by accident), by a half-empty Parliament.[92] Both works have achieved a remarkable longevity, though their merits lie in a certain terseness of expression rather than in the reasoned discussion of the law. What is significant about such approaches is not that they are irrational, but that there is an implicit rationality which we may call the jurisprudence of practice. This entails an elevation of the role of the courts and those who work in them. This has a consequence that is not normally acknowledged. At this practical level the 'balance of power' of legalism – between legislature and courts – has been unbalanced and the effects of this must be taken into account. Expressed in more theoretical terms we may say that this is a conception of law that elevates the importance of judgement or adjudication over that of legality or rules.[93] But before we can accept this position we are brought back once again to the need to examine the practice of this reason, that is to say the practice of criminal justice.

A corollary of the importance of practice was the authority of the common law as it was regarded as being of a timeless character, developing through native custom and bearing the 'testimony of experience'. This authority is central to the legitimation of judicial power. Hume accordingly goes to some lengths to present the common law pedigree of the criminal law. When he discusses the sources for his work he explains that he has drawn primarily on native sources such as the Books of Adjournal.[94] He echoes Viscount Stair in arguing that the principal non-native sources, the Civil (Roman) law and English law, can only be regarded as authoritative when they are in accordance with the particular stage of development of the people and the practice of the law.[95] This is to present a complex argument about the sources of the law. It was principally an argument against the civilian tradition, as represented by the work of Mackenzie, which had a radically different approach to the question of authority. For Mackenzie, sovereign power expressed through statute was regarded as the primary source of law. Thus Mackenzie was led to argue, when introducing his discussion of crimes, that, 'It were to be wisht, that nothing were a Cryme which is not declared to be so, by a Statute; for this would make Subjects inexcuseable, and prevent the arbitrariness of Judges'.[96] When this was silent the Roman law could be followed, for these laws 'are of universal use, for crimes are the same almost everywhere'.[97]

---

[92] Macdonald 1915, ch. 35.   [93] Ewald 1987 and 1988.
[94] i.e. the old Justiciary Court records.
[95] Hume 1844 I, pp. 15–18. He prefaces his general lectures on the law of Scotland with a similar set of remarks, 1939, pp. 2–3.
[96] Mackenzie 1678, p. 3. See also MacQueen 1986 (in particular the abstracts of papers by MacQueen and MacLean). For a similar argument, though without the appeal to Roman law, made by Hume's legal contemporary, see McLaurin 1798 II, p. 38.
[97] Mackenzie 1678, p. 7; see also Bayne 1748, pp. 1–2.

In arguing against this, Hume was able to draw on a set of arguments that had become commonplace in eighteenth-century Scotland, to the effect that the laws had to suit the particular situation and stage of development of a country. Thus he argued that the changes 'in the manners, and temper and way of thinking of the nation' which had occurred over the past century in the criminal law and its application to 'real business' had superseded existing texts on criminal law.[98] Criminal jurisdiction was a question for the courts of particular countries. The argument was that Scotland had to be left to develop on the basis of her own experience. It should not be surprising in the light of the argument of the previous section that, in order to sustain this, Hume also drew on a set of beliefs that were the English orthodoxy in the late eighteenth century. What is significant is the way which these were again inverted in order to produce an argument against English interference. His argument echoes the claims of Blackstone that the timeless qualities of the common law and the 'Ancient Constitution', as ratified by the events of 1689, were the primary safeguards of liberty[99] – although in this case it is to maintain the timeless qualities of Scottish institutions in protecting the rights and liberties of the individual. This can be seen most clearly in his comparison of the relative merits of Scottish and English procedure.[100] He points to the advantages of a system of public prosecution under the direction of the Lord Advocate as opposed to the English system where the 'care and cost' of obtaining a prosecution is placed on the aggrieved individual. The Scottish system is one of 'singular and constant moderation, which has prevailed, time out of mind, in the administration of this part of public justice'.[101] This cannot be regarded as an arbitrary system in Scotland,

where such is the care of freedom, the love of justice, and such the high influence of the popular part of the constitution, that any person holding the office of Lord Advocate who should strain his powers, or pervert them to oppressive purposes, would injure alike his own reputation and fortune, and the service of the Crown.[102]

This is followed by an account of the relative leniency of the Scottish sentencing, based on judicial discretion, compared to the punitive English

---

[98] Hume 1844 I, p. 2. Cf. W. Forbes 1730, p. v: 'Human nature having arrived to its present height of deprivation by degrees, the increase of crimes and offences was the just occasion of multiplying criminal laws, which are different in different countries, suited to the genius of the people, the publick exigencies and the situation of affairs'. See also Cairns 1993, pp. 166–8.

[99] Lieberman 1989, ch. 1; Pocock 1987; Lobban 1991; Postema 1986, ch. 1; Kidd 1993. A similar sentiment is expressed by Macdonald above, n. 79.

[100] Hume 1844 I, pp. 3–13.

[101] *Ibid.*, p. 9. The Lord Advocate and the system of public prosecution, incidentally, were far from being timeless but were established in the late sixteenth century as royal power struggled to control the practice of bloodfeud. See K. M. Brown 1986.

[102] Hume 1844 I.

system where there were numerous capital statutes and a correspondingly high use of pardons.[103]

The Scottish penal system almost certainly was lenient but, at the same time possessed a massive repressive capacity – a 'native vigour' – that was more readily available because of the concentration of political and legal control. At the time Hume wrote, the Scottish system had ably demonstrated this capacity in the repressive campaign of the 1790s against political radicalism.[104] Hume, as an active supporter of the Tory party at the time of the Dundas administration of Scotland, was defending the criminal law against criticisms that it was too repressive. It is perhaps also unsurprising that he failed to point out that in the unreformed political system the Lord Advocate was the effective holder of political power through the control of patronage – and so a direct representative of the executive.[105] His argument is therefore more convincing as a justification of the adaptability of the Scottish law and its capacity to maintain the political order established by the settlement of 1689, than as a defence of the liberties of the subject. None the less, the argument against the severities of the English system was not without significance. As Lieberman has recently pointed out, this severity was widely acknowledged, even in England, where contemporary debate, influenced by continental writers such as Beccaria and Voltaire, centred around the means of improving the statute law and reform of the penal system.[106] Hence, Hume's argument that statutes are necessarily harsh and that discretion (including the discretion to create laws) should be left with the judges was also an argument against liberal penal reform – which he refused to discuss.[107] As we have seen, Hume was not concerned with the formal limiting of state power, for the political strength of the common law was that it was to be self-limiting. By a repetition of the English orthodoxy, he was able to use the leniency of the Scots as a particularistic argument for the timeless qualities of the Scottish system.

These connections to controversy about the location of political power

---

[103] See generally Hay et al. 1975; E. P. Thompson 1975; Langbein 1983a. On the leniency of the Scottish system, see also the introduction to Syme's Justiciary Cases 1826–9 claiming that out of the fifty capital cases reported in the volume, there had only been one capital sentence.

[104] Lenman 1981, ch. 9. The repressive capacity of the system was also revealed in the treason trials between 1815 and 1820.

[105] This was the major criticism of H. Cockburn 1824 and 1825. It is instructive to compare the softer views expressed in his 1846 article.   [106] Lieberman 1989, chs. 9 and 10.

[107] This evasion is clearer still in a passage in the first edn of Hume 1797 I, pp. 2–3 which was omitted from subsequent editions: '[S]till less shall I think it any part of my duty, to enlarge at this time in observations on the due measure, proportion or application of punishments, or on the style, the objects, and proper qualities of penal laws, which are rather the business of the political philosopher, than of the lawyer.'

were gradually lost following the breaking of the Dundas system of patronage, the parliamentary reforms beginning in 1832 and the declining fear of political radicalism and disorder. By 1833 we have a settled definition of the Scottish common law: 'This general reference to the laws of the realm is held to imply the whole common law, and such statutes as, by their antiquity and universal usage, have passed, as it were, into the known and customary law of the realm'.[108] That the common law was the best means by which civil liberties can be protected was argued to have been a principle approved by no lesser authorities than the English themselves.[109] This is echoed in Lord Cooper's defence of the principle of legality: 'Unless a system of law and legal administration is maintained in a state of high efficiency and allowed to develop freely in harmony with its own distinctive principles and methods, the Rule of Law in that country will inevitably languish, and it will be the ordinary citizen who will be the victim'.[110] The rule of law, the principle of legality, thus depends not only on the autonomy of the law, but on its relationship with the community, the people of Scotland. We have already seen how the criminal law has been connected with the spirit of the people and so we must now, in considering the relationship between community and wrong, examine how the reasoning of the common law is justified and the judges have come to conceive their role.

Community and wrong

Analyses of the declaratory power have argued over the right of the court to punish any new and extraordinary wrongs, any act that is obviously wrong, or any old wrong that is committed in a new and previously unforeseen manner. This clearly requires that we be able to distinguish between acts that are 'right' and acts that are 'wrong'. Recent discussion devoted to this question has, in the main, attempted to draw principled distinctions between different categories of actions and values in order to determine the limits of the law. We have therefore been presented with the argument that when conduct is simply 'im-moral' then intervention is unjustifiable, but that when it is harmful to persons or property or is dishonest, intervention may not only be justified and necessary, but almost certainly covered by the existing principles of the law.[111] In moving away from the sphere of rules we are moving into the realm of principles, policies and values. But the choice between principles and policies is to be based on other principles and

---

[108] Alison 1833, p. 228.   [109] *Ibid.*, p. xxxi.
[110] Cooper 1957, p. 200. See also T. B. Smith 1961, p. 196; Gibb 1950, pp. 128–9.
[111] T. B. Smith 1962, pp. 124–31; G. H. Gordon 1978, pp. 41–3.

policies,[112] removing the question ever further from the practice of the law. Not only is the 'choice' that we are supposed to possess nugatory – to discuss making the 'right' or 'wrong' choice between competing principles and values is merely to repeat the argument without possibility of resolution – but we are left with the somewhat arbitrary boundary that has been drawn between these different spheres. This requires that we examine the way that this boundary has been drawn within the tradition. In this final section I want to argue that, regardless of the way in which these particular distinctions are drawn, the important element in the reasoning since the time of Hume, encompassing even those whose defence of legality appears to set them outside the dominant tradition, is that 'wrong' is conceived of as a predominantly secular notion. Moreover, its meaning is to be found embedded in the idea of a relation between the 'community' and the law – and 'community', of course, in its widest sense is the nation.

We have already noted that Hume's view of the common law required that the law change with the 'manners and temper of the age'. This claim was underpinned by a more sophisticated argument in which we can see a rejection of the universalising position of the Scottish speculative philosophers. These had sought to argue that society developed in a series of 'stages' towards commercial society, and that the state of the laws would therefore reflect the state of development.[113] In the hands of Kames, at least, these were arguments for changing the law, and in particular for the assimilation of English and Scottish law on the grounds that they had reached a common stage of development. The historically minded Hume accepted the argument about the development of commercial society, but neatly deflects its implications by distinguishing between civil and criminal law. In the former general laws may be necessary for the promotion of free trade, but in the latter the spirit of the laws is strictly national.[114] In civil business, 'it cannot be a matter of any concern to the State, or the administrators of public affairs by what rule the justice of a claim of debt, or the right flowing from any sort of ordinary contract shall be tried . . . But it is quite otherwise as to the law respecting crimes . . .'[115] The criminal law has a much closer dependence on the circumstances of

---

[112] e.g. A. T. H. Smith 1984, p. 58. See, for example, Ashworth 1995, ch. 3 where there is an A–Z of the different principles and policies that inform the modern law. Each principle (a,b,c, etc.) is matched by an opposing one and we are (presumably) supposed to locate ourselves somewhere on the resulting matrix. The end result is highly confusing.

[113] See principally Kames 1792, Preface and Tract I; A. Smith 1978, pp. 103–40, 397–437 and 475–85. See also Stein 1980, ch. 2; Cairns 1988 on Hume's teacher John Millar.

[114] This was also, of course, an argument against the idea of a *ius commune* or civil law. See text supra at pp. 42–3.

[115] Hume 1844 I, p. 16. See also Alison 1833, p. xxxi and T. B. Smith 1961, p. 216. Smith and Cooper take this argument to its furthest extreme by arguing, as we have seen, that the nation survives through its law – hence, if the legal system is assimilated to the English one, the possibility of a Scottish national identity would be lost. Cooper 1957, p. 199.

government and the people because of its relation to, for instance, social rank, the functions of magistrates, the institutions of society, religion, the state of government, the threats posed by foreign enemies and so on. A crime is then defined as 'an infringement on his part of that social regard, which, as a citizen, he owes to the community', as this has been determined by established practice and the collective rationality or wisdom of common opinion.[116]

This obviously idealised vision of community has persisted in the law, in spite of increasingly tenuous links to either notions of political community or the practice of legal institutions. The precise form of this survival will be discussed at greater length in chapter 4, and for the present it is sufficient that we discuss the significance of community to judicial reasoning. The problem is not that this community is represented by the judiciary and not the legislature: it does not bear any relation to an actual community, and so does not raise the issue of political representation.[117] The point is that it is a representation of judicial reasoning, and so must be analysed in terms of the particular judicial practices. Institutionally it is represented by the jury, though this plays only a negligible role in bringing community attitudes into the law.[118] Doctrinally it is represented by the 'reasonable man' – the imaginary jury member or representative of the community. In practice, community is instituted by means of the same process that it must serve to justify.

We can see perfectly how the idea of the community becomes central to the legitimacy of the Scottish law in Sheriff Gordon's account of the law of recklessness. He explains that we should differentiate between the reasonable man used as a 'standard' – in effect as a general way of making objective judgements about community standards – and the reasonable man used as a 'test' – where particular subjective assessments are made about the 'wrongful' character of actions.[119] Regardless of where the

---

[116] Hume 1844 I, p. 21. In this it may be that Hume was influenced by the views of his uncle, David Hume the philosopher, with whom he had a close relationship. The elder had supervised his education (Paton 1958, pp. 327–410). For an exposition of the elder Hume's views on law, see Postema 1986, chs. 3 and 4 esp. at pp. 133–4. Cf. also Blackstone 1765 IV, p. 5: 'a breach and violation of the public rights and duties, due to the whole community, considered as a community, in it's [sic.] social aggregate capacity'.

[117] See e.g. Styles 1993 where the issue is somewhat bizarrely discussed as though it were a question of the representativeness of different political institutions. Since Parliament is not truly representative we should not mind that the judiciary take liberties!

[118] It need hardly be stated once again that jury trial occurs in only about 3 per cent of all cases, the law tightly subscribes the types of issues that may be put to the jury, that the decisions that affect the outcome are all taken much earlier in the criminal process, and so on. For a discussion of all these issues, see McBarnet 1981.

[119] See G. H. Gordon 1978, pp. 244–54. Gordon's work represents the first major attempt to analyse Scottish criminal law in the terms of Anglo-American jurisprudence. It nonetheless remains firmly within the tradition, as this analysis of recklessness suggests. See below, ch. 5 for a more detailed analysis.

distinction might be drawn between subjective and objective tests, this merely demonstrates that judgements of right and wrong are made according to this representation of the community. The judges lay down the law by reference to the experience of the law. The ethos is the practice, and the question of right and wrong is always, emphatically, reduced to the technical legal question of what the courts should do in the particular circumstances. Thus, legitimacy in this account does not depend on an appeal to abstract, universal standards, such as the principle of legality, which could operate as an 'external' measure of the law,[120] but on the historical practice by the means of which the community is produced. In consequence, the criminal law has firmly locked itself into a circle of reasoning where, in an extreme form, the law is in fact precisely what the judges say that it is and legitimation is derived from the relation of the law, and thereby also from the judges as interpreters of the law, to the community.[121]

We can illustrate this point by returning once more to the debate over the declaratory power. We have seen that those who oppose the inherent powers of the court frequently appeal to the principle of legality. T. B. Smith tells us that the way that this principle operates in the Scottish system is by means of a 'plea to the relevancy' of the charge. What this means is that the accused person will ask for the court to consider, in advance of the trial, whether or not the charge sets out a crime known to the law.[122] In other words, the judgement of legality is not made by reference to a constitution, the European Convention on Human Rights or a democratically elected body, but is placed straight back into the hands of the judges. As Teubner has argued, however, such standards could never really be an external point of reference for the legal system.[123] Instead he argues that we should conceive of the social reality or practice of the law as composed of a number of such circular, self-referential relations, seeing the resort to 'external' standards as only ever an attempt to resolve the inevitable self-referentiality of the law. Criminal jurisdiction is founded on just this institutional and 'metaphysical' circularity.[124]

---

[120] Cf. Ewald 1991, p. 146: 'The theory of the average man, then, is an instrument that makes it possible to understand a population with respect only to itself, and without recourse to some external defining factor'.

[121] Although cf. Williams 1978, p. 5: '[I]n criminal cases the courts are anxious to facilitate the conviction of villains, and they interpret the law wherever possible to secure this.'

[122] T. B. Smith 1962, p. 131. See Forsyth 1858, pp. 372–5 for a succinct account of the origins of this process.   [123] Teubner 1989a.

[124] We see this circularity also in positivist definitions of the criminal law e.g. G. H. Gordon 1978, p. 15: 'The criminal law is probably, therefore, sufficiently defined as that branch of the law which deals with those acts, attempts and omissions of which the state may take cognisance by prosecution in the criminal courts.' The point here is not to produce an 'external' account of the law, but to produce an account that recognises the importance of this positivity. This argument is developed at greater length in Farmer 1996.

While this may allow the law to respond to changing social values and so on, the certainty or uncertainty that is produced by this is not the crucial issue for an understanding of criminal jurisdiction. The central point is that because the legal order is based on this relationship – that criminal law will always relate to a particular community at a particular time – it is able, paradoxically, to provide a measure of determinacy. This is the principle of legality, and it can only be understood within the complex of institutions, procedures, and legal and cultural values that we have been elaborating. It is a question that is neither purely technical nor purely abstract, in the sense which legal theory normally understands these terms. The problem is not that the law is unethical or without reason; it is that there has been a failure to reflect on the actual ethos of the law or the form of national isolation that it produces. By the failure to recognise this – which might also have required that they abandon the safe, traditional, view of national identity – the opponents of the declaratory power have merely reinforced the tradition.

Scots law and the case of marital rape

A striking contemporary illustration of the 'genius' of the Scots law, obliging us to reflect on the distinctiveness of Scottish practice, is provided by the celebrated case of *Stallard v. HM Adv.*[125] In this case the Scottish criminal appeal court held for the first time that a man could be guilty of the rape of his wife while the couple were still cohabiting. Prior to this case both Scottish and English law had accepted the general principle that rape within marriage was not a criminal act, so that the case was widely heralded as a breakthrough in the law. In Scotland the success of the prosecution was considered to demonstrate the flexibility that allows the law to change with the judicial perception of contemporary social attitudes. The fact that the English courts were subsequently to follow the same path[126] is more than an ironic footnote to the insularity of Scots law. A brief comparison of the style of reasoning in the two cases in fact offers an unparalleled opportunity for a consideration of the – usually unacknowledged – similarities between the two traditions.

Stallard offers a compelling demonstration of the operation of the principle of legality in contemporary Scottish practice. The stage was set by the accused challenging the relevancy of the charge. For both the trial judge and the judges of the appeal court, a statement in Hume was turned

[125] 1989 S.L.T. 469; 1989 S.C.C.R. 248. For a more detailed discussion, see Farmer 1989b.
[126] See principally *R v. R* [1991] 4 All E.R. 481. It is worth noting that the leading judgement was given by Lord Keith, a Scottish judge, although there is no reason to suppose that the results would have been different with an English judge.

to as the source of the rule. For the trial judge, Lord Mayfield, the question effectively began and ended at this point. Hume's authority could not be called into question. The task was to understand whether the actions of the husband fell within the scope of the general principle laid out by Hume. He concluded that the wife's 'surrender of her person' to her husband would always depend on the facts of the particular case, and could not support a rule giving the husband immunity. He deliberately added the disclaimer that to arrive at this conclusion was not to criminalise a new class of actions by use of the declaratory power, but simply to apply an existing principle.

The judgement of the appeal court shows off other aspects of the tradition. They began by arguing that while Hume is an authoritative source for the general principles of the law of rape, he provides no authority for the husband's immunity from prosecution. It was noted in passing that Hume appeared to have based his statement of the law on the work of an English writer, Sir Matthew Hale. This clearly discredits it since Hume, 'did not regard [English texts] as providing authority for any view he expressed about the law of Scotland'.[127] This antipathy towards England is echoed in the statement that English authorities were of no assistance in settling the case. It is suggested in even more disparaging terms that, 'any change or development in the law of England is likely to require the intervention of Parliament'.[128] It was thus established that there was no authority for Hume's view of the immunity, although his authority as a source of the general principles of the law remained intact. Thus the function of the court, as the true guardian of the common law, must be to determine the potential justifications for the rule: 'In our opinion, the soundness of Hume's view, and its application in the late twentieth century, depends entirely upon the reason which is said to justify it'.[129] The principles of the common law, as expressed by Hume, are subject to alteration according to the exigencies of the social, or legal, situation.

The question of justifications was then reduced to that of changing social attitudes. The low status of women, and their subjection to the domination of their husbands, in the time of Hume was pointed out. By contrast, '[b]y the second half of the twentieth century, however, the status of women, and the status of a married woman, in our law have changed quite dramatically'.[130] The index of change, of course, was a series of alterations in the law of marriage. The answer was then delivered by linking the law to a 'common sense' standard.

A live system of law will always have regard to changing circumstances to test the

---

[127] *Ibid.*, p. 472I.   [128] *Ibid.*, p. 473I.   [129] *Ibid.*, p. 473c.   [130] *Ibid.*, p. 473f.

justification for any exception to the application of a general rule. *Nowadays it cannot seriously be maintained that* by marriage a wife submits herself irrevocably to sexual intercourse in all circumstances.[131]

The question was thus transformed into the practical legal one of 'whether or not as a matter of fact the wife consented to the acts complained of'.[132] In this case the court has not laid down a general rule abolishing the marital rape exemption but only declared broad general guidelines as to what might constitute rape and might apply, depending on the circumstances of the case, to husbands charged with raping their wives.

It should not have come as a great surprise – except to Scots lawyers – that less than two years later the marital rape exemption was to be abolished in England, by a decision of the House of Lords. This court, no less than the Scottish courts, strenuously denied that by doing so they were thereby creating a new crime, claiming instead that they were merely removing a 'common law fiction'.[133] That this claim does not ring true is of less significance than the fact that it chimes with a lengthy historical chorus of such disavowals. Creativity and flexibility have played no less a part in the English than the Scottish criminal law over the last 200 years. The general features of this, in relation both to the common law and to statute, are evident in the case of *R v. R*.[134] The judgement had two limbs, the first concerned the general status of the marital rape exemption in the English law, the second the interpretation of the word 'unlawful' in s. 1(1) of the Sexual Offences (Amendment) Act 1976. The first part of the judgement closely followed the argument in *Stallard*, tracing the exemption back to the statement by Hale and arguing that, due to the changed status of women, the marital rape exemption was no longer justifiable. Hale's statement, it was concluded, is both unacceptable and unjustifiable to 'any reasonable person' in modern times.[135] The difficult question of whether s. 1(1) of the 1976 Act presented an 'insuperable obstacle' to the 'sensible course'[136] of departing from Hale's principle was briskly dealt with by arguing that the word is 'mere surplusage' in the Act.[137]

---

[131] *Ibid.*, p. 473g–h (my emphasis).   [132] *Ibid.*, p. 473k.

[133] [1991] All E.R. 481 at pp. 489–90 – a distinction which is not easily grasped! The defendant's appeal to the European Court of Human Rights on the grounds of the breach of the principle of legality (Art. 7 ECHR) was rejected. See *Times Law Rep*, 5 December 1995.

[134] [1991] All E.R. 481. For general reviews of this, see Ashworth 1995, chs. 2, 3; A. T. H. Smith 1984.

[135] p. 484b. Rather than discussing the justification of the rule at any length, the judgement simply includes a lengthy portion of Lord Emslie's discussion in *Stallard*, pp. 484f–485f.   [136] p. 488c–d.

[137] pp. 488e–489h. Cf. the pre-existing orthodoxy. See e.g. Smith and Hogan 1983, p. 405: 'The phrase 'unlawful sexual intercourse' has been held . . . to mean 'illicit intercourse', that is, intercourse outside the bonds of marriage.'

Although the general argument is unquestionably open to criticism, there is a more interesting process of displacement going on. Even while the court was accepting that Hale's statement was regarded as 'an accurate statement of the common law of England',[138] the authority of the principle was being carefully dismantled. Hale could be depicted as safely anachronistic by the reference to changing social attitudes, represented as we have seen by an appeal to the 'reasonable person'. The authority of the common law is greater than that of any particular writer. Indeed, this allows the indeterminacy of the law to be depicted as a strength rather than a weakness, by suggesting that the authority of the law is specifically derived from its ability to adapt to changing social conditions. The virtual absence of case law is consequently not taken as evidence of the widespread acceptance of the rule, but as implying a mysterious absence of consensus throughout a period of rapid social transformation. Notwithstanding the absence of cases, Lord Keith was able to construct a line of dissent through the cases from *Clarence* (1888) to the present, in order to illustrate 'the absurdity of the fiction of implied consent',[139] and 'the contortions to which judges have found it necessary to resort in face of the fiction of implied consent to sexual intercourse'.[140] The removal of this troublesome fiction, unthinkingly imposed on the common law by Hale, represents an advance, freeing the modern law from the constraints of the past.

If these initial strands of the judgement emphasise the flexibility and maturity of the English common law, the final strand would seem to run contrary to these themes. In dealing with the question of whether the word 'unlawful' in the 1976 Act had embodied Hale's proposition in statute, thereby placing the removal of the exemption beyond the competence of the courts, Lord Keith gave implicit consideration to the relative authority of common law and statute. He argued, somewhat unconvincingly, that to interpret the word 'unlawful' so as to mean 'outside the bonds of marriage' would mean that Parliament had implicitly abolished the common law exceptions to the exemption. It was, he concluded, 'in fact inconceivable that Parliament should have had such an intention'.[141] The strength of this argument relies on the presumption of the primacy of the common law: it pre-dates statute law and can only be altered by the explicit words of

---

[138] p. 483j. Although the rather random citation of early authorities at this point (Hale, East, Archbold) produces the implication that Hale was not representing a common opinion.

[139] p. 486g–h: 'that although the use of force to achieve sexual intercourse was criminal the actual achievement of it was not.'

[140] p. 487c: 'in general acts which would ordinarily be indecent but which are preliminary to an act of normal sexual intercourse are deemed to be covered by the wife's implied consent to the latter, but that certain acts, such as fellatio, are not to be so deemed.'

[141] p. 489c–d.

Parliament. In an inversion of our normal conception of the sovereignty of Parliament – the rule of law – statute law is prevented from making any encroachment onto the territory of the common law.[142]

This creativity and flexibility in interpretation has long been supplemented by an implicit belief by the courts in the existence of a power to punish new and immoral actions.[143] Without undertaking a general review of judicial law-making in the English criminal law or getting entangled in arguments as to the current status of these powers, it is clear that such declaratory theories of law rely on the idea of a residual jurisdiction of the courts of common law, derived in turn from a traditional authority that is a curious combination of beliefs in the age and modernity, but above all the superiority, of the common law. The apparently contradictory nature of the themes is once again resolved by reference to community standards and the importance of finding practical solutions to problems as they arise. Thus, although the English criminal law works within different constraints – principally the fact that most of the common law of crime has been consolidated by statute – it would appear that the elements of creativity and flexibility are no less important to its conception of legality. There are, therefore, important similarities with the Scottish legal tradition.

We might be tempted to conclude by simply pointing out, or bemoaning, the lack of distinctiveness of the Scottish legal tradition. Perhaps the only truly distinctive feature of Scots law lies in the formalisation of the existence of the power. It is unsurprising, then, that the Scots should be slow to acknowledge the similarities with the English! Equally, it is clear that the significance of the principle of legality has been over-exaggerated. Creativity was, and is, part and parcel of the English law, though the issue has never occupied such a central position – the modern English law being largely preoccupied with questions of the conditions of responsibility, rather than the scope or content of the law. The criminal law in Scotland, as we have seen, does not conceive of itself as a branch of philosophical or ethical reasoning in this way. This, though pointing to the possibility of shared misunderstandings of the nature of the modern law, serves principally to underline our earlier conclusion that ideas of creativity and flexibility are vital to the imagination of Scots law.

[142] See the discussion in Goodrich 1986, pp. 40–2. Note also that the normal presumption of statutory interpretation that penal statutes should be construed in favour of the accused person is discarded here.
[143] Celebrated recent examples include *Shaw v. D.P.P.* [1962] A.C. 220 (conspiracy to corrupt public morals); *Knuller v. D.P.P.* [1973] A.C. 435 (conspiracy to outrage public decency); *R v. Brown* [1992] 2 All E.R. 552 (on defence of consent to assault); *R v. Manley* [1933] 1 K.B. 529 (public mischief, wasting the time of the police). For historical reviews, see Jackson 1936–8; Allen 1931, pp. 244–6.

Conclusions

The debate on the inherent powers of the High Court is thus important precisely because it is so central to the self-understanding of the identity of the Scottish tradition. It sets an external boundary that also orders the internal space of the law in the ways that we have explored. The central orientation is towards practice and the avoidance of the abstract. Hence a recent attempt to argue that the inherent power could be surrendered by the court because it is only a practice rule and not a legal principle, fundamentally misses the point.[144] The practice is the principle in the Scottish system and it makes no difference what distinctions we attempt to draw between the various activities of the High Court. While it is ironic that the 'foundational' passage in Hume on the inherent power is drawn from the Introduction, normally cited badly out of context, and treated as a legal principle, this is not an adequate explanation of the practice. We should not be distracted by academic commentators repeatedly pointing to instances where Hume is taken out of context by the High Court. It is not enough to argue for 'more correct' readings of Hume or any other text in the absence of an understanding of the encompassing criminal law tradition – within which the question of the significance of Hume remains largely unexplored.

Through the idea of tradition, we have thus arrived at a more complex version of the criteria of legality, which was the primary object of this chapter. This is clearly a broader notion than that of legal principles, since we have seen that the understanding of principle is related to a wider set of legal and cultural values. The Scottish legal tradition is one of the experiences through which was built the sense of national identity that it claims to represent. As our analysis of the tradition moved between a historical account of its origins and specific examples of judicial reasoning, it became clear that these values do not lie behind or outside the law, as romantic but harmless idiosyncrasies of the Scottish system, but are also 'the unsung precondition of practical lawyering'.[145] The Scottish criminal law's reconstruction of an 'invented tradition', which is its own imaginary past,[146] is essential to the everyday operation of the law. The boundary that is sought to be drawn between text and context thus dissolves even as we become aware of the significance of national boundaries. It is a rationality which offers a reflexive account of its own past, of a particular legal order. The picture that emerges is of a tradition that is narrow, conservative, and inward-looking. It has been shaped, even distorted, by

---

[144] Willock 1989.   [145] Krygier 1986, pp. 237–62 at p. 246.
[146] Hobsbawm 1983. Cf. Macintyre 1985, ch. 15, who has the less conservative notion of tradition as an argumentative retelling of history.

its continual need to display its ability to maintain or sustain order, driven by a fear of the intervention of the Anglo-British state. Its 'sturdy nationalism' rests continually on the verge of a descent into paranoia. The concern with limits exhibited within the Scottish tradition is hence a concern with national borders and competences and the encroachments on these, rather than the typical modern concern with the limits of state power over the individual. The tradition holds the exercise of power out as something that is self-limiting, but this form of self-limitation is questionable. No doubt it is harder to be concerned with the limits of state power when you do not possess a state, but crucially, perhaps, it is harder also to limit state power!

But if this is a picture of a closed system of law, a number of questions remain. In our examination of the features of the dominant tradition, mapping the criteria of legality, we were in each case drawn to conclude that they are in some way unusable or limited, beginning a series of displacements that challenge in a more explicit way the boundaries and divisions of the law. The sense of maturity conflicts with understandings of the modernity of the law; the sense of national identity is muted and conservative; the finding of practical solutions has been elevated over an understanding of our practices; and generally there is the failure to reflect on the ethos of the law. We have repeatedly come up against these further boundaries. This requires that we undertake some form of reconstruction. The tradition can also be read as making a series of claims – about the nature of the criminal law, about the past, about the practice of law, about national identity and so on. In the next three chapters we will investigate some of these historical claims, specifically in relation to the nature of the criminal justice system, the substantive law and finally, by taking the specific case of the law of homicide, the conceptual structure of the law. In each case we will attempt to construct a historical account of legal practice that also addresses the question of how the particular reflexive account of the legal system developed. These alternative histories, or conflicting interpretations,[147] open the possibility of challenging the legitimacy of a tradition and this is what we must do by developing our analysis of the assumptions that underlie much legal doctrine.

An example of how this type of reconstruction might be brought into critical engagement with the law, in the manner that was discussed in the introductory chapter, emerges from the analysis in this chapter, and it is worth considering it briefly. We have seen that the question of community is central both to the substantive law and the wider conception of national identity. The critical force of our argument for legal practices could rest,

[147] Macintyre 1977, pp. 453–72.

then, on its leverage at precisely this point. We would envisage this operating in three principal respects. First, having argued that the principle of legality is intimately linked to the understanding of community, it would be unrealistic to argue for an understanding of either legality or community that was removed from these practices. Accordingly we must seek to reconstruct the place of community within the legal practices and institutions rather than relying on an idealised notion of political or ethical community that exists outside the law.[148] Second, we would need to build a more complete understanding of the operation of the idea of community in Scottish legal thought, specifically in the definition of particular crimes and concepts such as responsibility, and in the construction of moral arguments. The very vagueness of this notion may then allow for the presentation of 'better' ideas of community in legal arguments – in the sense of being more democratic and accountable than present practices. The force of the argument can derive from the fact that it utilises a concept that is already centrally lodged in legal doctrine. This is not to privilege community over legality, but to attempt to keep both ideas in play and to exploit the relation between them. Third, at a more general level, the idea of community allows for the possibility of a debate over the identity of our legal institutions. We have been able to open up the connections between legal practice and a conservative version of nationalism. Legal change would not necessarily entail the loss of separate identity, as we have been taught to assume, but it would entail the replacement of this backward-looking form of self-knowledge with alternative versions. There may be no absolute standards by which we can judge the law, but this provides us with the opportunity, provided that we orient this to current practices, to put a greater range of ideas about the law into play. The point is that we should not condemn out of hand but recognise the potentialities of such a system. It should be stressed above all that this is not a grand attempt to restore fundamental principles or a lost sense of community, that may never have existed outside the minds of a narrow legal elite. It is instead an argument for a better historical understanding of the criminal law and legal institutions.

[148] Rose 1995, esp. at p. 483.

3   The judicial establishment: the
     transformation of criminal jurisdiction
     1747–1908

Introduction

Beginning his treatise on the trial and punishment of crimes, Hume uses
the term 'the judicial establishment' to describe the nature and powers of
the various criminal courts in Scotland.[1] One of his principal concerns is
that of establishing the ancient and independent lineage of the central,
royal courts, in order to underline their contemporary status as sovereign
and independent courts of law. That this goes so clearly beyond the
declared remit of the work, that of the mere practical exposition of the
rules governing the jurisdiction of the various courts, should no longer
surprise us. By establishing their historical pedigree, and by presenting the
account as a series of practical legal questions, the argument seeks to place
the courts beyond history – that is to say, beyond political pressures and
demands and into the universal and particularistic present of the law. The
term is thus particularly apt, conveying the sense not only of the structure
but also of the permanence of the courts. In this chapter, we shall also take
up the analysis of the 'judicial establishment'. In particular, we shall
examine developments in the area of criminal jurisdiction – understood in
the loose sense of the spatial ordering and application of the criminal law –
in the century following the publication of Hume's work.[2] But in doing
this we shall go beyond the Humean account of jurisdiction in more than
the temporal sense, for we shall elaborate an additional sense of the
'judicial establishment'. The phrase also suggests that legal order is

[1] Hume 1844 II, pp. 1–31. The second volume of the fourth edition was originally published
separately in 1800 in two volumes as *Commentaries on the Law of Scotland respecting Trial for
Crimes.*
[2] Questions relating specifically to the substantive jurisdiction of the law will be dealt with in
the next chapter.

something that is judicially established, or founded on judicial practice. It is not timeless and universal, but is part of a process by which a complex of ideas and institutions is brought into being and continually renews itself. This directs our attention towards the judicial role, in case law and legal doctrine, in the drawing of the boundaries and divisions that constrain legal practice. By elaborating the process of 'judicial establishment', not only can we open out Hume's account, but also establish the basis for a broader historical analysis of criminal jurisdiction based on the development of legal practice. It is this that is central to the argument of this chapter.

This particular area has been chosen because it is the point of intersection of a number of important questions. In conventional modern usage the term jurisdiction refers to technical legal questions, and along with issues of procedure is generally ignored by legal theorists and historians alike. Historically, however, the term designated the power of law as such. It raised questions of the political ordering and administration of a territory. It was conceived of as a form of royal or individual property, rather than as a legal or administrative unit. It measured the extent and limits of sovereign authority, demarcating national boundaries. The transition to the specifically legal or administrative sense of the term can thus be seen as a decisive moment in the modernisation of the law, raising questions of the ordering and distribution of political power in the nation state. The concept of jurisdiction also denotes questions of legal ordering. It regulates the legal competence to judge or punish. It links questions of substantive law and questions of procedure, for, at the most basic level, the type of court and the procedure used are central elements in the categorisation and proof of crimes. Additionally, it is specific to the modern understanding of jurisdiction that it can denote different types of procedure, which fact, I shall argue, is central to developing an understanding of the modern legal order. Finally, it should be recalled that the concept of jurisdiction provides a link between our empirical and theoretical concerns, when it is used in the sense of the rationality by which a certain field of law is ordered or brought into being.[3] The development of criminal jurisdiction is in part the history of the development of the imaginary space that is occupied by the territory of the law. If the argument so far has drawn attention to the failures of the tradition to explain the boundaries of the modern law, in this chapter we go on to develop our own critical understanding of these.

We have two distinct aims in view. The primary object is to trace the formation of the modern, and specifically legal, understanding of criminal

[3] See chapter 1, at pp. 12–18.

jurisdiction. The second is to look at the formation and development of the tradition as this articulates itself in relation to developments in legislation and practice in the area of jurisdiction. The discussion will accordingly be divided into two parts. In the first we will look at criminal jurisdiction in Scotland between the passing of the Abolition of Heritable Jurisdictions Act in 1747[4] and the Summary Jurisdiction (S.) Act 1908.[5] The former has been chosen because it is conventionally regarded as the statute which established the modern Scottish criminal justice system. The latter is an appropriate finishing point because, together with the Criminal Procedure (S.) Act 1887,[6] this Act effectively codified Scottish criminal procedure, and consequently our modern understandings of jurisdiction. Although the emphasis will be firmly on the Scottish case, it will, however, be argued by reference to parallel developments in England that there was a more general transformation in the nature of legal power. In the second section we shall go on to look at the ways that the tradition has attempted to make sense of, or rationalise, these changes. In particular we will look at the reception of the statutorily created area of summary criminal jurisdiction, which presents an apparent threat to the vision of order represented by the tradition, to see how the tradition responds to and explains these developments through the manipulation of already existing terminology and categories.

Mysteries of the lower courts: criminal jurisdiction 1747–1908

Jurisdiction is a power conferred on a judge or a magistrate to take cognisance of and determine debateable questions according to law, and to carry his sentences into execution. Taking the widest construction of the terms 'judge' and 'magistrate' jurisdiction necessarily implies the existence of a power conferred by the state and vested in functionaries sanctioned for that purpose by the state.[7]

The Law of Scotland commits summary criminal jurisdiction to all Inferior Judges . . . [They] try by virtue of it the whole of the minor crimes recognised by the common law and most of the punishable offences created by Acts of Parliament. The number of persons affected by procedure of a summary character thus exceeds by many times the number of those arraigned before the more solemn tribunals . . . [This] necessitates an examination of the principles controlling its exercise . . .[8]

Between the beginning and end of this period the criminal justice systems of both Scotland and England underwent a radical transformation. In its

---

[4] 20 Geo. II c. 43.   [5] 8 Edw. VII c. 65.   [6] 50 and 51 Vict. c. 35.
[7] From *Dunbar v. Skinner* 1849 11D 945, quoted in Dalrymple and Gibb 1946, p. 161.
[8] H. H. Brown 1895, p. xix.

broadest terms, the shift is from a system composed of a number of overlapping feudal jurisdictions where central control and formal ordering is weak, to a system of hierarchical courts with increasingly detailed rules of internal ordering and a relatively high degree of central control. The broad lines of this transformation are generally interpreted as part of the movement towards centralisation and formalisation – of policing, prosecution and so on – and indeed the growth of criminal justice that is said to be characteristic of the modern state. However, few of the historical accounts have sought to analyse the emergence of summary jurisdiction more systematically, or to assess its significance to our modern understanding of criminal justice.[9] The increase in the use of summary procedures is generally seen as contributing to the expansion of criminal justice by facilitating the prosecution of crimes. The decrease in formality is said to be offset by decreases in the amount of punishment inflicted and the increased efficiency of summary process. However, by portraying it solely as a small element in this movement, the larger significance of summary criminal jurisdiction has been lost. In this section it will be argued that, as the system of criminal procedure was formalised, the legal understanding of jurisdiction moved from being that of who had the authority to order and control geographical areas of the country and its inhabitants towards being strictly a technical legal question. It comes to be defined in terms of procedure and powers of disposal, linked only in a secondary way to questions of geography or the nature of the offence. As the modern system of criminal justice has come to be dominated by the statutorily created area of summary criminal jurisdiction, this has transformed its character. In short, rather than understanding the modern system in terms of a process of rationalisation with its origins in the mid-eighteenth century, it will be argued here that it is characterised by the transformation that occurred in the second half of the nineteenth century.

The establishment of central organisation

The Abolition of Heritable Jurisdictions Act 1747 is regarded as the point at which the transition from the pre-modern to the modern criminal justice system is made. With this Act, it is argued, the old system of feudal courts was abolished, and the foundations of the 'centralised and formally

---

[9] Very little has been written about the rise of summary criminal jurisdiction in spite of its obvious impact on the functioning of the modern criminal justice system. For the little that there is, see Radzinowicz and Hood 1986, pp. 618–24; Gattrell 1980, pp. 274 and 302–5; Manchester 1980, pp. 160–2; McBarnet 1981, pp. 138–143; Jackson 1937, pp. 132–8; see Davis 1984 and 1989 for an account of the business dealt with by police courts in London. There are basic general accounts in Philips 1977, ch. 4 and Emsley 1987, ch. 7.

structured order were laid'.[10] It is thus an appropriate starting point. The Act was passed as a result of English pressures to place the Highlands of Scotland under government control following the Jacobite Revolt of 1745–6. Although Scotland was theoretically protected against legislation of this type by the Articles of Union 1707 (Arts. XVIII and XIX), there was sufficient consensus among the Scottish governing classes about the contribution of the jurisdictions to Jacobitism and the need for reform that the legislation was passed without difficulty – to the extent of being drafted by the principal Scottish law officers.[11] One of the aims was to subject the administration of justice to central control by breaking the traditional structures of feudal authority that bound the courts and their officials to the local nobility. This is stated in the first section of the Act where, under the rubric of making more effective provision for the administration of justice, three separate justifications are offered. These are,

for restoring to the Crown the Powers of Jurisdiction originally and properly belonging thereto, according to the Constitution, and for extending the Influence, Benefit and Protection of the King's Laws and Courts of Justice to his Majesty's Subjects in Scotland, and for rendering the Union more complete.

Although couched in terms that imply that this process is in fact the restoration of the property of the crown in jurisdiction, it is clear that the Act is an assertion of the right of the Crown to control and administer the country. One member of Parliament expressed this purpose concisely as 'to carry off the King into every part of the United Kingdom'.[12] The principal effect of the Act was to gather the control of jurisdiction into the hands of the Crown where it had otherwise been sold or granted in perpetuity to certain families. Certain courts and offices were abolished altogether, in particular the jurisdictions of justiciary and regality whose power had vied with that of the royal courts.[13] The hereditary office of sheriff was abolished, and the judicial powers of the high sheriff removed (s. 30). The jurisdiction of the sheriff survived, with the powers and duties of the sheriff being assumed by a new body of professionally qualified sheriff deputes. In this form the sheriff court was destined to become the centre-piece of the system of legal administration. The remaining feudal courts either had their jurisdiction reduced or more clearly defined. The capital jurisdiction of the baron courts, which in theory had meant that

[10] Davies 1980, p. 120; J. I. Smith 1958; see also Young, forthcoming, ch. 3.

[11] For reports on the passage of the bill, see Scots Magazine 1747. See also Phillipson 1990, ch. 1; Kidd 1993, pp. 150–60; Lenman 1981, pp. 1–2, 24–5. A footnote to the passing of the Act is contained in a letter from Walpole to Seymour Conway: 'The majority was 233 against 102. Pitt was not there, the Duchess of Queensberry had ordered him to have the gout' (quoted in Agnew 1893 II, p. 331).   [12] Quoted in Colley 1992 at p. 119.

[13] See McNeill 1984, pp. 90–3 for a detailed account of the powers of a regality. Cf. Hume 1844 II, p. 30.

they had powers of punishment equal to those of the supreme court, was abolished – although it had long fallen into desuetude. Its remaining competences were to deal with 'Assaults, Batteries and smaller Crimes' with a power to punish limited to twenty shillings, putting the delinquent in the stocks for a period of up to three hours or, under certain circumstances, imprisonment for up to a month in cases of default (ss. 17–19).[14] The remainder of the Act laid down mechanisms of central control.

This was to be done by means of the improved regulation of the inferior courts. This took place at two levels. First, the Act established the central role of the sheriff court. At a national level the network of sheriff courts was to be the means by which the other local courts were to be supervised.[15] The sheriff's powers over the lower courts included such things as the control of their records and the legality of their practices in the committal of persons to prisons (ss. 18 and 19). This link to the central power was subsequently reinforced by the requirement that the sheriff depute attend the circuits of the Justiciary Court.[16] Sheriff deputes were to be appointed on a more professional basis, according to their level of legal qualification, rather than their local connections. The post was to be held *ad vitam aut culpam* and the judge was made subject to legal penalties for neglect of duty or abuse of position (s. 29).[17] Courts were to be held more regularly and on a more public basis, and a requirement that sheriff deputes were obliged to be resident in their sheriffdoms for at least four months in every year was intended to prevent the appointment of poorly qualified local substitutes who would merely perpetuate the inadequacies of the previous system.[18] By the end of the century this, and the provision of more adequate salaries, seems gradually to have had the effect of forging stronger links with the centre.

The second level of supervision was exercised through the circuits of the High Court (ss. 31–40).[19] The Crown had been trying for many years to extend the influence of the Justiciary Court by providing for annual journeys to certain larger provincial towns in order to try the more serious cases (which would otherwise be settled by local courts) and to review the

[14] See Erskine 1871 I, iv, 28, p. 107: 'These restrictions lie so heavy on the baron, that they amount nearly to a prohibition of this branch of his jurisdiction.'

[15] Whetstone 1981, p. 9.   [16] 25 Geo. III c. 45.

[17] Cf. Claim of Right 1689; Hume 1844 II, p. 66.

[18] Whetstone 1981, pp. 5–11; Young forthcoming, ch. 3; Lenman 1981, pp. 24–5. The residence requirement was widely regarded as impractical, there being insufficient work or money to entice qualified lawyers to leave Edinburgh. It was eventually repealed in 1838 (1 and 2 Vict. c. 119 s. 9).

[19] The terms High Court, Justiciary Court, and High Court of Justiciary are used interchangeably to refer to the central and supreme criminal court of Scotland. The modern usage is to refer to it as the Justiciary Court.

decisions of the lower courts. This procedure was formally instituted with the establishment of the High Court of Justiciary in 1672 and purported to be a continuation of the old, and largely ineffective, system of travelling royal justices (Justice Ayres). In spite of further legislation the system had never fully taken root.[20] The new provisions were finally to be successful in establishing this function of the Court. They provided for twice yearly circuits (s. 31), for an appeal in less serious cases to the High Court on circuit rather than in Edinburgh (s. 34), and for the alteration of circuits as the circumstances of business and population demanded (s. 39). The foundations for the central control of criminal justice had thus clearly been laid by 1750 – although it is also clear that the practice still lacked uniformity. Yet I think that, in their rush to recognise this point, Scottish historians have created two blind spots. The first is that it has led historians to overlook the sense in which the Act is also part of a much older movement towards centralisation. The second, of greater importance for our argument, is that by the failure to place the Act in this context we have been prevented from seeing what is specific to later developments.

The abolition of heritable jurisdictions has been accorded considerable significance by both contemporaries and later historians. Following on the defeat of the Jacobites in 1746, and the end of the political threat to the Union, the Act was seen as a decisive movement towards modernisation. It swept away the barriers of feudalism that were seen to have both encouraged Jacobitism and blocked economic development. In certain circles this has even been seen as marking the completion of the Union and hence the starting point of modern Scottish history.[21] However, if we look more closely at the terms in which the Act deals with jurisdiction, the changes in the administration of justice can appear as much less radical. It is quite clear that there was no desire completely to sweep away feudal jurisdiction. Most obviously, in sections 20–2 there are a series of provisions stating that the jurisdiction of the proprietors of fairs, markets and mines (coal works and salt works) is to be preserved except in cases inferring the penalties of loss of life or demembration.[22] What seems peculiar to us in this instance is that such proprietorship should be regarded as 'jurisdiction', which we conceive of in predominantly legal terms. It seems stranger still that this 'jurisdiction' should be preserved if the Act were indeed the foundation of the modern order. There are other

---

[20] For an account of these failures, see Hume 1844 II, ch. 1 part 1; Cameron 1988; cf. Davies 1980, p. 150 which has them already on a more regular basis by 1709.

[21] Kidd 1993, pp. 150–60.

[22] This is a reference to the servitude of colliers which was not to be abolished until 1799 (39 Geo. III c. 56).

clear continuities with the older system. As we have already noted, many of the old courts and jurisdictions remain, albeit with their powers somewhat diminished. Some, indeed, survived well into the nineteenth century before being abolished or restructured. The Admiralty Court still possessed and occasionally used its power to try for all criminal offences 'upon the seas, and in all ports, harbours or creeks of the same, and upon fresh waters and navigable rivers below the first bridges, or within the flood marks',[23] and it was not abolished until 1830.[24] At the level of the burghs, as we shall see shortly, feudal powers survived well into the nineteenth century, and it would also appear that institutions such as the army and the church continued to exercise some separate jurisdiction.[25] From this point of view, then, the scope of the Act must be regarded more narrowly. It limited feudal jurisdiction only when it appeared to threaten the claim to universal jurisdiction of the central sovereign power. It only introduced reforms into two courts, albeit with the aim of establishing a national network of control over the others. The provisions relating to the regularisation of circuit courts were only the fulfilment of a long existing project. These moves established broad similarities with the administration of justice in England.[26] Just as the central supervisory role of the sheriff court was similar to the operation of the courts of Quarter Sessions, the circuit courts were equivalent to the system of Assizes that had existed for a long time in England. Although there were also important differences, notably in the much earlier centralisation of royal justice in England and in the professionalisation of the Scottish system, these similarities should not be overlooked. Even if it would not do to exaggerate the level of central control over criminal justice in the late eighteenth century, in both systems there was a two-tier system of control in place, operating at the county or burgh and at the national level, gathering the control of

[23] Statute 1681 c.16 restating existing powers. As late as 1827 this court tried a case of culpable homicide, *McHaffie* (Hume 1844 II, p. 192). This was clearly unusual. Statistics for the years 1805–10 show that there were no criminal trials in the Admiralty Court (PP.1812.X.217).   [24] 11 Geo. IV and 1 Wm. IV c. 69.

[25] Hume 1844 II, p. 34. Cf. England, where J. S. Cockburn 1991, pp. 87–90 suggests that military jurisdiction over common law crimes survived until the 1820s.

[26] The Quarter Sessions were meetings of the JPs for each county or borough that dealt with minor felonies and remitting cases of a more serious nature to the Assizes. This court also supervised the actions of justices acting individually or in pairs who committed the more serious cases that were brought before them to trial before the Quarter Sessions, but also through a review of the summary convictions that they handed down. See e.g. Landau 1984, esp. chs. 8 and 11; Bláckstone 1765 IV, ch. XIX; Stephen 1883 I, ch. 4. Although the Quarter Sessions theoretically possessed capital jurisdiction over all felonies excluding treason, commentators are agreed that by the eighteenth century this had narrowed to cover only petty larcenies and misdemeanours. Its jurisdiction was subsequently formally limited by 5 and 6 Vict. c. 38 (1842).

jurisdiction into the hands of the crown.[27] There is thus a definite sense in which the Act should be read alongside the earlier history of attempts by the sovereign power to impose its authority on, or to 'civilise', the unruly peripheries of the nation.[28]

It is interesting to assess the significance that Hume, as a near contemporary, accords the Act. He regards it as having simply regulated the behaviour of sheriff deputes and circuit courts rather than as having introduced radical changes in the legal organisation of jurisdiction.[29] While he might properly be viewed as someone with other political axes to grind, the clear implication of his work is that the Act should be seen, along with the Claim of Right 1689, the Act regulating unlawful imprisonment (1701), and the abolition of the Privy Council (1708) as steps taken for the legalistic curbing of despotic (Catholic) absolutist monarchy.[30] From this perspective, provisions professionalising judges, protecting them against arbitrary removal and the influence of local barons, while at the same time attempting to ensure their freedom from monetary corruption (s. 43) and ensuring their loyalty by making them take an oath of allegiance, make perfect sense. Placing the origins of the jurisdiction of the Scottish courts in the period before the Union, this is another example of the 'safe' nationalism that was discussed in the last chapter. The familiar litany of dates suggests that the Abolition of Heritable Jurisdictions Act is viewed as a step in the improvement of liberties protected by the Anglo-British constitution. Scottish liberties are to be protected by emphasising the historical role of Scottish institutions in their protection. Thus, it would appear from the means by which central control is sought that the 1747 Act was aimed at streamlining the operation of the system established in the late seventeenth century rather than introducing something new. This system was to resist further

---

[27] Blackstone 1765 IV, ch. XIX, lists eleven different courts of criminal jurisdiction but notes that practically all were obsolete or purely ceremonial at the time of writing. See also Landau 1984, ch. 12 on the rule of law and the changing practice of JPs in the eighteenth century.

[28] Scots Magazine 1747, p. 58; see K. M. Brown 1986, pp. 269–72 for the earlier history of this project. In this connection it is also interesting to note that the mid-eighteenth century was the period in which the Highlands of Scotland were comprehensively mapped for the first time, see Withers 1992, p. 147. Cf. Blomley 1994, pp. 75–105.

[29] Hume 1844 II, ch. 1.

[30] Note also that one grievance of the Claim of Right was against the assertion by Charles II, in an Act of Parliament (1681 c. 18), that the Sovereign had an absolute power over the other jurisdictions (i.e. cumulative jurisdiction). Cf. Scots Magazine 1747, pp. 129–33 condemning the 1747 Act for undermining the Claim of Right and the Act of Union. See also Inglis 1863 for a celebratory view of the growing strength of the legal profession in seventeenth century Scotland. Also see D. Forbes 1975, p. 179 on the reaction of David Hume, the philosopher, to the 1747 Act.

transformation until the 1830s because of legislative inertia and the entrenched power of the political and legal elite in Scotland.[31]

The issue up to the end of this period was clearly viewed as one of the control and regulation of the various forms of legal jurisdiction. This was a struggle over the 'Power of the Sword'[32] – that is to say over the question of the source of the power to judge and punish crimes. The principal concern was, thus, with the existence of other sources of power rather than with an intensive control over the exercise of that power.[33] That this was also conceived of as a question of the political control of territory, and consequently of its inhabitants, merely serves to underline the fundamental connection between juridical sovereignty and territorial space.[34] This was done by the means of creating a single law, and hence a single source of authority – though with the result that the sovereign was also to be bound by the law that they had created. By the late eighteenth century this sovereignty was all but unchallenged. The Justiciary Court could claim an 'almost universal' jurisdiction over the territory and inhabitants of Scotland.[35] Or, as Alison was to put this in more extravagant terms: 'The Court of Justiciary is the Supreme Criminal Tribunal over all Scotland, and its jurisdiction in criminal matters is both universal in point of extent and supreme in point of degree'.[36] To be sure, insofar as the object was to regulate the inefficiencies of the existing economy of power, we can see the origins of the modes of administration that were to characterise the modern criminal justice system.[37] But these were secondary concerns. There was little interference with the substantive jurisdictions of the courts, in the sense of dealing with the internal questions of the regulation of overlapping jurisdictions. This was not yet a system of criminal justice in the modern sense. Reform of the burghs and other inferior criminal jurisdictions was a matter that only came to be addressed in the early years of the nineteenth century.

The reform of the inferior courts

The 1747 Act reinforced lines of control between the central and local courts – a loosely hierarchical system – which to some extent still exist today. The jurisdiction of the High Court was universal but the jurisdiction of the other courts at this stage, if it could be defined precisely at all,

[31] Cf. Beattie 1986, Conclusion, where a similar periodisation is suggested for the English system.   [32] W. Forbes 1730, p. 215.
[33] Murphy 1991, pp. 196–7 points to the importance of establishing exclusivity of jurisdiction.   [34] Foucault 1991a, p. 93.   [35] Hume 1844 II, p. 31.
[36] Alison, 1833, p. 1.
[37] See Scots Magazine 1747, p. 58 where the reform is justified in terms of the speed, economy and utility that it would offer. Cf. Foucault 1977, pp. 78–9.

was defined negatively – in terms of the cases they could not handle or the powers that they did not possess. Following the purported rationalisation by the 1747 Act, there remained four principal courts of inferior jurisdiction: the sheriff court; the justice of the peace (JP) courts; burgh courts, which could be either royal or baronial in their grant of jurisdiction; and barony courts. By 1800 these began to be joined by a fifth, of increasing importance. These were the police burgh courts, created by local statutes from 1797 onwards.[38] The jurisdiction of these courts was certainly surrounded with great confusion. Writing contemporaneously Hume stated that, 'the application and extent of their powers are very liable to controversy, and has not been settled by any uniform or consistent practice'.[39] Jurisdiction appears to have been roughly cumulative. Different courts might, and did, exist within the same geographical area, and their powers depended more on the particular statute or charter that had brought it into being than on any rules of general application. Even then jurisdiction would, in practice, simply depend on what was deemed expedient or on the social or economic status of a particular district or parish.[40] In the absence of records from these courts, and the consequent absence of detailed historical research, we continue to know little about either the competences or the operation of the inferior Scottish courts at the beginning of the nineteenth century.[41]

The sheriff court appears historically to have had a slightly wider jurisdiction than the other inferior courts, something preserved and reinforced by the 1747 Act. According to Hume, they were able to try all transgressions against the common or ancient statute law, and held this power cumulatively with all other courts in the sheriffdom.[42] At times this had been considered to extend to even murder or robbery provided that the trial and sentence was carried out within a single day of the offence. By the eighteenth century, however, this had fallen into desuetude for, as Hume pointed out, 'it is difficult to imagine, how any trial can possibly be absolved, with the observance of those forms which are now esteemed material to justice'.[43] Procedure limited jurisdiction. As a consequence, although the sheriffs still possessed the power to pronounce sentence of death, they were unlikely to have occasion to use it, 'there being an

---

[38] See Carson and Idzikowska 1989. In England stipendiary police magistrates were established in the metropolitan area of London in 1792 (32 Geo. III c. 53). See also Beattie 1986, ch. 6 and (1835) 5 and 6 Wm. IV c. 76 s. 99.   [39] Hume 1844 II, p. 70.

[40] Houston 1994, ch. 2 discusses the relationship between jurisdictions and the perception of space in Edinburgh between 1660 and 1760.

[41] By far the most lucid account is to be found in Moncrieff 1877, chs. 1 and 2; see also Spens 1875, ch. 2.   [42] Hume 1844 II, pp. 60–1.

[43] *Ibid.*, p. 63. Cf. Stephen 1883, I, ch. 4 arguing that the capital jurisdiction of the Quarter Sessions gradually narrowed in the course of the seventeenth and eighteenth centuries to cover only petty larcenies and misdemeanours. See also (1842) 5 and 6 Vict. c. 38.

obvious propriety in reserving trials, likely to terminate in so serious a result, for the supreme criminal tribunal of the country'.[44] While the use of the newly created punishment of transportation was reserved to the High Court,[45] there appears to have been no formal limit to the power of the sheriff to punish at common law, the rule being that 'every judge who is made competent to a crime has an implied power of inflicting that degree of punishment which is adequate to the circumstances attending the offence'.[46]

The position of the justice of the peace courts in Scotland presented a stark contrast to England and Wales where lay magistrates shouldered the burden of criminal justice. There, although their most important role in criminal justice was considered to be the holding of the Quarter Sessions, individual JPs holding a commission for the peace also dealt with a large amount of criminal business – to the extent that Blackstone bemoaned their role in the decline of the ancient common law jurisdictions of Courts Leet and the Sheriff's Tourn.[47] Later the role of JPs in dealing with minor offences was formalised when, particularly in busy urban areas, the practice developed of holding petty sessions. These regular, public sittings of two or three magistrates without a jury, concentrating business into a few hands, became in time the main summary courts.[48] In Scotland, the office of the justice of the peace was practically moribund. The few JP courts which had survived from James VI's attempt to introduce the institution to Scotland exercised a genuinely minor criminal jurisdiction. They had jurisdiction over riots and disorderly conduct, together with various powers conferred by statute, of which the power to enforce excise laws and laws against the poaching of game were the most important.[49] Whetstone has argued that criminal justice was one of the areas in which the JPs had least impact, and that they mostly preferred to pass cases on to the sheriff. The practice of even this limited jurisdiction was to decline during the nineteenth century as other courts developed – although some of the more active JPs were apparently valued because they could relieve

---

[44] Alison 1833, p. 39.   [45] *Ibid.*, pp. 36–8.

[46] Erskine 1871 I, iv, 21, pp. 88–9; the power to punish would also depend on whether or not a jury was used, Hume 1844 II, pp. 66–70; see also Spens 1875, p. 20: 'What are the powers of the Sheriff Court with reference to criminal cases at common law without the intervention of a jury, has probably never been accurately ascertained or defined.'

[47] Blackstone 1765 IV, pp. 278–9. He also complained (*ibid.*) that the increase in business meant that the office was no longer attracting the right sort of man.

[48] See Stephen 1883 I, pp. 122–6; Beattie 1986, ch. 6; Emsley 1987, ch. 7. Landau 1984, chs. 6 and 7 argues that the origins of the petty sessions are much earlier – in the seventeenth century – but suggests that this was largely for carrying out their administrative functions. A more active role in petty criminal business seems to have developed later. See Vogler 1991, chs. 2 and 4 on the later development of the English magistracy.

[49] Erskine 1871 I, iv, 13, pp. 95–6.

the pressure on the Sheriff by dealing with minor cases.[50] The baron court, we have already noted, retained a limited criminal jurisdiction over minor common law crimes after the 1747 Act. They had a very restricted power to punish and by the late eighteenth century no longer played a significant role in the administration of criminal justice.[51]

It is over the question of the jurisdiction of the burgh courts that we encounter the greatest confusion. The jurisdiction of a royal or baronial court would normally have been inferior to that of the sheriff, relating mainly to the keeping of 'good neighbourhood' or the maintenance of public order. Their powers in particular burghs, however, depended on the original grant or commission and could, if so specified, be equal to the powers of the sheriff. This, for example, was the case in Edinburgh, where the burgh had received a grant of Sheriffdom.[52] To confuse matters yet further, after 1800 many of the larger burghs obtained private Police Acts which, without specifying these exhaustively, substantially re-enacted their older powers.[53] The position was broadly similar in England where the powers of borough Quarter Sessions would vary with the original charter and additionally depended on whether or not the jurisdiction of the county had been ousted. Even after the passing of the Municipal Corporations Act 1835, different towns and cities were of differing status.[54] The Scottish burgh courts seem in practice to have exercised quite broad powers, something justified on the grounds that they were essential for the maintenance of order. Alison records that burgh courts retained the power to inflict physical punishment without a jury long after the propriety of this practice had been challenged in the sheriff court.[55] In the case of *Young and Wemyss v. Procurator Fiscal of Edinburgh*[56] for example, the burgh court sentenced two men to be whipped on a charge of riot and assaulting and wounding. The men appealed to the Court of

[50] Whetstone 1981, ch. 2.
[51] Willock 1966, p. 82. For a statistical demonstration of this, though for a slightly later period, see the Fourth Report of the Royal Commission to Inquire into the Courts of Law in Scotland 1870 app. II, tables 12 and 18 (PP.1870.XVIII.455, 511).
[52] Hume 1844 II, p. 70; Erskine 1871 I, iv, 21, p. 102; Alison 1833, p. 61; McNeill 1984, p. 90; for an example see *Maxwell v. McArthur and Stevenson* 16 December 1775 M.7381. See also the case of *Mag. of Paisley and Adam* 30 November 1790 M.7687 where a burgh of barony was found to be equal to a royal burgh by reason of 'inveterate and immemorial usage'. See also Houston 1994, pp. 105–21 for Edinburgh up to 1760.
[53] See e.g. Appendix to the Fourth Report of H.M. Law Commissioners, Scotland 1840 (Burgh Police Returns) PP.1840.XX.115.
[54] (1835) 5 and 6 Wm. IV c. 76. See Stephen 1883 I, p. 121 describing the situation as 'obscure and repulsive'; Eighth Report of H.M. Criminal Law Commissioners PP.1845.XIV.161 at p. 7: 'It will be seen . . . how much inconvenience has been experienced from the locally circumscribed economy of criminal jurisdiction.'
[55] Alison 1833, pp. 53–61. See *Piscatore v. Simpson* (1770) in McLaurin 1774, p. 772, where it was held that criminal process before an inferior judge must be tried by a jury if it concluded for corporal punishments.   [56] 19 March 1783 M.7301. See also M.3447.

Session on the grounds of the absence of a jury and informalities in the libel. After an inquiry by the court into the current state of practice, it was held that 'at no period of our law has the intervention of juries been required . . . [in the lesser crimes]' because the use of juries 'would often render unavoidable the impunity of offenders'.[57] For Hume,

such a privilege of sharp and summary coercion had been thought material to the quiet of those places, and the safety of their inhabitants, otherwise so much exposed to the evil practices of the many dissolute and profligate persons, who have their haunt and resort in towns'.[58]

The informal and summary practice of these courts was thus justified on the basis of expediency. It is clear that there were no definite rules of procedure. Prior to 1827 the only formal procedures applied to the High Court and thus only covered trial by jury.[59] In the inferior courts these could be taken as guidelines, especially in the more serious libels or those concluding for physical punishment, but they were not binding, and in the absence of lawyers acting for the accused were unlikely to be enforced. Hume makes it clear that 'a deviation from any of those precepts, is not to be pleaded peremptorily as a nullity of the process'.[60] His sole recommendation was that cases be conducted as far as possible in a fair and equitable manner.[61]

Rather than detailing the formal process of reform of the inferior courts, a brief consideration of the two main developments can best show the nature of the transformation of criminal justice. The first is that central government tightened its grip over criminal justice as the sheriff court was consolidated in its role as the most important of the inferior courts. The levels of professional qualification required were increased as it gradually took over the appointment and payment of court personnel.[62] The reorganisation following the Burgh Police (S.) Act 1892 consolidated the influence and supervisory role of the sheriff in the general sphere of police administration.[63] The jurisdiction of the sheriff court expanded, increasing the number of cases that were dealt with under both solemn and summary procedure. By 1870, it exercised common law jurisdiction over

[57] *Ibid.*, p. 7301.   [58] Hume 1844 II, p. 149.
[59] A.P.S. c. 16 1672. The forms of process substituted following the 1747 Act also made limited provision for trial before the Sheriff without a jury. See Moncrieff 1877, esp. ch. 1 below. Also Cairns 1993, pp. 142–5. For the contemporary development of procedural rules in England, see Langbein 1978 and 1983b; Baker 1977.
[60] Hume 1844 II, p. 67.
[61] *Ibid.* See also case of *Banks and Sutherland* 1735 and other cases cited there.
[62] See generally Whetstone 1981, ch. 1; e.g. Acts (1825) 6 Geo. IV c. 23; (1828) 9 Geo. IV c. 23 s. 22; and (1838) 1 and 2 Vict. c. 119 s. 28. By 1877 all substitutes were appointed *ad vitam aut culpam* by the crown.
[63] 55 and 56 Vict. c. 55. See Carson 1984–5, pp. 215–16.

all cases which could be disposed of by a maximum fine of £50 or two years imprisonment. Its jurisdiction had also been increased by statute.[64] Some granted jurisdiction in new areas, while others expanded its common law jurisdiction.[65] The same process of consolidating the importance of the Quarter Sessions occurred in England, where various indictable offences – principally certain categories of larceny and damage to property – along with juvenile offenders were gradually either removed entirely from the jurisdiction of the superior courts or were made so in practice by making them triable either way.[66] The seriousness of a crime was coming to be assessed in material terms rather than in terms of the wrong of a class of acts, and the relationship between the seriousness of an offence and the court in which it was tried was beginning to take on significance. A final consequence of the better defined roles and more regular practice of the sheriff court and Quarter Sessions was that the other inferior courts began to deal with even lesser offences. As a hierarchical understanding of jurisdiction was gradually replacing the cumulative and overlapping system, the gradation of the seriousness of offences was being brought simultaneously into line with this new system.

Notwithstanding the growth of the sheriff court, the business of the lower courts and the overall numbers of summary convictions were increasing throughout this period, and this was only possible as a result of the reorganisation of these lower courts. This complex process has been little studied. In Scotland it was brought about by the gradual introduction of a system of 'police courts'. The complexity derives in part from the fact that this was carried out in a very piecemeal fashion, and in part because in many instances these new courts took over from the existing burgh courts in such a way that it is difficult to be precise about the changes that were introduced. This factor, no doubt, has contributed to their neglect. None the less a number of points can be made that underline the radical nature of this transformation. It is clear that the emergence of these courts was connected with the establishment of police forces and the reform of burgh administration and local government. Burgh councils had always been responsible for the provision of 'police', in the traditional sense of looking

[64] See Fourth Report of the Commissioners on the Courts of Law in Scotland 1870, PP.1870.XVIII.455.

[65] (1887) 50 and 51 Vict. c. 35 s. 56 allowing the Sheriff to deal with cases of robbery and wilful fire-raising – two of the original four 'Pleas of the Crown'; see also *Criminal Procedure (S.) Act* 1975 (c. 21) s. 291 (3) allowing summary trial of these same offences.

[66] See e.g. (1827) 7 and 8 Geo. IV c. 29 (abolishing distinction between grand and petty larceny); (1847) 10 and 11 Vict. c. 82 and (1850) 13 and 14 Vict. c. 37 (allowing juvenile offenders to be tried summarily); (1855) 18 and 19 Vict. c. 126 (allowing larceny under a certain value to be tried summarily); (1879) 42 and 43 Vict. c. 49 ss. 12 and 13, schedule I (increasing the upper limit of cases that might be tried summarily). For a discussion of this, see Wiener 1990, pp. 279–85; Radzinowicz and Hood 1986, ch. 19.

after drainage, street lighting and so on, and from 1800 onwards many of the larger and expanding burghs began to introduce specialised police forces as a natural extension of these traditional duties.[67] Initially only royal burghs were given the power to establish a police force,[68] but later, following the reform of the franchise, this provision was extended to allow new centres of population to establish forces.[69] A series of enactments followed, providing for the creation and financing of police forces, as well as creating a series of 'police offences' and summary procedures by which these could be tried.[70] Most of these were related to the maintenance of the burgh amenities, such as roads, lighting, drainage and licensing, but a number of minor crimes against the good order of the burgh were also formally defined and penalised.[71] Thus breaches of the peace and other types of disorderly conduct punishable at common law became also statutory offences. Normally the grant of jurisdiction was confined to these specific offences and their penalties; however, many of the statutes would be additional to the existing local provision rather than replacing it, with the result that even within a single burgh it took a long time for a uniform system to develop.[72] This occurred not least because the laws creating police forces brought their own internal pressure for centralisation and uniformity as quite specific problems could be created by the patchwork of provisions. Thus, for example, the punishment of banishing individuals from the burgh or county in which they had committed an offence was abolished in 1830, not only because it did not fit with emerging conceptions of punishment, but also because the problem of the displaced persons would remain.[73] Equally, problems of order were caused when vagrants moved, or were moved, to areas where they were dealt with more leniently.[74] Social problems were perceived at the national as well as the local level, and concern shifted to dealing with problems of internal order

---

[67] Carson and Idzikowska 1989. This tradition may explain why the introduction of police forces met with less resistance than in England, where historians have drawn a sharp distinction between the organisation and reception of the 'old' and the 'new' police e.g. Storch 1975; Gattrell 1990; cf. Davis 1984. The almost complete absence of Scottish research makes it difficult to know whether developments in Scotland are as different as they appear to be.   [68] 3 and 4 Wm. IV c. 46.

[69] 10 and 11 Vict. c. 39. See Lenman 1981, pp. 162–4 on electoral reform. The connection between the extension of the franchise and the more intense regulation of social life could hardly be clearer!

[70] e.g. (1850) 13 and 14 Vict c. 43; (1856) 19 and 20 Vict. c. 48; (1862) 25 and 26 Vict. c. 101.

[71] See e.g. Burgh Police (S.) Act 1892 ss. 380–453. Police jurisdiction could also normally cover the minor common law crimes, provided that they were not committed with certain aggravations e.g. serious assaults or property crimes over a certain value.

[72] See e.g. Moncrieff 1877, p. 48 where he points out that Edinburgh's regulations were derived from at least five different sources. Cf. Houston 1994, ch. 2 suggesting that a more uniform system had been established as early as 1760.

[73] 11 Geo. IV and 1 Wm. IV c. 37.

[74] Dove Wilson 1895; See also Carson and Idzikowska 1989, pp. 288–97 on the policing of Lanarkshire.

produced by inconsistencies and imbalances in the distribution of powers. As the century progressed, these were gradually eradicated, although the process of centralisation was constrained by the absence of a government department, such as the Home Office in England, that could take overall responsibility for the collection of information and the initiation of new legislation.[75] A more general provision was finally made by the Burgh Police (S.) Act 1892. As part of a wide reform of burgh administration, this Act laid down rules to govern the scope of police jurisdiction, as well as adopting the general procedural standard that summary police jurisdiction should be limited by providing for a maximum amount of punishment.[76]

The overall effect of these two developments was that prosecution became much easier and that there was a massive increase in the number and types of crime that were dealt with summarily.[77] Not only did the overall number of cases increase, but there was also a shift in the locus of judicial activity and the way in which cases were dealt with. The Justiciary Court came to play an increasingly insignificant role in the day-to-day business of criminal justice, as the percentage of cases dealt with under solemn procedure became an ever smaller part of the total. In England the year 1855 is conventionally cited as the turning point, when the number of recorded cases dealt with summarily for the first time exceeded those dealt with on indictment.[78] In Scotland, by 1898, of a total of almost 166,000 prosecutions, only about 2,500 were dealt with under solemn procedure, and only about 200 of these by the Justiciary Court.[79] In part this was probably due, as Blackstone had complained very early on, to the increasing numbers of statutes providing for summary punishments.[80] Other factors were of equal significance, though. Changing attitudes towards violence and disorder meant that towns and cities were becoming more active in their attempts to police and order public space.[81] The

---

[75] A situation that did not change immediately with the introduction of the Scottish Office in 1885 since the Lord Advocate retained overall responsibility for the criminal justice system. See Hanham 1965 and 1969.

[76] Imposing a limitation of sixty days imprisonment or a fine of £10, following the Summary Procedure (S.) Act 1864 (27 and 28 Vict. c. 53). Although this Act did not extend to the rural areas of Scotland and the larger cities (Aberdeen, Edinburgh, Glasgow, Dundee, Greenock) which meant that provision was still not completely uniform.

[77] Cf. Stephen 1877; Gattrell 1980, pp. 274 and 302–5 on the easing of prosecution in England.

[78] Following 18 and 19 Vict. c. 126 ('An Act for diminishing expense and delay in the administration of Criminal Justice in certain cases') allowing certain simple larcenies to be dealt with summarily. The effect is analysed in Jackson 1937.

[79] See Judicial Statistics for 1898 (PP.1900.CIII.447 at p. 38).

[80] Blackstone 1765 IV, ch. XX; see Landau 1984, p. 346 and 348 quoting an estimate that by 1776 there were over 200 offences punishable by summary conviction.

[81] J. S. Cockburn 1991; Beattie 1986, pp. 132–40. Landau 1984, chs. 6 and 7 suggests that justices were becoming a little more withdrawn and formal in their dealings with the public, adopting the role of the disinterested judge.

advantages of summary processes – cheapness and speed – were being
recognised in the practice of charging many lesser offences in such a way
that they could be dealt with summarily by the local courts. The costs of
proceedings could be reduced, encouraging the prosecution of larger
numbers of people, and crucially, given the lower penalties, it became
easier to obtain convictions.[82] Finally, new justifications were being
offered for these summary practices:

Jury trial is of inestimable importance in all political cases, and in all cases
whatever where a grave sentence, decisive of the prisoner's fate . . . is to be
pronounced; but in smaller cases, where imprisonment only, or fine, is to be the
result . . . it may well admit of doubt, whether a privilege introduced for his benefit
does not too often practically become an aggravation of his sufferings'.[83]

Views such as these were to predominate as the traditional model of
criminal justice bowed to the demands of efficiency and economy.

The defining feature of the system that took shape in the later years
of the nineteenth century was the summary trial of large numbers of
offenders for minor crimes. This not only affected the treatment
of individual offenders, but also had an enormous impact on the
understanding of criminal law and criminal justice. The main difference
from the older system, then, is not to be seen in the expansion of summary
convictions alone, for this had obviously long played some role in criminal
justice. The administration of the summary courts was developing in a
way that became increasingly estranged from a traditional model of
criminal justice that placed the jury trial of indictable offences at its core. A
qualitative shift had occurred in the operation of criminal justice.

The creation and regulation of summary jurisdiction

An increasing amount of the business of criminal justice was being dealt
with summarily; but there is a further element of this development that is
of considerable interest. Along with the rise of the new police courts there
came a reform of the existing summary processes which led in turn to a
transformation in the way in which jurisdiction was conceived. It moved
away from being a question of legal competence relating to geographical
space, the nature of the crime and the power of the particular court to
punish. Jurisdiction came to be defined primarily in terms of procedure. It
is not being suggested that the other questions cease to be important, for
that is clearly not the case, but it is undeniable that at a conceptual level, as

---

[82] See, for example, Radzinowicz and Hood 1986, ch. 19 and the literature cited there. They
also argue that in England the expansion of summary process was justified because it was
seen as a way of keeping juvenile offenders out of the system.
[83] Alison 1833, p. 58; see also appendix to Fourth Report of H.M. Law Commissioners,
Scotland 1840, PP.1840.XX.115 at pp. 325–31.

in practice, these become secondary to the question of procedure. This is most obvious in the growth of 'summary courts', cutting across the 'old' jurisdictions, and defined in terms of the procedure that they use. The nature of this transformation was neatly captured by a commentator on the 1908 Act:

The forms that must be observed and the steps or proceedings that must be taken to enable a judge to exercise his jurisdiction in a case, are known and referred to as the 'proceedings' or 'procedure' in the case . . . Jurisdiction is thus exercised through what is known as 'procedure'.[84]

Summary forms of process thus gave rise to a new conception – that of 'summary criminal jurisdiction'[85] – which is central to the organisation of the modern criminal justice system.

The rise of summary criminal jurisdiction may be divided into three stages.[86] The first, the period before 1820, is the 'pre-history', which we have already looked at. It is sufficient to reiterate the point that, while summary procedures were not a nineteenth-century innovation, before this there were many different types of process and courts and that there was perceived to be, 'a strong necessity for the introduction of uniformity of procedure and the suppression of such irregularities which could only be effected by statutory regulation'.[87] In the second period, between 1820 and 1864, there were the first statutory attempts to set these procedures on a more regular footing as the use of summary forms expanded dramatically, although they were of only partial success. Finally, in the third period, between 1864 and 1908, rules of uniform application were developed and the idea of summary jurisdiction emerged.

The first statutes covered a wide range of legal matters of which the reform of summary criminal process was only a small part, and these reforms should be understood against the background of this more general reorganisation of legal administration.[88] There was a determined effort to set both civil and criminal procedure in the sheriff court on a more

---

[84] Trotter 1909, p. 3. Stephen 1883 I, pp. 123–4 was the only contemporary commentator to remark on the significance of the emergence of the concept of summary criminal jurisdiction e.g. '[A]s a formal procedure was established they came to be invested with the name of courts of summary jurisdiction.'

[85] The earliest use of the expression 'summary jurisdiction' was in (1850) 13 and 14 Vict. c. 37. It is used more consistently after the Prevention of Crime Act 1871 (34 and 35 Vict. c. 112) where it was defined for the first time (s. 17). It was not used in Scotland until the Summary Jurisdiction (S.) Act 1881 (44 and 45 Vict. c. 33). It is misleading to refer to the earlier acts as the summary jurisdiction acts rather acts relating to summary procedure, and I have used their official citations rather than subsequent short titles.

[86] H. H. Brown 1895, pp. xxi–ii with slight modifications. The reforms in England were broadly similar, with a movement away from partial to increasingly uniform provision.

[87] Moncrieff 1877, p. 8.

[88] See generally Whetstone 1981; on the state of the legal profession and the political climate in which these reforms were carried out, see Phillipson 1990.

regular footing. Civil procedure was completely reformed,[89] and the recognition of the requirements of economy and speed led also to the establishment of a summary procedure for the recovery of small debts,[90] mirroring the recognition of summary criminal process. Sheriff courts were required to compile statistical returns of business, enabling a more detailed monitoring of legal administration.[91] These statutes produced three types of summary process. The first was that provided for by an Act of Adjournal of the High Court.[92] Although purporting to be an entirely new procedure, this was in fact an attempt to reinforce procedures that had been introduced, and ignored, following the 1747 Act.[93] Notwithstanding, this form remained unpopular and soon became obsolete.[94] The Act provided for two different periods of *induciae* (the period between citation and trial), depending on whether the trial was with or without a jury (not less than fifteen and six days respectively). In both cases the libel was in the form of 'criminal letters', that is, one of the forms of libel that was used before the High Court. With a jury, the procedures of the High Court were to be used with the court retaining its full sentencing powers. Otherwise the process was simplified and the libel could conclude only for limited punishments. The second form was of only limited application and was provided for under the Small Debts (S.) Act 1837.[95] Here it was laid down that the civil procedures for the recovery of small debts might be used in prosecutions for statutory penalties where the penalty did not exceed the sum of £8 8s 8d.[96] The most popular procedure was provided under a statute of 1828.[97] Here it was laid down that inferior courts might try offences 'in the easiest and most expeditious manner' (s. 19) where the libel concluded for punishment not exceeding £10 or sixty days' imprisonment. The libel was to be in the form of a short complaint (Schedule C), procedure was greatly simplified and requirements for the written recording of evidence were relaxed in order to speed up the procedure. The forms of this Act appear to have been widely adopted in preference to the 1827 forms. Their application was extended to some police burghs,[98] and they were used by royal burgh and JP courts.

---

[89] See (1838) 1 and 2 Vict. c. 119. See also (1836) 6 and 7 Wm. IV c. 56 and (1839) 2 and 3 Vict. c. 41.   [90] (1825) 6 Geo. IV c. 24; (1837) 7 Wm. IV and 1 Vict. c. 41.

[91] e.g. 1828 ss. 24 and 25; (1830) 1 Wm. IV c. 27 s. 15.

[92] PP.1826–7.XIX.689, under the authority of (1825) 6 Geo. IV. c. 23 s. 5. See also Alison 1833, pp. 39–43 where the text of the Act is reproduced in full. Further provision was made in (1828) 9 Geo. IV c. 29 s. 18.   [93] See Moncrieff 1877, ch. 1; Cairns 1993.

[94] On its unpopularity, see Trotter 1909, p. 4 (note). Macdonald second edn (1877) states that it is 'practically obsolete'; by the third edn (1894) it 'is obsolete'.

[95] 7 Wm. IV and 1 Vict. c. 41 s. 2.

[96] Later extended to £12 by (1853) 16 and 17 Vict c. 80.

[97] 9 Geo. IV c. 29 ss. 19–20 and schedule C; see also (1830) 11 Geo. IV and 1 Wm. IV c. 37 ss. 4–5. For case law on the 1829 Act, see Bell's Notes II, pp. 151–2.

[98] Those taking advantage of the Act of 1833 (3 and 4 Wm. IV c. 46 ss. 134, 136).

In many burghs, however, the reform of summary process was a direct consequence of the implementation of the various Police Acts. Although the forms of process were all probably 'extremely similar' to those used under the 1828 Act, as Alison notes at the beginning of the period,[99] we can still identify three different types of provision. The first, as we have noted, was that police courts might use the forms of the 1828 Act under the provisions of the Act of 1833. By an Act of 1856 the powers of burgh courts still using these procedures were reduced by half.[100] The general Police Acts of 1850 and 1862[101] limited the jurisdiction of the court to police offences and the penalties that were specifically provided for, and all common law crimes with the exception of certain more serious and aggravated crimes (ss. 350 and 413 respectively). There appears to have been no specific limitation of the power of the courts to punish common law crimes.[102] It was provided that all process before the police courts was to be summary – that is to say on complaint and without written pleadings (ss. 348 and 411 respectively) – and that the burghs could make such rules of procedure as they saw fit, provided that this was done 'with the advice and approbation' of the senior judges (ss. 349 and 412 respectively). The third type was where the burgh had simply obtained its police powers under a local act, as was the case for the largest towns. The forms of process, if they were specifically provided for, and power to punish would be subject to further variations.

We can gain a better idea of how this complex of regulations worked in practice by looking at an account of the local courts in Glasgow, written in 1840 by the assessor of the burgh and police courts.[103] We learn that there was both a police court and a burgh court. The former operated under a Private Act of Parliament which specified no forms of procedure, although certain maximum penalties were established ($£5$ or sixty days' imprisonment). The latter operated under its original charter, trying those offences that were considered to require greater punishment than the police court could give. Other cases still were remitted to the sheriff court, where the forms of procedure of the 1827 Act of Adjournal were used. No part of the general Police Act had been adopted. The writer complained about the lack of general provision:

[99] Alison 1833, p. 50.
[100] 19 and 20 Vict. c. 48 ss. 1 and 2. i.e. $£5$ or thirty days' imprisonment. Parliamentary burghs that had already adopted the 1828 procedures could continue to use the old powers, since they were not mentioned by the Act – 'probably by oversight' Moncrieff 1877, ch. 1. After 1850 new police burghs no longer had the option of using the forms of the 1828 Act.
[101] 13 and 14 Vict. c. 33 ss. 345–74; see also (1862) 25 and 26 Vict. c. 101 ss. 408–38. Cf. in England (1835) 5 and 6 Wm. IV c. 76 ss. 127–32 which laid down some general provisions for the trial of offences punishable on summary conviction.
[102] Although this was presumably subject to the maximum provided for royal burghs.
[103] App. to Fourth Report of H.M. Law Commissioners PP.1840 XX.115.

In the Courts in which summary procedure takes place, such as the Police Courts held by the magistrates of burghs and justices of the peace throughout the country, the form is different; and even in the same court in some places the same form is not invariably observed. The difference of form . . . arises from the absence of any enactment or authoritative order or regulation on the subject, for the general Police Act does not universally apply'.[104]

He went on to argue that in the police court matters were dealt with in terms of expediency rather than legality: 'the practice is rather acquiesced in than sanctioned – rather tolerated than authorised'.[105] He concluded by giving his clear support to the development of summary procedure, provided that it was through the use of rules of general application.

In England the situation was no less complex, with problems deriving from the lack of formal organisation of the system of justices. Prior to 1848, justices of the peace acting out of sessions had no formally recognised court – statutes providing only that certain offences had to be tried before one or two magistrates – and, though the practice of holding petty sessions was acknowledged, this was still often done on an *ad hoc* basis without records of the jurisdiction of particular sessions. Much confusion, it seems, resulted from the uncertainty over the distribution of powers between different boroughs, counties, divisions, ridings and so on.[106] Equally, statutes provided for summary conviction without specifying the forms under which the crime was to be tried.[107] Much was left to the discretion of the magistrate, and procedure and punishment were consequently irregular.[108] The first major reform came with a series of three Acts passed in 1848, better known after their sponsor, Sir John Jervis.[109] These Acts reformed criminal process for justices acting out of sessions by attempting to collect together existing provisions on committal for trial, summons, adjudication and conviction, as well as protecting justices against litigation for acts carried out in the course of their duties. Although the Acts undoubtedly represented a great improvement on the existing situation, a certain amount of disorder and uncertainty seems to

---

[104] *Ibid.*, p. 325.   [105] *Ibid.*, p. 326.
[106] See Eighth Report of H.M. Commissioners of Criminal Law PP.1845.XIV.161 at p. 7.
[107] On the question of the form of summary convictions, see Landau 1984, pp. 348–62 and chs. 6, 7. The earliest statutory attempt to regulate this was an Act of 1822 (3 Geo. IV c. 23) which provided for a general form of conviction (i.e. a record of proceedings) in cases before a magistrate.
[108] 'We have also to observe, that the numerous provisions contained in the mass of statutes affecting criminal jurisdiction are at present confused and perplexed' (Eighth Report of H.M. Commissioners of Criminal Law PP.1845.XIV.161 at p. 7).
[109] (1848) 11 and 12 Vict c. 42, 43, 44. For a brief history and account of the Acts, see Freestone and Richardson 1980. Notable here is the emergence of the modern form of the caution against self-incrimination in (1848) 11 and 12 Vict. c. 42 – the modern form of the presumption of innocence. Also 1865 (28 and 29 Vict. c. 18) instituting a common procedure for all trials on felony and misdemeanour.

have remained. Not all existing statutory provision was repealed, and subsequent statutes seem to have carried on providing for summary convictions as before without necessarily specifying that the forms of the 1848 Act should be used. There was no clear limit on the jurisdiction of JPs since a range of penalties continued to be available. As Stephen pointed out, the Acts also reformed the procedure without formally constituting the court. It was only as a result of this, 'as a formal procedure was established [that] they came to be invested with the name of courts of summary jurisdiction'.[110] This is the process that was to be completed between 1864 and 1908.

Before going on to consider this process, it is helpful to draw attention to the characteristic features of the reforms in this period. Most obviously we can see that, in spite of certain similarities in the practice of various courts and a number of provisions that appear to have achieved more general application, the provision was still very piecemeal. Different regulations were provided by a number of different acts, which normally applied only to specific courts. This provided in effect for a certain level of local variation, given that provisions did not usually supersede prior local arrangements. Additionally, both the level of regulation and the degree of specification of the new statutory forms remained very low. In this period the aim was to facilitate prosecution and conviction by endorsing the removal of the more formal requirements of the traditional legal process. This required that summary practices receive some formal recognition, even encouragement, but the procedures appear to have been regarded as simply the absence of formalities. There was as yet no attempt positively to designate summary process. Finally, we should stress that, although the legislation was to a limited extent formalising existing courts and practices, what was emerging was a new system of courts and procedures that was of a markedly different character.

In the latter part of the nineteenth century this patchwork of provisions was gradually consolidated under the rubric of summary jurisdiction. This was brought about by a series of statutes that were of increasingly general application and which introduced increasingly specific rules for the conduct of summary prosecutions. In England, general provision effectively arrived with the Summary Jurisdiction Act 1879[111] which sought to supplement the 1848 Act. The Act provided a range of more detailed general provisions on penalties (s. 4, up to £25), proceedings (s.

---

110 Stephen 1883 I, p. 124. Petty sessions were recognised in an Act of 1855 (18 and 19 Vict. c. 126) s. 9 which held that they should be an open court and that public notice should be given of when the court was to be held.

111 42 and 43 Vict. c. 49. Completed by Summary Jurisdiction Act 1884 (47 and 48 Vict. c. 43) repealing a large number of statutes or parts of statutes dealing with summary convictions but preserving the jurisdiction of justices to act summarily.

39) and appeals (ss. 31–3). Crucially, it also laid down that the provisions
of the Act were to apply to future statutes (s. 51). In Scotland, the
Summary Procedure (S.) Act 1864[112] was the first statute to deal
exclusively with summary procedure, introducing a system of prosecution
that was to be available for all offences punishable by summary conviction
(ss. 2–3). It did not yet, however, aim for uniformity, because the new
procedure remained optional, and courts could continue to use any
pre-existing processes (s. 31).[113] The Act provided more detailed forms to
be used for complaints and for the recording of proceedings. The next step
towards uniformity was taken with the Summary Jurisdiction (S.) Act
1881,[114] under which the option of using the old forms was removed,
subject to certain exceptions (s. 3). The exceptions, though, still en-
compassed a significant area of operation – all local and general Police
Acts. The exact scope of this exemption became clearer with the Burgh
Police (S.) Act 1892,[115] which, while it made uniform provision for police
for the first time, still provided a different source of procedural rules
(although in other respects it substantially re-enacted the provisions of
earlier Police Acts). The uniform system of procedure was established
with the Summary Jurisdiction (S.) Act 1908 which repealed and
consolidated all previous statutes on summary procedure.[116]

With the passing of this Act we see that what has emerged is a
positively defined summary jurisdiction. Differences remained between
the English and the Scottish procedure – the English system at least
formally retained the possibility of choosing trial by jury – but these were
largely insignificant in the face of the broader changes. There was now a
dense body of regulation covering procedure before, during and after the
trial in the event of the occurrence of various likely and less likely
situations.[117] There was, in addition, a special procedure of review or
appeal which, though it did not entirely supersede existing forms, was
especially tailored for summary trials.[118] Finally, while the negative

---

[112] 27 and 28 Vict. c. 53. For a discussion of this, see Moncrieff 1877, ch. 2; Anon 1865, pp. 51–9.

[113] For a graphic illustration of the survival of the old procedures, see the Fourth Report of Royal Commission to Inquire into Courts of Law in Scotland 1870 app. II. Table 16 'Burgh Courts' in column headed 'Statutes or Acts of Adjudication Regulating Procedure' PP.1870.XVIII.455, 511.

[114] 44 and 45 Vict. c. 33 which also applied some provisions of the English 1879 Act.

[115] 55 and 56 Vict. c. 55.   [116] For discussion see Renton 1908; Trotter 1909.

[117] The 1908 Act, for example,. runs to seventy-seven sections and eighteen pages of schedules.

[118] See Summary Prosecutions Appeals (S.) Act 1875 (38 and 39 Vict. c. 62); and 1908 Act ss. 60–73. The original version of the 1864 Act had contained provisions for review that were substantially the same as these. These were rejected by the House of Lords for fear that they would provide opportunities for magnifying the defects of form (Moncrieff 1877, ch. 2). See Royal Commission Fifth Report 1871 (PP.1871.XX.257 at pp. 16–17)

limitations on the common law power to punish of the judge were still important,[119] these had been joined by a series of penalties for offences specifically created by statute. These general provisions flattened local differences between the various types of courts, for the primary differentiation was and is in terms of procedure. It is, from this point, possible to speak of 'summary courts' and a domain of summary jurisdiction. This jurisdiction, it is clear, is not organised around the question of sovereignty or the power to punish. Rather, jurisdiction and the order of law is now organised around procedures designed to ensure an equal distribution of powers around the system. Procedural safeguards were not modelled on the criminal trial, but on a calculus that weighed the cost to the individual against the cost to the system. The imperative of this system was not the presumption of innocence but the demand for an internal order based on efficiency and speed. This has enormous implications for our modern understanding of criminal justice – though these have rarely been faced – and in the remainder of this and in the following section we will begin to draw these out.

Historians of legal systems have long pointed to the relationship between procedural rules and the formation of the substantive law. This is particularly true of the common law which is seen as having been shaped by the forms of action and the availability of remedies. What is surprising to us, therefore, is the relative neglect by historians of the development of procedural rules in the modern period,[120] for the transformation of criminal procedure in the nineteenth century has certainly had a great impact on the substantive criminal law. At the beginning of the period no procedural rules existed for the conduct of trials outside the superior courts. By the end there was a large and technical body of statutory rules covering procedure in the superior and inferior courts, and an increasing amount of case law devoted to their discussion and elucidation.[121] In spite of the supposed informality of summary procedure it is increasingly an area that is only comprehensible to those with a professional understanding. In summary procedure, where it was expressly provided that there could be no appeal on the grounds of informality alone, increasingly

recommending reform. Under the 1864 forms of process no note of evidence needed to be kept, making review impossible. Recommended instead that a system of appeal by stated case be developed. In England, see 1879 Act s. 33 and 1884 Act s. 6.

[119] e.g. 1864 s. 29; increased by 1892 s. 490; and 1908 ss. 7 and 11. In England there remained special provisions for indictable offences triable summarily e.g. 1879 Act ss. 12–14; Summary Jurisdiction Amendment Act 1899 (62 and 63 Vict. c. 22); Criminal Justice Administration Act 1914 (4 and 5 Geo. V c. 58) ss. 14, 15.

[120] There are several remarkable studies of the eighteenth-century English criminal trial. See Langbein 1978 and 1983b; Beattie 1986.

[121] Solemn procedure was also consolidated by the Criminal Procedure (S.) Act 1887 (50 and 51 Vict. c. 35).

specific forms and rules provided detailed grounds for challenge – to the extent that one of the aims of the 1908 Act was to provide for rectifications of errors, and the upholding of convictions, where there had been no miscarriage of justice.[122] In spite of the claims of successive statutes to be simplifying the forms of procedure, the overall effect is one of increasing complexity as longer, and more specialised, statutes attempt to deal with every foreseeable situation. Equally, with the rise of summary procedure, solemn procedure also became more 'solemn'. Records from the middle of the nineteenth century show the Justiciary Court dealing with large numbers of cases in very short periods of time.[123] By the end of the century the overall numbers of cases dealt with by that court had diminished, although there is no record of less time being spent on criminal business. It is from this tension between the summary practice of criminal justice and the increasing legalism of the higher courts that the modern criminal law emerges. This had an impact on the practice of criminal law but also, as we shall argue in the next chapter, on the understanding of crime and criminal law.

We shall develop this point further in the next section, by looking at the way that the modern distinction between civil and criminal jurisdiction is grounded in procedural rather than moral categories.

The distinction between criminal and civil jurisdiction

The existence of a clear distinction between civil and criminal jurisdiction has long been regarded as a feature that differentiates modern from more primitive legal systems.[124] In early modern Scotland the distinction between private and public wrongs was not clear, although with the establishment of the office of public prosecutor (1579 and 1587) and the development of a separate central criminal court (1672) there were signs of its emergence as part of the establishment of juridical sovereignty.[125] In this section I want to suggest that even as late as the middle of the nineteenth century this distinction was still in the process of being clarified, something which lends force to our argument that there was a qualitative shift in the nature of criminal justice in the course of the nineteenth century.

In the early years of the nineteenth century the Court of Session still

---

[122] Trotter 1909, pp. 1–2.

[123] Quicker, indeed, than under our conception of summary procedure. See D. B. Smith 1978. Cf Langbein 1978 and 1983b suggesting an alternative genealogy of the criminal trial in which the lengthy modern jury trial is but a relatively recent innovation. See also Hostettler 1992, ch. 4.

[124] See e.g. Kames 1792; discussed in Young forthcoming, ch. 3.

[125] See discussion in, ch. 2, pp. 30–1.

possessed a criminal jurisdiction. This was partly derived from statute, as in the cases of deforcement of messengers or fraudulent bankruptcy,[126] and partly from 'ancient custom and usage', in cases of perjury or forgery for example. This was largely a procedural leftover from the period before the establishment of the Justiciary Court, and in spite of more recent memories of interference by the Court of Session in criminal prosecutions,[127] this jurisdiction was clearly diminishing. Between 1805 and 1810 it is recorded that three people were prosecuted, for perjury, in the Court of Session.[128] Alison stated that by 1833 the practice of the Court of Session, when facts of a criminal nature emerged before them, was to remit the case to the public prosecutor for trial in the Justiciary Court.[129] Conversely, both Hume and Alison considered that the jurisdiction of the Justiciary Court excluded actions for damages only ('patrimonial interests'), even if these stemmed from actions that were, on the face of it, criminal. The existence of these doubts suggests that the distinction was not yet firmly settled.

More importantly, in the late eighteenth century the Court of Session was still acting as an appeal court to all the inferior criminal courts.[130] Although this was only supposed to occur in cases of a minor character and where the penalty was only pecuniary, Hume had reluctantly to admit that in practice the civil court also reviewed cases involving penalties of a more serious character, 'although it has the appearance of an irregularity'.[131] He concluded that the inducement to interpose was possibly due to the need for a 'speedy and unexpensive course of review'[132] – although this does not explain why cases should not have been reviewed by the Justiciary Court on circuit. This situation was changed in the early nineteenth century, 'in consequence of the practice of later times, when more correct ideas have come to prevail as to the great lines of distinction between civil and criminal practice'.[133] Indeed the same writer attributed the change to the influence of Hume, who had so strongly disapproved of the former practice. It is also clear that this new practice arose from an active restraint on the part of the civil court: it began to refuse to intervene in the more serious criminal cases, or those involving a jury.[134] Hume later argued that the new practice, even in police offences, was that if the prosecution was

---

[126] Statutes A. P. S. 1581 c. 118; 1696 c. 5. [127] Hume 1844 II, pp. 29–30.
[128] PP.1812.X.217. [129] Alison 1833, p. 65.
[130] See e.g. cases cited above, at notes 46–50, and Hume 1844 II, pp. 72–4; see also Stair 1832 IV, i, 35. The Court of Session was the only court that could advocate or suspend sentences of inferior courts. Cf. England and the existence of Appeals of Felony where the civil court was competent to inflict capital punishment. See Kenny 1902, pp. 18–19.
[131] Hume 1844 II, p. 72. [132] Ibid., p. 73. [133] Alison 1833, p. 68.
[134] And when they did make a decision, it involved the interesting situation of stating that they were competent to say that they were incompetent. See e.g. Bruce v. Linton and MacDougall (1861) 24D 184.

brought by the public prosecutor, or with his concourse, and the penalty was in the public interest, then the 'course of review shall, for the future, be confined to what is certainly the more proper natural channel'.[135]

However, this was insufficient to settle the question of where the distinction properly lay. Difficulties persisted over such questions as which was the proper court in which to bring a suspension, or whether the offender was a competent witness in their own defence.[136] These questions arose particularly in relation to the new administrative offences that were being created by statutes such as the Police Acts, where the traditional categorisations of crimes as 'wrongs' broke down, chiefly because of its circularity. Whether or not a penalty was in the 'public interest' could only be determined by reference to the nature of the offence; the definition of 'proper' criminal offences could only be determined by reference to the practice of the criminal courts.[137] While these would appear to be minor technical questions and of little apparent importance to the development of the 'great lines' of distinction in jurisdiction, they are nonetheless revealing. The clarification of the questions of public and private right was not sought in moral categories, but through the development of stricter procedural rules. The determining factor was not taken to be the nature of the offence, but 'the style of the libel and the character of the proceedings'.[138] This point was reiterated by section 28 of the Summary Procedure (S.) Act 1864. This provision referred to 'the Uncertainty which exists as to the Nature of the Jurisdiction conferred by the various Acts of Parliament authorising Convictions for offences, and the Recovery of Penalties . . . upon summary Complaint'. Jurisdiction was accordingly held to be of a criminal nature when the court was authorised to pronounce a sentence of imprisonment *in modum poenae,* either as the original sentence or by way of enforcing other pecuniary penalties or orders in cases of default. All other proceedings by way of complaint were considered to be civil.[139] It does not escape circularity, but it roots the solution to the administrative problem in the newly developing procedural rules. Jurisdiction is defined in terms of procedure.

We can point to two further nineteenth century developments that are

[135] Hume 1844 II, pp. 73–4, and case of *Johnston* 1810 cited there.
[136] e.g. *Campbell v. Young and ors* 1835 13S 535; *Stevenson v. Scott* (1854) 1 Irv. 603. Generally, see the discussion in Anon 1858, pp. 276–84. Permitted in England after the Criminal Evidence Act 1898.
[137] Anon 1858, pp. 277–8. See also cases cited in Williams 1955; Allen 1931.
[138] *Robt. and Alex. Gray* 1820 in Hume 1844 II, p. 74 (note).
[139] For a commentary on the point, see Moncrieff 1877, pp. 108–11; H. H. Brown 1895, pp. 1–5 although note that he attempts to refer to 'quasi-criminal' jurisdiction. See also (1848) 11 and 12 Vict. c. 43 s. 1 and (1879) 42 and 43 c. 49 ss. 6, 35. A sum of money recoverable on a complaint, not information was deemed to be a civil debt.

relevant to the building of the modern distinction between civil and criminal jurisdiction, although we lack the research necessary to trace their influence in full. The first is the emergence of a system of public prosecution. While it is probable that from the early nineteenth century all prosecutions in the Justiciary Court had been at the instance of the Lord Advocate,[140] the development of a system of public prosecution for the inferior courts occurred later and more gradually than is commonly supposed. Hume makes hardly any mention of procurators fiscal, a feature which is broadly consistent with his scanty treatment of the inferior courts. Alison, who was an enthusiastic supporter of the idea of public prosecution, gave more space to a discussion of their duties, but was sparing in his praise. He claimed that they 'are selected in general from a subordinate class of men, and are not to be presumed in every case to be . . . so thoroughly exempt from improper motives'.[141] The changes in the nature of prosecution – in the sheriff court, at least – appear to have derived from the increasing willingness and financial ability of the fiscals to undertake prosecution in the public interest.[142] From being a local attorney, appointed by the sheriff, by the 1870s county procurator fiscals had been placed on salaries and were under the active supervision of the Lord Advocate.[143] From 1907 these fiscals were appointed by the Lord Advocate.[144] This professionalisation of the system was reinforced by statutory provisions limiting the liability of the public prosecutor to damages, along with the recognition that the common law protection of the public prosecutor against civil damages applied also to procurators fiscal.[145] In the police courts, various town and police officials were enabled to prosecute, as well as aggrieved individuals.[146] These prosecutors were not formally brought within the centralised prosecution system until 1975.

While it is clear that in England many prosecutions continued to be carried out by private individuals during this period, it has also been remarked that there was a clear relationship between the development of summary courts and the growth of police prosecution. The police took

---

[140] See Alison 1833, p. 88 (note); Hay and Snyder 1989, pp. 28–9. For an account of the early history of public prosecution in Scotland, see Normand 1938.

[141] Alison 1833, p. 93.

[142] Whetstone 1981, pp. 19–22. It appears that it was necessary to have the concourse of the fiscal to bring a prosecution.

[143] See Report of the Select Committee on Public Prosecutors PP.1854–5.XII.1, qn. 120; PP.1860.LVII.231.   [144] 7 Edw. VII c. 51.

[145] e.g. 1864 Act s. 30; commentary in Moncrieff 1877, pp. 111–19; Alison 1833, ch. 3.

[146] e.g. under the local Act in Aberdeen the Inspector, Clerk and Treasurer of Police were entitled to prosecute PP.1834.XLVIII.357; more normally it would be the Chief Constable of the force. Select Committee on Police (S.) Bill PP.1890.XVII.69 at p. 107; see Hallard 1878; Trotter 1909, pp. 107–11.

responsibility for the prosecution of summary offences including small thefts, common assaults and any other offences created by the Police Acts.[147] To a great extent, then, they were effectively acting as public prosecutors long before the creation of the office of Director of Public Prosecutions in 1879.[148] Additionally, in many of the statutes enlarging the scope of summary jurisdiction, provision was made for the justices to make payments to assist the prosecutor in the bringing of the complaint.[149] It seems clear that this combination was undermining the presumed constitutional centrality of private prosecution, in the same way that summary jurisdiction was undermining trial by jury. It did so in both jurisdictions by means of a new, formally defined, 'public interest'. This was signalled by the growing involvement of public prosecutors and the police, and in the facilitation of the prosecution of new types of crime and offence. Although a large amount of discretion was placed in the hands of these new state institutions,[150] it is commonly considered that this professional involvement was decisive in the formalisation of the law. In 1856 the Lord Advocate thus praised the beneficial effects of the centralised system, arguing that frequent consultations methodise the law and that 'the whole criminal procedure is now reduced into a very good and uniform system'.[151]

This gradual assumption by the state of the central role in the prosecution of all crimes, great and small, clearly had an enormous impact on the development and maintenance of rigid distinctions between civil and criminal jurisdiction. This points to the second development, the increasing differentiation of the fine or pecuniary penalty from other patrimonial interests. As the prosecution system was centralised, the previously flexible boundaries between fines and damages were subjected to more formal administrative controls. We have already seen, in the discussion of the powers of the Court of Session, that the existence of a pecuniary penalty was formerly considered to throw the case into the jurisdiction of the civil court because of the existence of a patrimonial interest. By the end of the period the public character of the fine had been made clear – and in fact under the 1864 Act it became the determining

---

[147] Davis 1989, pp. 399–400 and pp. 419–24. Although it is also clear that there could be wide regional variations.

[148] Prosecution of Offences Act 1879 (42 and 43 Vict. c. 22) and Prosecution of Offences Act 1908 (8 Edw. VII c. 3).

[149] eg. (1826) 7 Geo. IV c. 64; (1847) 10 and 11 Vict. c. 82 s. 14. This is not to overlook the fact that summary proceedings were encouraged because they were cheaper both to the private prosecutor and to the system. See the review by Hay 1989.

[150] The Scottish system confers a great deal of discretion on the public prosecutor over the choices of procedure, court and penalty. See *Clark and Bendall v. Stuart* (1886) 1 White 191 at p. 208.

[151] Report of the Select Committee on Public Prosecutors PP.1856.VII.347–394 at p. 353.

feature of criminal jurisdiction. Its reception and use in the system is clearly related to both the new 'administrative' offences, and the administrative demands of the new criminal justice system.[152]

This has been a lengthy account of the transformation of criminal justice – although in many respects it is still incomplete. It is worth, therefore, drawing the main threads of the argument together. I have argued that, in spite of certain continuities, we cannot regard the process of development since 1747 as the continuous evolution of a centralised system. On the contrary, the nineteenth century saw a qualitative shift in the nature of criminal justice. Along with the movement of the primary locus of operation to the summary courts, which brought many more people into the system, there was a concomitant shift in the way that jurisdiction was conceived. It has now taken on a distinctively legal meaning, referring primarily to decisions about the administrative distribution of people within the criminal justice system. Substantive issues are determined by reference to procedural standards. The concern with territory is displaced by a concern with population,[153] the concern with sovereignty by the demand for internal ordering and regulation. These are the principal characteristics of the modern legal order.

Legal competences

Thus far we have concentrated almost exclusively on the development of new courts and legal structures, presenting the evidence of massive changes in the nature of legal practices. But to leave the story here would also be to leave it incomplete. Our next step must be to look more closely at the way that the concept of jurisdiction was discussed and reflected upon in the legal doctrine, in such a way as to neutralise, or reduce, the potentially radical impact of the changes. This is, to be sure, an artificial distinction, and we must be wary of simply reproducing the distinction between law and practice. That said, it is important to bear in mind the extent to which the High Court can be said to constitute its own jurisdiction. To put this slightly differently, we should bear in mind that the High Court, as a consequence of its position as the supreme court, was often called upon to determine questions relating to the scope of its own jurisdiction. Its legal authority was constituted by reference to the system whose activities it reviewed. But, at the same time, it constructed a

---

[152] Young forthcoming, ch. 4.
[153] Foucault 1991a. Cf. the analysis in Feeley and Simon 1994, esp. at pp. 181–2 arguing that a certain Supreme Court decision represents 'the expansion of the mentality of the border to virtually *all* the interior spaces of the United States' (emphasis in original).

reflected version of this system, in legal concepts and reasoning, which was essential to the practical solution of the problems that came before it – and, hence, was no less important to the exercise of its authority. In settling the questions that come before it, the court has continually to provide an authoritative account of its own authority. This offers us a precise guide to the terms in which the territory of the law was marked out, and it is this that concerns us in this section. If we are to recover something of the origins of the tradition and the limits that it imposes on our contemporary understanding of criminal justice, it is a necessary prelude to establish the terms in which jurisdiction has been thematised over our period. We shall divide this into two stages. First, we must establish the categories in terms of which the question of legal competence was formulated between 1747 and about 1830, the days of the 'old' system. We shall then go on to look at some of the ways in which the 'new' system was written about in the contemporary case law and doctrine.

Natural jurisdiction 1747–1833

In our first period, the prime concern was that of establishing exclusivity of jurisdiction. Indeed, it is a measure of the authority of the law that such questions of political ordering were conceived of in predominantly legal terms. The discussions of jurisdiction and the perception of related problems were couched in a language that stressed and reinforced the sovereignty of the Justiciary Court over all matters criminal within the national boundaries of Scotland. Just as the law was to be a universal code for the people, the supreme court had a jurisdiction that was to be universal over territory, persons and crimes. Hume accordingly set the tone by arguing that the jurisdiction of the High Court was 'almost universal'.[154] It could try all crimes, whatever their degree of seriousness and regardless of whether they were committed against private individuals or the public economy and police. It was only necessary that they should be 'infringements of our ordinary . . . universal code of law; that which is administered by the secular courts of justice, and is common to all the inhabitants of the land'.[155] The point was underlined by Alison who, in phrasing his justification of public prosecution in similar terms, also made clear the need for a proper machinery of enforcement: 'He [the Lord Advocate] is now invested with [these powers] in the fullest and most unlimited extent – so that his title to prosecute crimes is now universal; embracing not only public crimes of every description . . . but also those of

[154] Hume 1844 II, p. 31. Cf. the discussion of the appellate jurisdiction of the House of Lords over criminal law in Scotland, ch. 2 above, at p. 36.
[155] Hume 1844 II, p. 34.

a private nature, which more immediately affect the welfare of individuals'.[156]

Both writers offered lengthy discussions of the sources of criminal jurisdiction, arguing for the replacement of the ideas of jurisdiction derived from Roman law.[157] Both, rejecting the efforts of previous writers (principally Mackenzie), argued that it could not be based on either birth (*forum originis*), domicile (*forum domicilis*), or the place of arrest (*forum deprehensionis*). They declared that such principles were not relevant to the practice of 'independent sovereignties', although perhaps being of some application between inferior and limited jurisdictions. It was argued that, 'no such doctrines have ever been fully received into the practice of this country'.[158] Jurisdiction was therefore to be based solely on the place where the crime was committed (*forum delicti*). The reception of the *forum delicti* and the rejection of the other grounds was grounded in the same principles. Indeed, Hume's argument was constructed in such a way that by eliminating the other possibilities, first on theoretical grounds and then because there was no record of them in the practice of the law, the *forum delicti* stood alone. The reasons for this were stated in the rejection of the *forum originis*:

[T]he peace of the land has not been broken, and the society of its inhabitants has not been shocked or disturbed by his deed, as they are by one which passes at home; nor are they likely to feel so much the propriety or necessity of executing the vengeance of the law on him in such a case'.[159]

The authority of the law was thus based on a combination of the right moral sentiments of the people and a compact between states and those individuals to whom the protection of the law was offered: 'This power is universally recognised by the laws of all civilised countries; since every foreigner who comes to a state, and, *pro tempore*, obtains the benefit of the protection of its laws, is bound, in return, to yield obedience to them'.[160] Hume concluded in terms that stressed the supervisory role of the High Court in the administration of jurisdiction. He pointed out that the inferior courts 'receive the aid of the Supreme Court towards explicating their jurisdiction', because they are connected by a 'common interest and mutual regard' in the enforcing of one law in every part of the country.[161]

The terminology of this argument is important. It clearly founds criminal jurisdiction within the bounds of the sovereign and independent nation state. This universal jurisdiction is presented as the natural state of affairs and yet, as the language of the common law demands, an age-old

[156] Alison 1833, p. 85.   [157] Hume 1844 II, pp. 49–57; Alison 1833, pp. 70–83.
[158] Hume 1844 II, pp. 49–50. This echoes his rejection of the Roman law as a source for Scots law, discussed in ch. 2 above, at pp. 42–4.   [159] Hume 1844 II, p. 51.
[160] Alison 1833, p. 81.   [161] Hume 1844 II, p. 57.

practice that is part of the 'ancient constitution' of Scotland. The issue of independence does not raise itself directly here, since the boundaries of legal sovereignty were not considered to have been affected by the Act of Union. This was due to the fact that legal authority was considered to derive from the sovereign, rather than Parliament. The Act of Union had dissolved the Scottish Parliament but left the 'kingdom' intact.[162] A further nationalist twist comes with the reference to the moral sentiments of the people which, as we have already had cause to note, were not to allow the development of universal principles but to entrench the differences from England. It is a further index of the concerns of these writers that there is virtually no discussion of the inferior courts. There was little interest in discussing particular powers in particular localities. This points to an important shift in the purpose of the law. With the privileging of the *forum delicti* the law was moving away from the control of individuals as possessors of a biography, towards the control of actions within a particular legal space. Within the boundaries marked out by the law, space is to be homogenised and the legal subject abstracted from particularities of place, time and history. Yet, as the indigenous and particularistic jurisdictions were being swallowed up, we see in the same period the staking of an ever greater claim to particularism by the Scottish legal tradition.

But we must note that there is a continuing tension between the normative claims of the extent of the jurisdiction of the High Court, and a recognition of certain practical limitations. In Hume this is signalled by the admission that the jurisdiction of the High Court was only 'almost universal'; in Alison, the large declarations of principle are eaten away by exceptions. This further underlines the argument that jurisdiction was still conceived of in terms of political sovereignty. This tension and the awareness of it also determined which situations were regarded as problems for the theory. But in the handling of these questions we also find clues to understanding the future development of the tradition. We can draw an example from each of the three categories of territory, persons and crimes.

One of the first broad exceptions discussed by Hume is the practically obsolete jurisdiction of the Admiralty Court.[163] In his handling of this question there is a clear sense of a need to explain why it should not be seen as compromising the jurisdiction of the High Court. In order to do this he had to draw a number of distinctions. The first distinction was that which was drawn between 'proper maritime causes' and 'ordinary crimes'. The

[162] See, for example, Hume 1844 II, pp. 1–16 where he works hard to dismiss the suggestion that the office of Justiciar had derived its authority from the Scottish Parliament.
[163] Hume 1844 II, pp. 34–7.

former were considered to be the proper province of the Admiralty Court, the latter fell within the cognisance of the High Court. The distinction was important because it allowed him to argue that the criterion of jurisdiction was not to be found, 'in the circumstances of the bounds or territory where the thing complained of happens, (for that would be no sufficient reason for sending such trials to a peculiar court), but in the nature of that thing, as an offence against the laws of navigation or seafaring business'.[164] Thus, most of the business of the court could be regarded as legitimate because of the quality of the cases that were dealt with. This led in turn to the second distinction. This was between 'old' jurisdiction, based on the controlling of order within the bounds of a particular territory, and 'new' jurisdiction, which distinguishes particular categories of offences within the universal sovereign jurisdiction. This enabled him to discount those cases where the court had clearly exercised jurisdiction based on territory alone as either obsolete or an abuse of power – notwithstanding that the original grant of jurisdiction to the Admiralty Court, cited in the text, appeared to be of a remarkably territorial nature.[165] This therefore clarified the nature of the *forum delicti*. It could clearly not be of a specific local application, for that would be a principle of the 'old' jurisdiction. It related, rather, to the nation, and only within that could a distinction be permitted on the basis of the nature of the crime. The principle of universal jurisdiction was thus preserved – although ironically the Admiralty Court was abolished shortly afterwards.[166]

We see a similar exercise being carried out in the discussion of jurisdiction over persons. The concern was once more to establish the secular sovereignty of the High Court over other bodies or 'states' in society, such as the military or the clergy, which had their own internal disciplinary bodies and had, at various times in the past, claimed to be subject to a different or 'higher' authority. This led Hume to launch an extraordinary diatribe against the Catholic church. He argued that common sense demands that the clergy be subject to secular authority for breaches of the good order of the state. Then, 'such were not the maxims of former times, while all the Governments of Europe lay sunk and humbled, under the tyranny of the Roman Catholic Church'.[167] Even with the passing of these 'ignorant and superstitious ages' following the Reformation,[168] the situation did not improve. Many reformed clergymen 'struggled hard for a total independence on all temporal authority'.[169] Resolution came only with the Settlement of 1690, when the independence of the church was secured at the cost of submission to secular

[164] *Ibid.*, p. 35.   [165] See also above, n. 23.
[166] (1830) 11 Geo. IV and 1 Wm. IV c. 69 s. 21.   [167] Hume 1844 II, p. 44.
[168] *Ibid.*   [169] *Ibid.*, p. 45.

authority on certain matters. Once again the message is clear: there is a single law and the courts that administer it have universal authority. 'The competency of jurisdiction turns . . . on the nature and grounds of the charge',[170] and if these are part of the national law then only one court is competent to judge. All other bodies are subordinate to the High Court; no one is outside the law.

Both these examples, then, are backward looking in character. They are concerned with establishing the exclusivity of jurisdiction against other historically powerful institutions – in the one case a feudal institution, in the other against the ideological threat presented by the church and its doctrines. The third example, while containing similar features, refers to more contemporary threats. It concerns the question of the jurisdiction of the High Court over 'new' crimes, particularly those created by statute, many of which specified an inferior court in which the offence was to be tried.[171]

In this case we should take special note of the form in which the argument is presented. It was stressed from the start that the High Court had 'a natural pretension to take cognisance of all offences'.[172] The principle thereby followed automatically that this common law jurisdiction remained unless removed by statute 'either by direct words or unavoidable inference'.[173] A statute might grant a particular power of jurisdiction, but it could not thereby render a crime a creature of statute.[174] The laws conferring jurisdiction on particular judges for particular offences would thus always be cumulative with the jurisdiction of the High Court. An example, approved by both writers, is that of an attempted prosecution under the Combination Acts outlawing strikes and other industrial action.[175] The accused questioned whether the particular statute could apply in Scotland. The decision of the High Court was that, even if the statute extended to Scotland, it would not remove the common law jurisdiction of the High Court under which they could try the offences anyway, awarding higher penalties if they chose. The example is revealing because the prosecution of strikes at common law was something that was already controversial because it was said to involve the use of the declaratory power (the inherent jurisdiction over crimes whether or not they were already known to the law). It thus shows that the jurisdiction of

---

[170] *Ibid.*, p. 42.
[171] Cf. Blackstone's much-cited criticism of statutes creating summary offences (1765 IV, pp. 278–9); see also Landau 1984, ch. 12 esp. at pp. 350–1.
[172] Hume 1844 II, p. 37; cf. Alison 1833, p. 10; 'as soon as statute, or custom, or the increasing depravity of the age, has given them birth'.   [173] Alison 1833, p. 8.
[174] *R v. Dick and Lawrie* (1832) 4 S.J. 594.
[175] *Falhouse, Wilson and Banks* (1818) in Hume 1844 II, pp. 37–8; Alison 1833, pp. 8–9. Discussed in ch. 2 above, in relation to the declaratory power.

the High Court at common law was stated by the court in the widest possible terms. This has a number of important consequences. It placed the statute law in a particular relationship to the common law. It had always to be subordinate to the common law or re-enacting it. Alternatively, if statutes created new courts, procedures or offences these were clearly marked out as being less serious or 'in aid of' the common law.[176] Finally, the Justiciary Court, as in all the questions deriving from natural jurisdiction, was placed in a particularly good position to judge. Such questions as related to the scope of their own jurisdiction were to be referred to them for them to determine for themselves. And they were not slow to seize these opportunities, thus establishing the conceptual machinery that was able to absorb the challenge posed by summary jurisdiction.

Reconceiving jurisdiction 1833–1908

As we would expect, in the later period the practical significance of the concerns of Hume and Alison receded. In place of an overt concern with the sources of sovereignty, discussions of jurisdiction took on an increasingly technical character. Jurisdictional issues became more involved with the interpretation of the new statutes and the internal management of competences in the criminal justice system. However, the transformations wrought by summary jurisdiction were not, at a doctrinal level, to be the main, or even a significant, object of reflection. It appears that to recognise this would have been to require recognition of the changes brought about by summary jurisdiction. Theoretical reflections on the changing nature of the system tended to focus on problems of the relationship between common law and statute law. Here, the breadth of the concept of universal jurisdiction was to be important in minimising the impact of the developing summary jurisdiction.

As I have already pointed out, the growth of legislation regulating criminal procedure led to an increasing body of case law on the interpretation of these statutes. Without attempting an exhaustive study of this case law, we can instead analyse those cases that have been considered to offer authoritative statements of the law, and therefore begin to see how the High Court constructed a particular understanding of the summary courts and their role in the operation of the criminal justice system. This works to reinforce their own superior status by a continual reference to the idea of the universal and natural scope of the territory of the common law. A prime example of this sort of argument is

---

[176] Alison 1833, p. 11; Hume 1844 II, pp. 39–40.

to be found in the case of *Bute v. More*.[177] This case, which concerned a summary conviction in the burgh court for offences against the laws against trading on a Sunday, raised the question of the scope of summary jurisdiction. Although in the particular case it was held that the prosecution was incompetent, the leading judgement by Lord Justice-General Inglis gave what was subsequently to be accepted as the authoritative version of the origins of summary jurisdiction. This, it was considered, was not a statutory creation. All inferior courts had practised, and therefore possessed, a summary jurisdiction at common law,[178] even if the later statutes had purported to confer jurisdiction on those courts. The statutes, from the 1828 Act onwards, had merely defined and regulated that procedure. This is in part, of course, an accurate picture of the history of summary procedure. Its significance lies in the general conclusions that this argument is then allowed to support. It is at least arguable that the 1828 Act and subsequent changes had created new processes that superseded the earlier, irregular ones,[179] and that with the 1864 Act there was the creation of a new entity, summary jurisdiction. It cannot be argued that prior to the 1828 Act the inferior courts had possessed summary jurisdiction in this later sense. However, in the argument of the court there was a stressing of continuity, together with a reference to Hume[180] – which is all the more surprising considering that Hume made no reference to the burgh courts! The conclusion was that the origins of all jurisdiction are in the common law, and therefore the superior common law court had an implicit right to regulate the inferior courts, a right that could only be superseded by statute under limited conditions. This point was elaborated by Lord Justice-General Dunedin in the case of *McPherson v. Boyd*, an early case of 'speeding':

I have always understood it to be the law of Scotland that in the case of statutory offences, which are not offences at all until they are created by statute, the jurisdiction must be conferred on any courts which have not universal jurisdiction, and the only courts which have universal jurisdiction are the Sheriff Court and this Court . . . When I say universal jurisdiction, I mean an inherent universal jurisdiction, which may, however, be curtailed in many ways. But there is an underlying universal jurisdiction in both the Sheriff Court and this Court, and it seems to me, therefore, to be settled by quite long practice that, where Parliament

---

[177] (1870) 1 Coup. 495 at pp. 510–20.

[178] *Ibid.*, p. 515: 'It speaks of the jurisdiction as being conferred by the recited Acts. That is not the case, because it certainly belonged to these inferior Courts before the recited Acts were passed'.

[179] See e.g. the argument of Sheriff Logan in *Byrnes v. Dick* (1853) 1 Irv. 151: 'Previously to the passing of the Acts referred to the sheriff had no summary jurisdiction. They conferred it on him, but only under the restrictions imposed by them.' This was rejected by the High Court. See also the discussion in Spens 1875, ch. 2.

[180] *Bute v. More* (1870) 1 Coup. 495 at pp. 513–14.

is going to give jurisdiction to courts other than the Sheriff Court or the Court of Justiciary, it must say so.[181]

Statutorily conferred jurisdiction can only add to this independent and universal jurisdiction. Statutorily created crimes were, in the view of the court, in general a strengthening of this common law jurisdiction, rather than its replacement.[182]

Many problems arose in cases where statutes had provided for certain maximum penalties but that the prosecutor had attempted to either exceed or limit these by the choice of a certain court or procedure. The question was therefore that of the discretion of common law institutions in the face of specific statutory requirements. In these cases it was held that parliamentary legislation must be clear and unequivocal in its terminology if it was to encroach on the territory of the common law. These requirements, needless to say, were established by the practice of the common law courts. The case of *Clark and Bendall v. Stuart*[183] established that the discretion of the prosecutor over the choice of court and procedure could only be limited by the express enactment of Parliament. The same point was made in more general terms by Lord Justice-Clerk Macdonald in the case of *Cameron v. McNiven*.[184] Here an offence against the Burgh Police (S.) Act 1892 was tried before the sheriff. It was held that the 'inherent' jurisdiction of the Sheriff covered all offences unless these had been explicitly removed from his jurisdiction. Thus although it was acknowledged that the legislature might take away existing powers, this would have to be expressly stated in the language of the statute.[185]

The classic statement, and most telling summary, was made by the same senior judge, Lord Justice-Clerk Macdonald, author of the influential treatise on criminal law and procedure:

Here we come face to face with this difficulty, that there is nowhere any definition of summary procedure, or summary jurisdiction. It is assumed all through the Acts of Parliament that these words are perfectly well understood, and the statutes all refer to it as perfectly well understood, and as already existing.

He then discusses various modes of proceeding under Scots law, before going on,

181 (1907) 5 Adam 247 at p. 254.
182 *Clark and Bendall v. Stuart* (1886) 1 White 191 at p. 207; or Lord Justice-General Kinross in *Paton v. Neilson* 1903 (J.) 5F 107.
183 *Clark and Bendall v. Stuart* (1886) 1 White 191. Cf. Lord Justice-General Inglis in *Bute v. More*, above, p. 94.
184 (1894) 1 Adam 346; see also *Tasker v. Simpson* (1904) 4 Adam 495 at 502–4; see also *Stirling v. Dickson* (1900) 3 Adam 252.
185 For cases where it was considered that jurisdiction was excluded, see *HM Adv. v. Rowet* (1843) 1 Broun 540; *HM Adv. v. Duncan* (1864) 4 Irv. 474; cf. *HM Adv. v. Robinson* (1844) 2 Broun 176.

So far as I know, there is no other way to explain the term summary procedure, except that it means procedure where there is no *induciae,* no indictment, and no notice of the witnesses to be examined, and where there is no objection to the proceedings because no agent appears for the accused.[186]

That this remains the standard judicial definition of summary criminal jurisdiction is in itself worthy of remark, for the collection of negatives recalls the early history of summary jurisdiction. It implies, moreover, that it is something that has no proper existence, for it has yet to be called into existence by being named. It is hardly enough to point to the fact, as commentators usually do, that 'many of these negatives are superseded by positive statutory requirements'.[187] Rather, we have to concede that the picture is indeed, from the point of view of the common law, an accurate one. From this point of view it appears that summary process arose as a means of avoiding the formalities associated with the common law. It did so only in the inferior courts and for offences that were to be considered inferior. The practice only arose by leave of the common law and the jurisdiction that it granted.

It need hardly be repeated that such a picture is inaccurate. However, we must ask ourselves why a senior judge should produce such a negative definition, and why this definition should be so readily accepted. It is difficult to answer this question except in terms of the preceding analysis. There is a relentless privileging of the common law made possible by the wide contours of the concept of universal jurisdiction, and this amounts to a negative definition of all the other courts. Common law courts and rules, with their long history and royal connections are superior even to parliamentary legislation. This, it must be stressed, necessarily implies that there is a further privileging of the visions of community and order represented by the common law and its view of independent Scottish sovereignty. For these reasons, the emergence of summary jurisdiction never forced a·reconsideration of the bases of jurisdiction within the Scottish legal tradition.

Conclusion

The modern history of criminal justice has been told as a story of centralisation and displacement. The process of centralisation occurred as local and particular jurisdictions were annexed by the common law institutions. In this account, hierarchy and homogeneity were imposed as necessary adjuncts of the process of modernisation. Then there was displacement as stately common law institutions such as the trial were

[186] *Lamb v. Threshie* (1892) 3 White 261 at p. 271.
[187] H. H. Brown 1895, p. 7; cf. Trotter 1909, p. 4.

marginalised by new courts driven by the imperatives of speed, cheapness and efficiency. Whether told as a history of the decline in the quality of justice and the moral and social status of legal institutions or as a necessary trade-off between the demand for order and the historical rights and protections of the accused, its contours are deeply familiar. Aside from the apparently contradictory elements of this history – can the common law both centralise and be displaced? – we have seen that it is only partially accurate. The familiar story conceals as much as it reveals. The argument of this chapter has introduced a number of revisions. The concentration on centralisation, it was argued, had obscured the changing form of criminal justice in the nineteenth century. It is not enough to look merely for signs of growing central control. It is necessary to examine the forms of that control and the terms in which order is imposed or negotiated. To address these questions, as has been shown, is to reveal different stages in the process of centralisation. This process, moreover, is normally interpreted as the simple capture of inferior jurisdictions, with no attempt being made to understand whether or how this transformed the common law, or the ways that the law maintained or sustained its authority. In a similar manner, displacement has been regarded as a simple change of scale. The development of summary jurisdiction is viewed in negative terms, stressing the absence of formalities and the sense in which it developed out of the perceived failures or shortcomings of more formal institutions of policing, trial and punishment. It has been argued here that the emergence of summary jurisdiction should be understood in positive terms. In moving from being concerned with territory and sovereignty to procedure and order, it was not only the scale of criminal justice that was transformed, but also the nature of jurisdiction and the significance of criminal procedure. Certainly, there are important continuities with the older system, and we should be wary of overstating the degree of central control. Notwithstanding this, we have gained new insight into the nature of modern criminal justice by analysing it in terms of the shift that occurred in the late nineteenth century.

It is important to stress, however, that the institutions that developed in this period did not simply sit alongside the common law – they also transformed it, forcing a process of adaptation and adjustment. Thus, the account of centralisation begins to make sense when read in terms of the physical power of the central institutions to control the understanding of jurisdiction. The High Court has always been in the position to determine questions relating to its own jurisdiction and that of the other courts, and this is the means by which the Scottish legal tradition was in a position to construct a vision of itself and its history that deflected the potential impact of summary jurisdiction on the legal order. The existence of summary jurisdiction was accounted for and incorporated into the decisions and the doctrine as a vital part of the conceptual machinery that makes those decisions possible. The radical nature of the shift was not addressed, for that would have undermined the basis of the judicial establishment. The story of displacement then makes sense when it is read against the complex of ideas both legal and 'extra-legal' that are drawn on by the court in justifying its own authority by constructing an imaginary space within which the criminal law is to apply. The tradition, it can be seen, is not something that is rigid and monolithic, but is in a continual process of reconstruction in response to changing circumstances. It forms itself around other developments, using here the idea of universal and natural jurisdiction to explain the scope and nature of the legal order. It is a partial account that makes sense if it is understood as a means of controlling authority and meaning within the criminal law. Thus we see the significance of the ideas of maturity and the priority of the common law – replacing an understanding of legal modernity. Our critical analysis depends on developing our understanding of both the modernity of the law and the constraints the tradition imposes on our thinking about this modernity.

Our primary concern thus remains that of developing an understanding of this modernity. In this period the modern sense of legality became increasingly detached from the issue of sovereignty and indeed from traditional ideas of the criminal law. It was increasingly being conceived in terms of procedures and the internal order of the system. This new moral order was progressively harnessing normative questions of seriousness and danger to procedure and systemic demands for speed and efficiency – to the extent, indeed, that this is the defining characteristic of the modern law. While the impact of this development has not diminished, neither has its significance been thought through. The important point about these procedural rules, therefore, is not that they bypass or render insignificant the common law but that they are the means of its continuing application. The law is still a vital social institution, but in order to ensure its continuing social relevance it must respond to the new administrative demands that are imposed upon it. The procedural rules, as they become more complex and specialised, mediate between the administrative demands of the interventionist state and the more traditional juridical forms. The procedural rules are the essential techniques for the balancing of the differing demands of law and administration. The truth is that the modern criminal law is defined through these procedures rather than by moral categories. In the next chapter we shall continue to pursue this interpretation by looking at the transformation of the substantive jurisdiction of the criminal law throughout the same period, for it will be argued that the production of internal order in the courts was mirrored by a concern with the imposition of homogeneous standards of behaviour. We will look, in other words, at the sense in which the order of the court was to become co-extensive with conceptions of public order.

4 The 'well-governed realm': crime and legal order 1747–1908

> After this . . . follows the *major* proposition of the libel, which names, or at least describes the crime, and characterizes it as one which, by the law of this and all other well-governed realms, is accounted a heinous crime and severely punishable.[1]

Introduction

It tends to be assumed that the substance of the criminal law is something that is relatively stable. There is said to be a basic 'core' of crimes, comprising homicide, rape, theft and so on, that remains unchanged, protecting certain fundamental social values such as human life and property. Equally, it is assumed that the law has always recognised that the question of guilt or moral blameworthiness was bound to the intention of the accused person. Even if this were so, and it is an overly simple account of the law, it tells us very little indeed about criminal jurisdiction at a particular place or time. We do not know, for example, what actions were included within these broad categories or how liability was attributed for these actions. Such issues can only be determined by examining the theoretical and practical limits governing the application of the rules. Different patterns emerge in the attribution of criminal liability, and the overall significance of certain crimes within the criminal justice system changes over time.

The issue that this raises, then, is not so much the question of the values that the law seeks to protect, but one of how crime is perceived and prosecuted. The formulaic recitation, as described by Hume, that comprised the major proposition of the criminal libel, captures well the combination of forces that define the substantive jurisdiction of the law. It raises the question of the right or wrong of actions, and hence their punishability. It combines the universal and the particular, linking local concerns to broader issues of good government, and it was also an enabling formula, the means by which the force of the criminal law was

[1] Hume 1844 II, p. 164; see also Cairns 1993.

brought into operation. Indeed, we have already noted a particular application of this in our discussion of the declaratory power, in the commonplace belief that prosecutions did not have to fall within the existing categories of crimes. It thus combines procedure, substantive law and the question of good government. This, however, is to raise more complex questions about criminal jurisdiction than is done by simply questioning which fundamental values the law seeks to protect. The central issue might be described as that of how the criminal law governs, or of determining the place of law in the production of the 'well-governed realm'.

The question of substantive jurisdiction is thus located at the intersection of crucial questions relating to the ordering and imagination of the nation. We face questions of boundaries and legality, once again. These relate to the power to determine which acts will be punishable, and which permissible, by law. In a political sense this poses the question of determining the boundaries of public and private power, dealing with the issue of where the state can enforce private rights to property or personal autonomy in the name of a public good. This in turn raises the 'administrative' question of the means by which these boundaries will be policed, the processes of enforcement or the types of regulation that will be used. It also includes the familiar liberal problem of the limits of state power and individual autonomy, which we have already encountered in the discussion of the principle of legality. We face the questions of the legal conditions of applicability of state sanctions as criminal sanctions, the separation and definition of the private and public aspects of an event and so on. These are closely linked to legal procedures; perceptions of seriousness are not only moral questions but are determined by, amongst other things, patterns of prosecution, the standards of proof required and the severity of the sentencing. In this chapter we will attempt to reconstruct a picture of the substantive jurisdiction of the criminal law in Scotland.

We shall broadly follow the pattern of the previous chapter. In the next section we will look at changes in the organisation and practice of criminal law from the middle of the eighteenth to the beginning of the twentieth century – to coincide with the 'codification' of procedural law. However, in the final part of the chapter we will begin to explore two important and related problems. These are the relationship between the common law vision of order and the transformation in criminal jurisdiction, and the development of criminal law doctrine in the nineteenth century.

Tightening the bonds of society: substantive jurisdiction 1750–1908

A Crime is a punishable Act of Injustice, by committing what is forbidden, or omitting to do what is commanded by Law.[2]

We know very little about the history of the criminal law in the nineteenth century. Although there has been an explosion in studies of the law in eighteenth-century England, the substantive law has only a shadowy presence in the histories of the nineteenth century. While all commentators seem to be agreed on the centrality of the problems of crime and policing to the Victorian mind, studies of the criminal law do not go far beyond noting the political battle over the reform of the 'bloody code' and the recurring theme of codification. We shall look at these questions only very obliquely in this chapter. This is partly because such issues were of much less significance to the development of the Scottish law in this period,[3] but more because we are concerned to link the very substantial changes in the nature of the criminal law to the institutional changes that were described in the last chapter.

The consolidation of political order

From the Act of Union until the parliamentary reforms of the 1830s, for all but the briefest of periods, political and social power was concentrated in the hands of the same narrow political elite.[4] But if the political order had achieved a certain level of internal stability, its control over certain areas of the country and social life was, at best, precarious. It is only recently that historians have started to bring to light the extent of social conflict and disorder in late eighteenth-century Scotland – a period of rapid economic and social change.[5] New research suggests that there were high levels of popular protest – against food prices, in favour of political reform, and latterly due to increasing numbers of industrial strikes as the early trade union movement became active. If the stability of the political order has deceived historians into generalising about actual levels of order in Scotland, it would be easy to make the same mistake in relation to the

[2] W. Forbes 1730 II, p. 2.
[3] It should be noted that although the greater preoccupation with property and its protection in England in the eighteenth century was arguably as much to do with public order as property, this meant that property was thematised differently in the English law, occupying a much more central role.   [4] On political stability, see Murdoch 1980; Lenman 1981.
[5] For recent reviews, see Whatley 1990 and 1992 arguing that historians have paid too much attention to the apparent political stability. See also Houston 1994, ch. 5 esp. pp. 320–31; for specific examples, see Logue 1979; Fraser 1988b; Devine 1990a.

criminal law. It, too, appears to be very settled and accepted, apparently mirroring the political order that it protected; but this appearance could, on occasion, be deceptive, for in practice the authority of the law and of its officers was readily challenged. Illegality and disorder were tolerated, but when protests threatened to spread outside a particular locale this was frequently met by the use of military force and repression. The perceived ringleaders were charged with the most serious crimes – treason, sedition or mobbing – carrying the penalties of death or transportation for life. To take only the most notorious examples, the 1790s witnessed a series of show trials for sedition against members of the Scottish Societies of Friends of the People,[6] and between 1815 and 1820 charges of treason were brought against the radical leaders of political uprisings in the west of Scotland.[7] The use of these heavy-handed tactics was connected to the instability of the political order and the limited powers of enforcement that the state could deploy. The criminal law was lenient in comparison to England, but only when it could afford to be. When the political order felt threatened, the reaction would be harsh and repressive.

The criminal law of this period was the means of the expression and protection of a range of concerns that reflected the political and social interests of the ruling elite. The seriousness of these crimes was shown by the heavy penalties and trial in the central, superior, courts, but they dealt with a very small number of cases. There are no precise figures, but if we take the earliest ones readily available, between 1805 and 1810, the High Court and circuit courts together dealt with between only 80 and 115 cases each year[8] – a figure which reflects the lack of formal organisation of the criminal justice system. The principal concern was with those crimes that actually or potentially challenged the political order. Thus Erskine, in a work first published in 1773, made the following, conventional, distinction between crimes proper and delicts. Crimes were more serious, those breaches of the law which had a 'more direct tendency to subvert the government or constitution, or loosen the bonds of society'.[9] These were to be pursued by the King's Advocate, in courts of a proper criminal jurisdiction and punished for the terror of others. Delicts, on the other hand, 'are commonly understood of slighter offences, which do not affect the public peace so immediately; and therefore may be punished by a small pecuniary fine, or by a short imprisonment, as petty riots, injuries,

---

[6] See H. Cockburn 1888; Hume 1844 I, pp. 553–60.
[7] Though many of these collapsed. See Hume 1844 I, pp. 515–25; Fraser 1988a, chs. 5–6; Return of Persons arrested or detained on Treasonable Charges in Scotland 1817 PP.1818.XVI.155; Commission of Inquiry into the Courts of Justice in Scotland. Fifth Report (Court of Justiciary) PP.1819.XI.69. See also Jamieson 1994.
[8] Return of Number of Persons Committed for Trial in Scotland 1805–1810 PP.1812.X.217.   [9] Erskine 1871 IV, iv, 2.

offences against inferior jurisdiction etc.'.[10] The terminology, derived from Roman law, has caused a certain amount of confusion, not least because the modern action of delict is a branch of private law, and crimes used to be divided into public and private according to whether or not the state took an interest,[11] however, the distinctions as they were then drawn are sufficiently clear. Crimes were offences against the laws of God or the good government of the realm, tried in the superior courts – defining, in practice, the extent of their jurisdiction. Delicts were lesser offences against public order tried by the inferior jurisdictions for minor penalties. It comes as little surprise to find that the conditions of liability for these minor crimes had not been elaborated in any detailed way by either judges or treatise writers. A prime example of this is Hume's discussion of 'breach of the peace', a minor offence mainly within the jurisdiction of the burgh courts. This is dealt with in one paragraph where he writes that if a quarrel is carried out in such a way, 'as to disturb or alarm the neighbourhood, this *seems to be* cognisable at instance of the public prosecutor'.[12] The understanding of these minor crimes would clearly vary from place to place, and the level of enforcement would depend on the activity of the magistrates and constables of the local jurisdiction in which they occurred. The substantive jurisdiction of the law, no less than its territorial jurisdiction, was piecemeal and fragmented.

This connection between crime and the protection of political order is again obvious in the sub-division of the category of crimes.[13] From Mackenzie onwards, throughout most of the eighteenth century, the standard classifications sought to reflect the seriousness of the injuries done to the commonwealth.[14] Thus, for example, Erskine's title declared that 'the atrocity of crimes is measured by their consequences for society',[15] and he went on to treat, in descending order of seriousness, crimes against religion, crimes against the state and finally those against private individuals in either their person or their property.[16] We should

[10] *Ibid.* (my emphasis); see also Mackenzie 1678, p. 2. Crimes are those transgressions which tend to 'wrong the Common-wealth, and public security immediately' and therefore must be punished by express laws.
[11] See Mackenzie 1678, pp. 21–2. See also W. Forbes 1730 II, p. 2. Discussed in Young forthcoming, ch. 3.
[12] Hume 1844 I, p. 439 (my emphasis). Alison 1832 does not mention breach of the peace at all. See also Erskine on offences against the laws of police 1871 IV, iv, 38–9. See the discussion in Christie 1990, ch. 1.
[13] See Cairns 1988 for a detailed discussion of this point. We should also note that the early English writers on the criminal law, notably Hale, Foster and Hawkins, were dealing with the 'Pleas of the Crown', reflecting the concerns of the centralised, royal system.
[14] *Ibid.*, p. 382.   [15] Erskine 1871 IV, iv, 15.
[16] Cairns 1988 also suggests that some of the classifications, and particularly that of Mackenzie, were also based on a declining seriousness of punishment. This is not

also note that crimes against individuals were initially regarded as punishable as an aspect of the interest in good government and the security of property (Mackenzie), and it was only later in the century that private individuals were recognised in the criminal law as having interests that needed to be protected in their own right. That political order remained the primary category can be illustrated by looking at the definitions of certain types of treason, mobbing and deforcement.

At the beginning of the eighteenth century the content of the crime of treason was considerably wider than those acts that directly challenged the political order (or, to be more precise, there was a different conception of political order), for there were a whole series of 'constructive' treasons – crimes that had been elevated, by statute, into the category of treason. This included such actions as wilful fire-raising, murder under trust, parricide and some offences against the currency of the realm.[17] Since seriousness was measured in terms of the perceived threat to the social order, the category of treason could include acts that appear (to us) to be of very different natures, which could then be more severely punished. Seriousness attached to the category 'treason', rather than to particular acts or intentions. This distinction survived into Hume's treatment of homicide. He discussed a category of aggravated homicide, punishable with greater than ordinary severity. This comprised those cases where there was, 'some singular baseness or cruelty in the manner of the deed, or some peculiar relation between the parties'.[18] These types of killings were in fact those that had formerly been treated as constructive treasons, although by the time that Hume wrote the statutes that had made them so had been repealed in the revision of the law of treason that followed the Union.[19] Closely related to treason was the crime of mobbing. Its criminality lay in the fact that the violence of a mob was regarded as usurping 'those means which it belongs to the supreme power alone to employ'.[20] The danger was 'the appearance of power, as well as the disposition to execute their own unlawful purposes, of their own will and authority'.[21] In cases where the grievance of the mob was considered to be

inconsistent with the argument here since it was the central courts, those connected to royal authority, that were claiming for themselves the sole power to impose capital punishments. See above, ch. 3.

[17] Smith and Macdonald 1958, p. 284. See Townsend 1993, pp. 116–18 on the strange form of the modernisation of the law of treason.

[18] Hume 1844 I, pp. 286–91. In England these were petty treasons under the statute 25 Edw. III c. 2 covering three species of murder under trust. See Blackstone 1765 IV, pp. 203–4.

[19] (1709) 7 Anne c. 21. See Hume 1844 I, pp. 532–3 and ch. 27. In England (1828) 9 Geo. IV c. 31 declared that petit treason was to be treated as murder.

[20] Hume 1844 I, p. 418.   [21] Ibid., p. 416.

of national, rather than private or local, concern, it could be charged as treason by 'levying of war'.[22] As Hume admits, this is a fine, almost invisible, distinction, and in practice much would depend on the response of local magistrates and authorities rather than abstract definitions of the crime. The trial of these crimes could accordingly be difficult or embarrassing since the definitions placed the focus directly on the question of the legitimacy of the actions – of the state as well as the protesters. Local juries often would not convict and the trials would collapse.[23] A final example, that was also close to contemporary concerns, is the crime of deforcement – the obstruction of officers of the law in the execution of their duty. Whatley[24] points to the fact that a notable feature of the first half of the eighteenth century was the high level of attacks on government officers, particularly customs and excise officers, who were attempting to enforce the payment of new taxes and duties levied as a result of the Union. Deforcement was regarded as a serious offence, 'because it is a contempt of the authority of the King, as represented in his Courts of Justice, and in the course of legal process; and is thus a matter of evil and very dangerous example, which tends to the unhinging of government, and to intercept the benefits of the state of civil union'.[25] As we are returned repeatedly to these themes it becomes clear that the question of good government was seen to depend on the continuing efforts to instil a respect for the sources of the law and the authority of its officers.[26]

A final characteristic of this system was a certain informality that is most marked in the refusal to fix the definitions of particular crimes. The law recognised certain heads of action but retained a procedural openness to new ones. The conditions of liability were worked out, often in minute detail, for each individual crime only as a series of responses to situations as they arose. Thus to take a typical statement from Hume about the crime of mobbing: 'I shall not pretend to lay any definition of it [the crime] before the student; but shall rather attempt to convey some notion of it in the course of an inquiry concerning the several particulars, which are

[22] Hume 1844 I, pp. 418–19, 521–9. The examples of local concerns that Hume gives are the lowering of the price of grain in a particular place or rescuing a criminal from execution.
[23] For a frank recognition of the potential difficulties involved in charging treason in the case of mobbing, see the letter from Duncan Forbes, Lord Advocate, to the Secretary of State on the occasion of the Malt-Tax riots in Glasgow 1725. He argues for the use of a simple charge of mobbing in order to avoid the procedural difficulties involved in the treason charge. Quoted in H. Cockburn 1824 at pp. 389–90. See also Lobban 1990.
[24] Whatley 1990.
[25] Hume 1844 I, p. 336. It is also interesting to note the tolerance displayed by Hume towards soldiers or legal officers who were excessively violent in the execution of their duty, e.g. 1844 I, pp. 195–217. See also Mackenzie 1678.
[26] Whatley 1990, p. 10; see also Lenman 1984, p. 212.

necessary towards the conviction of any offender in this sort'.[27] Procedure
did not require a strict adherence to the existing heads of crime but merely
the libelling of an act that was 'plainly of a criminal nature'.[28] It is here, in
these procedural rules, that we find the origins of the flexibility so highly
prized by the Scottish legal tradition.[29] But if these formulations betray
some natural law origins in the belief that immoral acts were necessarily
illegal, they are also based in the weak formal organisation of the law.[30]
Procedure and remedies – the ability to respond to pressing or threatening
situations – were more important than formal definitions. The prosecutor
and judge were between them possessed of a large discretion, permitting a
response that might be lenient or repressive as the situation allowed.

Yet the system was not completely informal, but was constrained by
complex and rigid rules of procedure in the High Court.[31] The smallest
error or deviation could, and often did, lead to the complete acquittal of
the accused. To grasp this point it is sufficient to register the dire warnings
offered to lawyers about the consequences of errors in form. Hume sternly
reminds us that,

> any omission or inaccuracy that breaks the texture of the syllogism, and hinders
> the connection of sense, or even of language, shall, in strictness, vitiate the libel . . .
> It is not decent that the face of a criminal record should be slurred with these lame
> and disjointed accusations; and no allowance can be had of such slovenly
> blunders, in the preparing of this sort of business'.[32]

These were not empty threats, though they point rather to the need to
preserve the dignity (or decency) of the legal process than to any desire to

---

[27] Hume 1844 I, p. 416; see also e.g. I, p. 238 on assaults and real injuries; I, p. 386 on
deforcement and so on.

[28] Hume 1844 II, pp. 168–9 and I, pp. 12, 328; Alison 1832, ch. 34. This was a common
feature of other European systems in the same period. See for France, von Bar 1916, ch.
10; England, Manchester 1980, p. 209. Attempts to limit this by the codification of the
criminal law date from 1751 in Bavaria. See von Bar 1916.

[29] Above, ch. 2; it is significant that this flexibility was probably not confined to the criminal
law, but also applied to the law of reparation in the same period. See McKechnie 1931; D.
M. Walker 1952.

[30] Devine 1990b, pp. 53–4; Young forthcoming, ch. 3; cf. Connolly 1980. The royal
prerogative of mercy might also have played an important part in the operation of this
system – Edmund Burke quoted by Hume II, p. 495. See the classic account of Hay 1975;
cf. Gane 1980.

[31] See also Cairns 1993, pp. 142–5. For England, see Langbein 1978 and 1983b attributing
the growth of formalism to the intervention of lawyers in the criminal trial. The English
system of common law procedure was reformed by (1851) 14 and 15 Vict. c. 100.

[32] Hume 1844 II, p. 155 and cases cited there. Likewise Alison 1833, p. 211. These errors
would not necessarily prevent the prosecutor from starting again! For an example, see
case of *John Hannah* 1806 (Hume 1844 I, p. 8). A libel was dismissed when the
prosecution misdescribed the occupation of the murdered woman's father, and the court
refused to allow the prosecutor to start again.

protect the rights of the accused. The criminal statistics for the early nineteenth century show that between 10 and 20 per cent of cases were discharged or deserted every year for want of sufficient evidence or 'Informality of Execution by Messengers or on account of the Terms of the Verdict or other Cause' – there were acquittals in a further 15 to 20 per cent of cases each year.[33] Even bearing in mind the extremely small number of cases involved, these figures must qualify any claim that the Scottish courts could be depended on to convict those who were brought before them.[34] The legitimacy of the legal order may have been open to challenge, but we cannot properly characterise it as either wholly illegitimate or repressive.

This picture of a system of criminal law that is both highly flexible and highly rigid and that is central to legitimation of political and social order suggests direct comparisons with the English law where, if anything, the exercise of discretion was more marked. Recent histories of the English criminal law have dwelt on the combinations of mercy and severity, of discretion and formalism, and of order and disorder that characterised the criminal law of the 'ancien régime'.[35] The formal severity of the law, 'a system of punishment that depended fundamentally on hanging', was tempered by the use of the royal prerogative and the low levels of enforcement.[36] The procedure of the central courts was highly formal,[37] but gave room for a certain level of discretion in mitigation of the severity of the law. A complex balancing of central and local authority was achieved by means of the criminal law. Thus, while the country may have been violent and the people 'ungovernable', it has been argued that this was a form of social and political order and that government by the criminal law lay at its heart. This question of governability was to remain at the heart of the law. If the insecurity of the political order was greater in Scotland, it is no less the case that in both jurisdictions the legitimacy of the political order depended on the administration of criminal justice in the courts. These were in turn sustained by the network of local jurisdictions and the personal nature of the confrontation with the law. However, with industrialisation and the migration of population to the cities, the problem of crime and social order grew in significance. The problem was not simply that the ability of these traditional institutions to maintain order, or to govern,

[33] Return of Number of Persons Committed for Trial in Scotland 1805–1810 PP.1812.X.217.   [34] Connolly 1980, p. 121. Cf. E. P. Thompson 1975, pp. 259–65.
[35] The literature is enormous and cannot readily be summarised. For a review of the main themes and points of controversy, see Innes and Styles 1986.
[36] Beattie 1986, p. 632. The classic account is in Hay 1975; cf. Langbein 1983a.
[37] See Langbein 1978 and 1983b.

was being challenged, but that the very idea of order itself was being transformed.

From political order to public order

Over the last twenty years historians have drawn attention to transformations of policing and punishment in England.[38] The growing urban working classes were subjected to higher levels of discipline and surveillance through the more intensive policing of minor illegalities. The new police fought not only for the control of public space but for the ordering of public behaviour. There is every reason to suppose, following our account of the development of police courts, that the patterns of development are broadly similar in Scotland, though there has been little research in this area. What has been less remarked upon is the transformation that was brought about in the organisation and use of the criminal law as it came to be dominated by a preoccupation with 'public order'.

This is most obvious if we look at the remarkable changes in the use of the criminal law over the course of the nineteenth century. Not only was there a dramatic expansion in the number of cases – that parallels the development of summary jurisdiction and the growth of police forces – but there were also changes in the relative significance of crimes, in numerical terms, to the operation of the criminal law. This can be illustrated by a crude comparison of the criminal statistics over the course of the century.[39] We have already noted that in the early 1800s the Justiciary Court was only dealing with between 100 and 150 cases every year. These were mainly concentrated in the areas of murder, culpable homicide, theft and housebreaking;[40] there are no figures available for the inferior courts, but in the absence of systematic prosecution it seems unlikely that they would have been dealing with more than a few thousand cases every year. By the late 1830s, when some figures become available for the sheriff court, there was still a similar pattern, although the caseload of the Justiciary Court had almost doubled. From an overall total of 2,594 trials in both courts there were 2,332 convictions (about 75 per cent),

---

[38] For reviews of the revisionist history of policing and punishment, see Gattrell 1990; Philips 1985; Ignatieff 1985; Reiner 1985, chs. 1 and 2. See also Foucault 1977; Silver 1967; and for Scotland, Carson 1984–5. On the changing image of public order in the nineteenth century and its peculiar English form, see Townsend 1993, chs. 1 and 3.

[39] On the development of crime statistics in Scotland, see Young forthcoming, ch. 4. The following analysis is intended simply to report on the official statistics collected. The shortcomings of these statistics, notably in relation to the inferior courts, should be noted, though to the extent that we are concerned to register the growing importance of the inferior courts (something that is reflected also in the fact that their activities began to be recorded) these do not affect the overall argument.   [40] PP.1825.XXIII.523

once again predominantly in the areas of offences against property and against the person.[41] It was not until 1868 when there was a change in the method of collection of criminal statistics that the extent of the activities of the inferior courts begins to be revealed. The total number of persons arrested was a staggering 119,623, which produced a total of 87,156 trials with 81,901 convictions.[42] Around 3,000 of these were tried under solemn procedure in the High Court or sheriff court, with the rest tried summarily in the sheriff and burgh courts. Slightly less than half of the arrests fall into the category of miscellaneous statutory police offences (45,865), to which we should also add the arrests for minor assaults, breaches of the peace and disorderly conduct (42,014), statutory road offences (2,084), begging (1,375) and public house offences (2,173), which were all also 'police' offences.[43] The other major categories were theft (10,463) and assault (6,771), of which a sizeable proportion must have been tried summarily. Cases dealt with under solemn procedure were still mainly in the areas of crimes against property and the person, suggesting that certain species of assault and theft were of considerable symbolic importance.

This pattern was to continue with slight variations until the end of the century and we can briefly summarise the main trends.[44] Notwithstanding a slight decrease in the mid-1880s, the overall number of prosecutions continued to increase: in 1877, 142,346 persons were charged; in 1888, 137,920; and in 1898 some 165,903. Taking the year 1898 as an example, 163,613 cases were prosecuted summarily. Convictions were obtained in 119,811 instances with acquittals in only 5,222. Proceedings were dropped for various reasons in 35,656 cases, though normally with the forfeiture of pledges (bail), which in many police districts was regarded as equivalent to a conviction. The increases can be put down to the improved organisation of the police and the availability of summary modes of prosecution, rather than increasing depravity or viciousness – a fact recognised by contemporaries.[45] The overall number of cases tried in the Justiciary Court decreased to the level at the beginning of the century – to underline the point made in the last chapter that solemn procedure

---

[41] These figures do not cover cases tried under the new summary process. Table of Number of Criminal Offenders in Scotland 1837 PP.1837–8.XLIII.121 About 1,600 offences of various sorts against property; 125 cases of riot and breach of the peace.

[42] Report on Judicial Statistics of Scotland 1868 PP.1871.LXIV.477 (the figures for the individual offences are only broken down for the number of arrests not trials).

[43] These mostly came from the cities of Glasgow and Edinburgh.

[44] The figures in this paragraph have been drawn from the Reports on the Judicial Statistics for Scotland 1877, 1888, and 1898 in PP.1878–9.LXXVI.425; PP.1889.LXXXV.401; PP.1900.CIII.447.

[45] See the Report of the Departmental Committee on Habitual Offenders etc. 1895, in PP.1895.XXXVII.1–12; see generally Gattrell 1990.

became more solemn – although the number of cases dealt with by solemn procedure remained roughly the same (between 2,000 and 2,500 annually). Finally, from the way that the various offences were broken down in these statistics we can read off some of the major concerns of the law enforcers. There were steady increases in prosecutions for minor assaults, disorderly conduct and breaches of the peace (57,628 in 1877; 63,422 in 1888; 67,239 in 1898), so that proportionally these continued to be between one third and one half of the crimes prosecuted every year. In the later statistics the category of police offences was broken down to reveal that in 1877 28,893 people were charged with being drunk and incapable, a figure broadly consistent with the figures for 1888 showing 19,826 people charged with being drunk and incapable along with 8,219 offences against the Public House and Licensing Acts. By 1898 this had jumped to the overall figure of 40,977, and, since most breaches of the peace were regarded as having been committed under the influence of alcohol, a contemporary estimate was that drunkenness accounted for 71 per cent of the total apprehensions and citations in Scotland each year![46] Offences against property, by contrast, remained at a constant level (around 14,000 each year), decreasing as a proportion of the whole. These figures suggest very clearly that the major concerns of the nineteenth-century law enforcer were order and respectability. The new policing intervened in and controlled the activities of particular groups of the population, but it could only do so on the basis of a transformation of the concept of public order.[47]

An important feature of this development was the decline in the use of military force in the maintenance of public order. This marks an important shift in the use of the criminal law. The authorities became aware of the shortcomings of the use of naked military force in situations of political or industrial unrest. Troops could have no permanent presence in an area of unrest: the level of force was too high, they were expensive to maintain and, on top of everything, their use might inflame rather than calm disorder by heightening the sense of confrontation.[48] Instead, police were used, and their tactics aimed at prevention and the control of order. This was a more 'economical' use of force, both in the sense of costing less and of avoiding the grand confrontation. This is not to

[46] Report of the Departmental Committee on Habitual Offenders etc. 1895, p. 1.
[47] See e.g. *McAra v. Mags. of Edinburgh* 1910 S.C. 1059 Lord President Dunedin at p. 1073: 'The primary and overruling object for which streets exist is passage. The streets are public but they are public for passage and there is no such thing as a right in the public to hold meetings as such in the streets.'
[48] See Select Committee on Police PP.1852–3.XXXVI.107; Alison 1883, pp. 337–402, 492, 606; Carson 1984–5, pp. 5–8; Gattrell 1990, pp. 265–8; Townsend 1993, pp. 17–19. See also Vogler 1991.

say that troops were not used, indeed Carson provides examples of their use well into the 1880s, but they were used more sparingly as the political dangers of direct confrontation were recognised. This led to a more 'economical' use of the law. The grand semi-military confrontations of the turn of the century had produced trials for sedition and treason, many of which had collapsed because of difficulties of proof and the discussion required by these charges of the legitimacy of the actions of both protesters and the authorities. Even where convictions had been obtained it was not without cost, as the equation of the law with political repression was damaging to the legitimacy of the government. Instead, we find charges of the less serious crimes of mobbing, rioting and breach of the peace and an emphasis on the criminal nature of the protest. There is a striking illustration of this in the use of the charge of mobbing so that the definition no longer presented the drama of a political confrontation, but was reduced to its formal legal elements. We can see this in a string of cases arising from one of the most controversial episodes of the nineteenth century – the so-called 'Highland Land War'.[49]

These cases arose out of incidents on the Western Isles in which the crofting community had resisted attempts by the highland landowners to have them evicted from their homes. The conflict had escalated to the point at which the government had sent marines to assist in the delivery of eviction notices and the suppression of the revolt. The three reported prosecutions reveal an active restraint on the government side. The crofters' grievances were not discussed, though much was made of the fact that the landlords had gone through the correct legal procedures. The Crown was at pains to underline the principle that the law extended to the whole of the country and that no one, neither crofters nor landlords, was above the law. The state did not defend partisan interests, for the rule of law was derived from the community itself: 'The laws of the land are just the rules of society, prescribed by society for the common welfare of society, alike for all, and enforced in the same manner upon all'.[50] The juries were instructed that the crime of mobbing had been committed if an assembly of people had gathered with a common illegal or unlawful purpose, and had attempted to effect that purpose by the use of violence or intimidation. Finally, those found guilty were given light sentences for there was no need to run the risk of creating political martyrs. By the end

---

[49] HM Adv. v. Martin and ors. (Borniskitaig Crofters) (1886) 1 White 297; HM Adv. v. Nicolson and ors. (Garralapin Crofters) (1887) 1 White 307; HM Adv. v. Macdonald and ors. (Herbusta Crofters) (1887) 1 White 315.

[50] Lord Young, sentencing the accused in Macdonald and ors at p. 318. See also Lord Advocate Macdonald in Martin and ors. at p. 302: 'Without that there is no guarantee of the liberties and rights, either of those who have property, or those who have none.' See also Carson 1984–5, pp. 6–8.

of the century, high profile cases such as these were exceptional. Occasional charges of mobbing and rioting were disposed of summarily, but more commonly resort would be had to the charge of breach of the public peace, which obviated the requirement to prove unlawful purpose. The removal of the political element from the definition of these crimes marks the movement to a new legal order. Crimes against political order thus slipped unnoticed into obscurity.[51]

Equally significant to the formation of the modern criminal law was the more intensive policing and prosecution of minor delinquencies. This was aimed at the control and eradication of alternative forms of subsistence and, more generally, at ways of life that challenged Victorian visions of respectability.[52] Control of the streets and the cities was important because disorder was regarded as criminogenic, but also as an end in itself. Particular targets were vagrancy, unlicensed street trading, begging, prostitution and, the root of these evils, drunkenness. A notable feature of the law that emerged was that the obtaining of a conviction, and the recording and controlling of the offenders, came to be regarded as more important than the severity of the penalty.[53] This was facilitated by an impressive arsenal of common law and statutory powers, many of which developed out of the traditional categories of the burghal jurisdiction,[54] the best example of which is the crime of breach of the peace.

Breach of the peace was not of great significance to the criminal law of the early part of the nineteenth century, as befitted a crime that was largely the concern of the inferior courts. Although treated by Hume as species of the crime of mobbing and rioting, it was widely accepted that control of the public peace fell within the scope of the traditional police powers of the burgh and would not normally be prosecuted on indictment. The charge was so elastic to be capable of covering almost any activity that disturbed the sensibilities of Victorian Scotland, and this elasticity was exploited to

---

[51] G. H. Gordon 1978, ch. 39 notes that there were prosecutions for sedition in 1848 and 1921. The crime of mobbing had almost disappeared by mid-century. In the statistics for 1868, (n. 42 above), there were only thirty-eight arrests and most of these appear to have been prosecuted summarily. For the position in England, see Lobban 1990 who charts the decline of the use of the charge of seditious libel and the rise of the crime of unlawful assembly as an offence less than riot. This protected the public peace without putting the political claims of the protestors at issue.

[52] Carson 1984–5, pp. 8–15; see also Petrow 1994; F. M. L. Thompson 1988, ch. 8 at pp. 329–31; Radzinowicz and Hood 1986, ch. 3 and Wiener 1990, chs. 5–7 on the distinction between 'reformable' criminals and the irredeemably bad. It is also very important to note the abiding connection between indecency and public order recorded in B. Brown 1993, pp. 33–5.

[53] See the Report of the Departmental Committee on Habitual Offenders etc. 1895.

[54] Underlining the point made in the last chapter that there seems to have been a continuity between the 'old' and the 'new' police.

the full.[55] A brief survey of the reported nineteenth-century cases shows its use against 'disorderly conduct' ranging from fighting and brawling, to threatening or drunken conduct, to the throwing of a quantity of pease meal and soot into the air on a Glasgow street![56] A further striking feature of the use of the charge from mid-century onwards was its use against actions which could, on the face of the complaint or libel, have been charged as alternative, and more serious, offences.[57] Whether prosecuted under common law or statute, a choice that often depended on whether or not the town in question had adopted a Police Act, the vast majority of these offences were prosecuted summarily, at the instance of the local procurator fiscal of the police or burgh court, who would probably also be the local superintendent of police. All that was required was that the conduct have been such as might reasonably have produced alarm to members of the public.[58] The scope of the charge, and the ease with which it could be proved, can be illustrated by the case of *Ferguson v. Carnochan*.[59] The disturbance had taken place within a private dwelling house late at night. Two policemen alleged that they had heard shouting and arguing and, on gaining admittance to the house, that Ferguson was drunk and had sworn at them. This self-corroborating evidence was sufficient to produce conviction. When Ferguson appealed, on the grounds that he had been in his own house and that there was no proof that anyone had been alarmed, it was held that not only did the public peace include any disturbances emanating from private houses or premises, but also that the public need not have actually been alarmed. The focus was less on the particular conduct and its actual effects, than on the belief that what was being done caused, or might have caused, disturbance to members of the public.

The crime of breach of the peace was also sufficiently elastic to catch actions on the edge of illegality, where it might otherwise have been difficult to obtain a conviction. An affirmation of this power is found in the case of *Jackson v. Linton*,[60] in which a man was convicted for having

[55] See the excellent discussion in Christie 1990, chs. 1 and 2: '[N]o separate class of 'police offences' is now recognised at common law . . . since 'police offences' have largely been subsumed by breach of the peace' (p. 18).

[56] Christie 1990; *Stevenson v. Lang* (1878) 4 Coup. 76 is the case of soot throwing.

[57] *Fraser* (1839) 2 Swin. 436 (contravention of the statute against perturbing the order of the kirk in time of worship); *Ainslie* (1842) 1 Broun 25 (casting off clothes); *Duncan* (1843) Broun 512 (mobbing and rioting); *McKechnie* (1832) Bell's Notes, pp. 111–12 (contravention of the statute against duelling). Christie 1990, pp. 21–2.

[58] For an example of statutory provision, see Burgh Police (S.) Act 1892 s. 380(12) with a matching common law provision in *Macdonald* (1887) 1 White 315.

[59] (1889) 2 White 278; Christie 1990, pp. 24–9, 36–8. See also *Matthews and Rodden* (1860) 3 Irv. 570. Smout 1986, pp. 148–9 discusses the policing of overcrowded buildings. Breach of the peace inside a private house was also covered by various Police Acts e.g. the Burgh Police (S) Act 1892 (55 and 56 Vict. c. 55) s. 380(2).   [60] (1860) 3 Irv. 563.

attempted to pick pockets. He attempted to suspend his conviction on the grounds that the Justiciary Court had recently held that an attempt to steal was not a criminal offence. This argument was summarily rejected by the judge, in the following terms: 'As to its criminality I have never had any doubt. It is a breach of the peace, and a breach of the peace with felonious intent'.[61] This prompted the later observation that many offences prosecuted under other names 'are truly at the same time breaches of the peace'.[62] The case as reported implies, moreover, that the use of such powers was commonplace against those suspected of being of bad character or 'rogues and vagabonds'. The converse was also true. In an earlier case Lord Ivory had observed that it was a principle upheld by the court that a person should not be brought summarily before the magistrate, 'when a party accused is respectable, known to the police, law-biding, and not purposing to go abroad, and not caught in the actual commission of an offence'.[63] Most tellingly these cases reveal how the combination of broadly defined offences, informal summary procedures and the newly organised enforcement agencies was able to push back the boundaries of the criminal law.

This was matched by the prosecution of other activities regarded as having some nuisance value, notably prostitution, begging and vagrancy. Not only had none of these been offences at common law, but they were notable because of the importance of character, rather than simply conduct, to the definition of the offence. Prostitutes were punished under powers provided in local and general Police Acts and consequently were not punishable outside the burghs.[64] The offence was loitering and importuning by a 'common prostitute', a definition that placed considerable powers in the hands of the police and made it practically impossible for a woman, once charged, to escape conviction.[65] This combination of character and nuisance was also found in the provisions on vagrancy. This was regarded as a considerable problem in nineteenth-century Scotland, because few places were willing to bear the cost of supporting them – to the extent that by the end of the century the police had gone to the extraordinary length of compiling a regular census of vagrants.[66] In the burghs these were dealt with by penal provisions against those begging or

---

[61] Lord Justice-Clerk Inglis, *ibid.* at p. 566.
[62] Macdonald 1867, p. 214. And *vice versa* no doubt . . .
[63] *Durrin and Stewart v. Mackay* (1859) 3 Irv. 341 at p. 346. See also *Etch and Goff v. Burnett* 1849 Shaw 201.
[64] See 1892 Act s. 381(22) reproducing the provisions of the 1862 Act. For a recent account of the English position, with particular reference to London, see Petrow 1994 part iii; Steedman 1984 part i.
[65] Report of the Departmental Committee on Habitual Offenders etc. 1895 at pp. 12–14; Dove Wilson 1895, pp. 559–60.
[66] See e.g. Forty-second Report of the Inspector of Constabulary 1899 PP.1900.XL.431.

conducting themselves as a vagrant, with severer penalties for a second offence.[67] More stringent powers were provided under the Prevention of Crime Act 1871.[68] The common feature of these provisions was that a person found in suspicious circumstances or unable to prove that they were earning an honest living could be summarily prosecuted. The actual commission of a criminal act was no longer, if it ever had been, a prerequisite of punishment. The numbers of prosecutions under these powers were relatively small, but their effect must be looked for elsewhere – in the gradual concentration of powers in the hands of an organised police force,[69] and as a record of the introduction of a new social interest into the criminal law.

The concern with drunkenness and criminality appears to have escalated from the 1870s and 1880s onwards, when we begin to see the collection of separate statistics for offences involving drunkenness, and the specification of these in the general criminal statistics.[70] There can be little doubt as to the scale of drinking in Scotland throughout the nineteenth century, nor that the drinking habits of the urban poor were regarded as both a matter of disgust and concern to their social superiors.[71] Links had long been drawn between alcohol and the social problem of crime, fostering the belief that drink was indeed the root of evils as diverse as poverty, disease and bad housing. More specifically, though it was believed to precipitate violence and disorder by those who were already drunk and to encourage theft and dishonesty amongst those attempting to finance their drinking habits, drunkenness itself had not previously been regarded as criminal.[72] One response to this was the establishment of a general system of licensing to control the sale of alcohol. This brought breaches of licensing conditions within the scope of

[67] 1862 Act ss. 331–4; 1892 Act ss. 408–11; Dove Wilson 1895, pp. 557–8.

[68] 34 and 35 Vict. c. 112 s. 15. Amended by 39 and 40 Vict. c. 23; 42 and 43 Vict. c. 55; 48 and 49 Vict. c. 75 and the Penal Servitude Act 1891 (54 and 55 Vict. c. 69). On the background to this legislation, see Wiener 1990, pp. 148–51.

[69] Carson 1984–5, pp. 10–11.

[70] For the most detailed contemporary analysis, collecting statistics from 1870 onwards, see the Report of the Departmental Committee on Habitual Offenders etc. 1895 PP.1895.XXXVII.1; for examples of statistics, see Return of Number of Cases of Drunkenness in Burghs in Scotland PP.1857–8.XLVII. 631; Return of Arrests for Drunkenness in Scotland, 1882 PP.1883.LV.713; Return for each Burgh and County in Scotland of Number of Arrests for being Drunk and Disorderly 1892 PP.1893–4.LXXIV.Pt.1.145. See also Judicial Statistics 1898 PP.1900.CIII.447 particularly at pp. 20–5 where a map is drawn to represent the geographical distribution of the problem.

[71] Though these same superiors were happy to record the consumption of heroic amounts of alcohol! See for background, Smout 1986, ch. 6; Fraser 1990. See also Petrow 1994 pt. IV; Wiener 1990, pp. 294–306.

[72] See Hume 1844 I, p. 469: 'if it could effectually be restrained by penal laws, would well deserve the attention of the Legislature'; see also Dove Wilson 1895, p. 558.

the criminal law, and also aimed at the production of revenue.[73] Another was the singling out and policing of the disorderly effects of alcohol consumption. Initially this was done by means of the burgh's powers to enforce good order where drunkenness was causing a breach of the peace. Later, the specific offence of being drunk and incapable was introduced in both Police and Licensing Acts[74] – although this did not lead to a decrease in the numbers prosecuted for breach of the peace. The enforcement of these provisions was not uniform: in the counties it would appear that the payment of fines was not enforced; Edinburgh police and magistrates claimed to prosecute in every case; while in Glasgow, until 1875, convictions were not sought where pledges (bail) had been made, since the forfeiture of the pledge was itself regarded as equivalent to a conviction.[75] As serious crime was perceived to be decreasing, drunkenness was regarded as the major problem that the criminal law had to face, since practically all minor offences against public order were believed to have been committed under the influence of alcohol.[76]

By the end of the nineteenth century, then, the criminal law was being turned towards the solution of these social problems. The 'well-governed realm' was seen to require not only the simple suppression of unrest, but to be based on the construction of a positive vision of social order. The nature of this new relationship between criminal law and public order was captured in a memorandum presented by the Director of the Scottish prisons, Colonel McHardy, to the Departmental Committee on Habitual Offenders in 1895.[77] There were, he explained, a considerable number of people who frequently appeared before the police courts charged with minor offences for whom the law was not sufficiently deterrent since they were frequently recommitted to prison for short periods. He went on,

These persons cause – 1st. Immense trouble to Magistrates, Police and Prison Officials, 2nd. Considerable disturbance in the poorer districts of cities and towns, and 3rd. Largely prevent the improvement in the social state which is the great endeavour of modern government.

Connections had thus been drawn between the law, public order (especially in the cities), and the objects of good government. Threats to

[73] See Robertson 1878, p. 267–72 for a history of the various provisions.
[74] e.g. 13 and 14 Vict. c. 33 s. 97; Burgh Police (S.) Act 1892 s. 382 provided for more severe punishment on second and subsequent offences, although this was not enforced. Licensing statutes contained provisions on being drunk and disorderly from the Public House Act Amendment Act 1862 (25 and 26 Vict. c. 35) s. 23 onwards.
[75] See Report of the Departmental Committee on Habitual Offenders etc. 1895, pp. vii–viii.
[76] *Ibid.*, pp. lxvii–lix; Report of the Departmental Committee on Rules for Inebriate Reformatories PP.1899.XII.775; see also Inebriates Act 1898 (61 and 62 Vict. c. 60) and the Licensing (S.) Act 1903 (3 Edw. VII c. 25) ss. 70, 72 and 75; see A. M. Anderson 1904, pp. 7–13; discussed in Radzinowicz and Hood 1986, pp. 301–15.   [77] App. D.

order were perceived at the most mundane level – the costly, repetitive, demoralising petty offenders. The trouble and disturbance that they caused was regarded as a threat to social security which did not strike at the heart of the legal or social order. Indeed, legal (public) order had been differentiated from political or social order. These were seen as the ends of good government, providing the basis of policies in criminal justice,[78] but the maintenance of legal order had become primarily a technical question, the control of public order a question of management, and the criminal law a means to the fulfilment of a greater social end.

What is more, the means of operation of the law had changed. Through broad and flexible definitions it retained its openness to changing social circumstance, but the power to define the objects of legal regulation had been taken over by minor legal officials and police officers. The redefinition of public order also affected the criminal trial. A criminal population of unprecedented size had been created, and that brought related problems of dealing with large numbers of persons speedily and efficiently. From the 1850s, the trial was geared to the production of guilty pleas and the facilitation of prosecution, and the legal order of the courtroom mirrored the ordering of public space outside.

The administration of the criminal law

The policing of public order produced categories or classes of deviants who were treated as special problems. The attribution of guilt was based, as we have seen, on character, situation or history rather than responsibility for actions. Different classes of legal responsibility were specified, underlining the fact that the criminal law's professed concern for the rights of the accused had long been matched by an equal preoccupation with discipline and surveillance.[79] The relationship between individualism and the various forms of legal liability is complex, but it is important to see how it was shaped by the positioning of the criminal law in the emerging network of agencies and institutions of criminal justice. We shall look very briefly at the legal background of provisions relating to prior offences, juveniles and lunatics and 'regulatory' offences which, although differing in nature, together reveal important features of the modern law.

The practice of treating previous convictions of an offence as aggravations, increasing the severity of the punishment, was well established by

---

[78] See Radzinowicz and Hood 1986 and Wiener 1990 on the emergence of the idea of 'policy' in criminal justice.
[79] Indeed, as Foucault 1977 suggests, these seem to go hand in hand, esp. at pp. 102–3. See also Wiener 1990, pp. 52–83, 151–6, arguing that the early Victorian law was dominated by a concern with the building of character. See also Feeley and Simon 1994.

the early 1800s.[80] This had a special application in the law of theft, where the aggravation of being a 'habit and repute' thief, one who had the reputation of living in whole or in part by thieving, could render the accused liable to capital punishment.[81] This type of aggravation, based on character and previous convictions, became increasingly important not only for the degree of punishment, but also for the finding of guilt.[82] This can be illustrated by comparing two differing views on the question of the proof of the aggravation. For Burnett, writing early in the century, the evidence of neighbours as to the character of the accused was to be given more weight in the trial than that of the police.[83] Some thirty years later the opposite was true. Alison argued that, especially in the great cities,

In truth, the only persons, excepting those of their own gang, who keep their eye upon them, and can speak from personal knowledge of their profession and avocations, are the police officers into whose hands they frequently come on charges of theft and whose business leads them to be in a peculiar manner conversant with persons of their habits.[84]

This process was facilitated by improvements in the organisation of the courts and the keeping of records. Until the Criminal Procedure (S.) Act 1887 adopted the English law on this point, previous convictions were required to be proved as part of the prosecution case and before the verdict of the jury in both superior and inferior courts.[85] Following the Act, although they could only be brought before the court at the sentencing stage, they no longer had to be proved, the record of the court being sufficient proof. Notwithstanding this, in summary courts it appears to have been standard practice to read out the previous convictions as part of the charge, even after the passing of the 1887 Act.[86] The perception of 'danger' was removed from the experience of the community into the hands of the criminal justice organisations.[87]

This was accompanied by important changes in legal practice. By the late 1830s, theft was in practice no longer a capital crime in Scotland. This had a number of important consequences. As convictions became easier to obtain, the category of theft was expanded by the courts to include

[80] See Hume 1844 II, p. 219; Alison 1832, pp. 297, 304. *Campbell* (1822) Shaw 66.
[81] Hume 1844 I, pp. 92–7. It did not require that the person have been previously convicted of theft. [82] See Alison 1832, pp. 302–3.
[83] Burnett 1811, p. 131. Perhaps reflecting something of the original function of the jury.
[84] Alison 1832, p. 298. This sentiment was given the force of a legal presumption. In a case in 1838 it was held that to prove this aggravation it was sufficient that, 'two police officers depone that the prisoner is a habit and repute thief, even if they themselves do not think the repute well-founded . . .' (Lord Meadowbank in *HM Adv. v. Mackenzie* (1838) 2 Swin. 210). [85] 50 and 51 Vict. c. 35 ss. 67 and 71. Macdonald 1867, ch. 1.
[86] See Report of the Departmental Committee on Habitual Offenders etc. 1895, p. xv.
[87] On police, experience and danger, see Ladeur 1994, pp. 301–3; Murphy 1991, pp. 198–203.

constructive possession and forms of theft by finding.[88] This facilitated the gradual downgrading of the seriousness of theft which was increasingly being tried under summary procedures. More importantly for our present argument, however, the operation of this 'administrative and judicial discretion'[89] not only obviated the need for legislation to restrict the numbers of capital offences, but had the greater effect of blurring the distinctions between the different classes of property offences. Prior to this, for example, the aggravation of 'habit and repute' could only apply where previous convictions had been for exactly the same offence and, because of the potentially severe consequences of conviction, strict distinctions had been maintained.[90] Subsequently, the courts relaxed the strictness of the rule, allowing the more ready application of the aggravation. This practice was regularised by the Criminal Procedure (S.) Act 1887. This established first that charges of one type of dishonesty could lead to convictions for other types,[91] virtually destroying the need for strict definitions. Second, it laid down that a previous conviction which would be regarded as a relevant aggravation need no longer be for the same offence, but need only fall within certain broad classes of crimes.[92] The Summary Jurisdiction (S.) Act 1908[93] extended these provisions further by establishing that any convictions falling into the class of offences inferring disorderly conduct or breach of the peace would be regarded as relevant aggravations. The facilitation of prosecution and proof by these means has proved in the long term to be of much greater importance than any of the specific provisions on habitual criminality.[94] The broadness and flexibility of the common law concepts had been reinforced by the careful use of administrative and judicial discretion.

[88] For a brief history of this, see G. H. Gordon 1978, pp. 450–9 and cases cited there.

[89] *Ibid.*, p. 454 n. 32. Although the Criminal Procedure (S.) Act 1887 s. 56 finally abolished the death penalty for all offences other than murder, this was merely regularising the existing practice. Prior to this, Scotland had twenty-five capital offences to England's eight (figures cited in Radzinowicz 1968, p. 324). In England the use of the death penalty was either limited or abolished for offences not involving violence in a series of statutes in 1837, and abolished for all offences other than murder or high treason by the Offences Against the Person Act 1861. See generally Radzinowicz 1968, ch. 8.

[90] It had probably operated to mitigate undue severity. See the judgement of Lord Cockburn in *HM Adv. v. Falconer* (1852) Shaw 546.

[91] 50 and 51 Vict. c. 35 s. 59 e.g. a conviction for reset on a charge of theft, of theft on a charge of fraud etc. For a justification of this, see Macdonald 1891; see also G. H. Gordon 1978, p. 42 on the declining importance of distinctions between crimes.

[92] 50 and 51 Vict. c. 35 ss. 63–5. Offences inferring dishonest appropriation of property, personal violence, and indecent conduct. And applying also to convictions obtained in England; see also 31 and 32 Vict. c. 95 s. 12.   [93] 8 Edw. VII c. 65 s. 34(7).

[94] A habitual criminal was defined by the number of previous convictions they had, and as a result of this became subject to an additional indeterminate period of treatment or punishment. See Report of the Departmental Committee on Habitual Offenders etc. 1895; Radzinowicz and Hood 1986, chs. 3, 8; see also Garland 1985, ch. 7.

This blurring of the boundaries between guilt and character as a result of the development of new administrative procedures – a sort of diminished form of legal responsibility – is also to be seen in the provision for the treatment and punishment of children and lunatics. The increasing legal recognition of the juvenile offender was particularly connected to the growth of summary procedure, increasing legal responsibility by decreasing the penalties. However, as juvenile offenders were increasingly segregated from adults through the use of special procedures and punishments, responsibility was formulated in less absolute terms.[95] After 1850 the boundary between legal guilt and legal status was blurred by a range of provisions under which children were treated as less responsible. Juvenile offences were decriminalised while the prevention of crime was provided for by bringing up the young in habits of industry, sobriety and morality.[96] A similar pattern can be found in the law on lunacy. The definition of criminal lunacy was one of the controversial legal issues of the nineteenth century, giving rise to much scientific and pseudo-scientific speculation.[97] Yet Smith has argued that, notwithstanding the intense debates over the legal definition of insanity in the nineteenth century, decisions at the crime–insanity boundary became a function of administrative procedure. The 'criminal lunatic' was the formal administrative category that was used to resolve the ambivalence of the law in dealing with persons who were neither criminals nor patients, emerging as part of a wider regulation of mental and social health.[98]

Under the law of the early nineteenth century, proof of lunacy at the time a crime was committed freed the offender from liability to punishment. In these cases, in the absence of mental hospitals or prisons, the accused had normally to be entrusted to friends or family on the condition that they lodged a sum of money with the court as security for good behaviour.[99] Over the course of the century, provision for criminal lunatics was gradually assumed by the state. Initially this was done through the provision that insane prisoners should be taken into state-

---

[95] Early in the century juvenile offenders were barely recognised by the law. See cases in Hume 1844 I, pp. 30–7. See also Ralston 1980. Wiener 1990, pp. 51–2 argues that from mid-century magistrates were willing to treat young children as responsible adults.

[96] See e.g. Reformatory Schools Act 1866 (29 and 30 Vict. c. 112); Reformatory and Industrial Schools Act 1891 (54 and 55 Vict. c. 23); Reformatory Schools Act 1893 (56 and 57 Vict. c. 48); Reformatory Schools Act 1899 (62 and 63 Vict. c. 12); Industrial Schools Act 1866 (29 and 30 Vict. c. 118); Industrial Schools Act Amendment Act 1880 (43 and 44 Vict. c. 15); Day Industrial Schools (S.) Act 1893 (56 Vict. c. 12); Children Act 1908 (8 Edw. VII c. 61); see Report of the Departmental Committee on Habitual Offenders etc. 1895; Ralston 1988; Wiener 1990, pp. 285–94; Garland 1985, pp. 222–3.

[97] R. Smith 1981; N. Walker 1968; for a fascinating reconstruction of the McNaghten case, see Moran 1981.   [98] R. Smith 1981, ch. 2. See also Foucault 1988, esp. at p. 130.

[99] Hume 1844 I, pp. 37–45; Alison 1832, pp. 644–61; for an example, see *Douglas* 1827 Syme 184.

administered asylums for an indeterminate period,[100] but the most significant change probably came as state officials took control of the procedures for the definition of criminal lunatics, extending the range of offences in which lunacy was seen as a relevant factor. The question of the fitness of the prisoner to undergo trial remained a legal question – the plea of 'insanity in bar of trial' – although the increase in numbers falling into this category may have been a result of the centralisation of prison administration. Prison doctors, alert to the existence of mental illness, examined every patient, rather than leaving the question to the discretion of legal counsel.[101] Moreover, as the operation of the prerogative of mercy, the possibility of pardoning, mitigating punishment in the case of the death penalty, or releasing the prisoner, passed from the hands of the sovereign to those of the Secretary of State,[102] it is clear that the state was increasingly exercising an administrative control over what were perceived as social problems.

The most notorious challenge to the idea of individual responsibility came with the development of strict or absolute liability – less perhaps the administration of the criminal law than the criminal law in administration. In the second half of the nineteenth century there was a proliferation of new statutes regulating and licensing public trade, safety, pollution, revenue and so on.[103] While this type of offence was not completely new,[104] as is often assumed, there was a drastic change in the scale and quality of governmental intervention and a transformation of criminal liability. From the factory legislation of the 1830s onwards, central government became increasingly involved in legislating to prevent accidents, license certain types of activity, set standards of quality, and the

---

[100] The first provision was made in the Criminal Lunatics Act 1800 (39 and 40 Geo. III c. 94) although this was not compulsory and was not referred to by either Hume or Alison. Extended to all crimes and all prisoners by Lunacy (S.) Act 1857 (20 and 21 Vict. c. 71) ss. 87–9.

[101] N. Walker 1968. This reflected a more general transformation in the understanding of 'lunacy', see Foucault 1988.

[102] See e.g. 1857 Act s. 93; Criminal and Dangerous Lunatics (S.) Amendment Act 1871 (34 and 35 Vict. c. 55). Decisions on whether or not to release prisoners on licence were taken in the same way, see Radzinowicz and Hood 1986, pp. 676–81.

[103] For a list of such statutes, see A. M. Anderson 1904, pp. 98–145; Robertson 1878, pp. 267–72 and Lecture VII. For very brief accounts of the development of this process in England, see Cornish and Clark 1989, pp. 605–7; Manchester 1980, ch. 9. For a detailed study of the area of food legislation, see Paulus 1974; for early factory legislation, see Carson 1979.

[104] It had long been recognised that certain types of interference with public trade, for example speculation in times of famine, were serious crimes: Hume 1844 I, ch. 25. Also burghal jurisdiction was concerned with the regulation of trade and the general welfare of the burgh and its inhabitants, and in certain instances the Burgh Police Acts continued to provide for these functions of inspection and so on to be carried out. See Robertson 1878, p. 282.

criminalisation of socially harmful activities.[105] These new offences were normally prosecuted summarily. While certain actions were criminalised, just as often liability was imposed on the basis of an omission or failure to act or to comply with minimum standards of behaviour or with positive duties created by the law. Although directed at the protection of the public or specific sections of the public, and being in part a response to public opinion and pressure, by the end of the century these areas were viewed as largely technical matters, affecting the interests of producers, manufacturers and sellers.[106]

In undertaking these new administrative duties, the practice of the criminal law was transformed. In the most immediate sense this was a question of numbers; as the substantive law expanded, so the courts dealt with a greater number of people. But the more important consequence derived from the manner in which liability was imposed for these new offences. For many – though not all – of these offences it was not considered necessary that there should have been intent to do the act that was done or knowledge about a certain state of affairs (strict liability), and an employer could be held liable for the actions of their employee (vicarious liability). This amounted to a presumption of liability on the grounds that certain persons were in a better position to remedy the defect. A particular person was specified, such as the proprietor or license holder, who was to be held liable in all circumstances because of that position.[107] Statutes sometimes provided for the defences that the breach was outwith their control or knowledge, or that they had taken all reasonable precautions to ensure that the legislation was complied with, but the overall emphasis was placed on making the regulations enforceable.

The development of strict liability, proceeding as it did from a desire to promote the social interest in the effectiveness of the law, or social protection, above a concern with individual justice or injustice, is frequently portrayed as a development that is alien to the general principles of the criminal law.[108] These principles, it is argued, cohere around the central claim that it is necessary to prove the moral blameworthiness, or guilty mind, of the offender without which there can be no just

---

[105] At the end of our period, we see the introduction of the first legislation on the motor car, one of the most important developments for the modern criminal law – Motor Car Act 1903 (3 Edw. VII c. 36).   [106] Paulus 1974, ch. 1.

[107] As, for example, in the dual approach to the problem of drunkenness, discussed above at pp. 116–17.

[108] See, for example, the review in Richardson 1987. Indeed after an initial acquiescence in the development, the judiciary began to insist on the importance of *mens rea*. See the discussions in Edwards 1955 and Stallybrass 1936. For a summary of the main criticisms, see Norrie 1993.

punishment. A second version of this argument claims that modern legal justice is as much to do with criminals as with crimes, the crime signalling the presence of the 'dangerous element' in the social body.[109] According to this argument, the construction of the modern, reformed, act-based code of criminal liability carried the seeds of its own destruction as the criminal emerged from the interstices of the formal prohibitions – the need to know who was being punished was central to the idea of effective punishment.[110] Though both arguments beg the question of the actual importance of individual responsibility to the modern law, it is possible to see that, to the extent that they pick out the themes of social protection and efficiency, the claims are not necessarily inconsistent. If we take, for example, Fletcher's claim that the philosophical clarity of the modern criminal law is constrained by the institutional context within which the rules operate, we can begin to clarify the claims being made here.[111] He argues that prosecutors have discretion to screen the cases that are suitable for prosecution and to decide on the appropriate charge, denying the courts the opportunity to clarify and distinguish categories of wrongdoing. Questions of penalty and the handling of the case become issues of administrative discretion rather than formal law, as prosecutors can use the threat of a more severe penalty to produce a guilty plea. This is an important point but we can push it further.

We have seen that the expansion of the criminal justice system through the use of summary procedure created the demand for the efficient processing of large numbers of persons. This brought a pressure to bear on the criminal law, downgrading the 'seriousness' of a number of offences and blurring the distinctions between them. In this system, though, administrative discretion not only rests with the prosecutor, police and other enforcement agencies, but also in the rules of law where the procedures for the definition and proof of minor offences themselves facilitate conviction and control.[112] Formal (or philosophically clear) rules do not precede discretionary enforcement. Accordingly we should not see the administrative context and the substantive rules of the criminal law as antithetical, as Fletcher implies. Rather, they develop in such a way as to complement each other. We see a different aspect of this in the development of strict liability.

Many of these statutes had superseded attempts to criminalise certain types of behaviour at common law. This was particularly true of the regulation of safety on railways or in factories. The middle years of the nineteenth century saw a series of prosecutions for homicide arising out of

---

[109] Foucault 1988, p. 128; Foucault 1977.
[110] Cf. Weber 1969, pp. 880–90 on the inherent instability of formal rules.
[111] Fletcher 1978, pp. 319–21.   [112] Cf. McBarnet 1981.

industrial or transport accidents.[113] In these cases the courts had attempted to specify, through the device of individual responsibility, standards of behaviour for the carrying out of risky activities. This judicial intervention paralleled changes in civil law where there had been a similar response to the problems of accidents caused by the development of dangerous machinery and mass transportation.[114] It was frequently the case that minor errors by individuals not in a position to indemnify victims could produce ever more devastating consequences. The response of the courts reflected changes in the social conception of risk which was increasingly seen as something that could be measured and reduced, and where liability could be allocated to those best placed to bear it.[115] Just as in civil law this increasingly led to systems of strict liability and compulsory insurance, in the criminal law the number of common law prosecutions for negligent homicide declined rapidly in the latter part of the century as new, and more readily proved, statutory duties were introduced. The case by case approach gave way as the state took on the role of defining the levels of acceptable risk through statutes that created summary offences for the failure to comply with the relevant safety regulation.[116] Responsibility was distributed on the basis of penalising those who undertook risky behaviour, seeking to reduce it to acceptable levels. These may have reduced the symbolic importance of accidents and deaths in the workplace, but were based on the equally important realisation that such risks could never be entirely eliminated. The means adopted – the downgrading of seriousness, the penalising of conduct rather than intent, and the facilitation of prosecution – were entirely consistent with the spirit of the modern criminal law.

There is one final point that must be made. If we focus on this developing concern with the reduction and management of risk and the more efficient administration of an economy of illegalities, then the criminal law need not appear as antithetical to the order of administration. It is an institution that distributes different categories of social risk. And to the extent that this is a form of 'actuarial' justice,[117] this is not so much the displacement of individualised justice as its re-ordering. The intensified

---

[113] See the list of cases in G. H. Gordon 1978, pp. 790–4. See ch. 5, below, where this argument is developed.

[114] Wiener 1990, pp. 211–14. Cf. Foucault 1988, pp. 146–8 arguing that the changes in the criminal law were the result of the transformation of the civil law.

[115] Cf. Ewald 1986a, pp. 65–7 on balance in the modern law based on the socialisation of judgement, flexibility, distribution and allocation, and the production of generalised principles of equivalence.

[116] See e.g. Railway Employment (Prevention of Accidents) Act 1900 (63 and 64 Vict. c. 27) and Factory and Workshop Act 1901 (1 Edw. VII c. 22). Discussed in Cornish and Clark 1989, ch. 7 esp. at pp. 515–20; Bartrip and Burman 1983. See Murphy 1991 on the impact of statistics on the law.   [117] The term is taken from Feeley and Simon 1994.

government of the social body is accompanied by the demand that the individual meet higher standards of self-government.[118] As we shall see in the next chapter, these changes in the way in which responsibility is attributed and distributed suggest that the enduring importance of the criminal law is as a form of social, rather than moral, ordering.

From public drunkenness to the prevention of industrial accidents, the nineteenth century witnessed a massive expansion of the substantive criminal law, as an ever greater range of conduct was subjected to regulation. This brought a qualitative shift in the ordering of criminal jurisdiction, specifically in the way that legal liability was perceived and enforced. In certain respects the story is familiar, linking together the policing of public order, the discipline and classification of the 'dangerous classes', the bureaucratisation of punishment and the establishment of the 'penal–welfare complex'.[119] A common understanding of the development of modern policing and punishment has the retributive, moralistic and individualistic penal law taken over by new models of professional knowledge and forms of social intervention based around medicine, criminology and social work. These focused on the criminal character and the social origins of criminality rather than criminal actions alone. The 'criminal population' was divided on the grounds of reformability and manageability, sub-categories were identified and disciplined. A new 'bio-power' based on the management of population, the health of the social body, succeeded the juridical form of sovereignty.[120] There is, however, an important difference in the story told here. The development has been traced specifically through the criminal law, piecing together the origins of the legal mechanisms of enforcement and control. It has been demonstrated that the criminal law remained central to the definition of these categories of offenders and aggravations, and to the ordering of the criminal population. It was thus part of a continuum, these provisions clearly showing the possibility of interchange between the criminal law and the interventionist agencies. This points to the important conclusion that in neither Scotland nor England was the criminal law ever a purely formal or retributive system. The rules have always been more flexible, serving ends other than those of legal formalism. It has, in this form, been central to the new kinds of social organisation, enabling the growth of a

[118] Cf. Hume 1797 I, p. 23. Note also the shift in punishment towards the disciplining of individuals and the reconstruction of moral personality e.g. Foucault 1977; Ignatieff 1978. Cf. Wiener 1990 who argues that there is a decline in the importance of character building towards the end of the century as the idea of social protection emerges.

[119] See Garland 1985.

[120] The most succinct statement of this position is in Foucault 1979, part v. See also Garland 1985, chs. 1, 8.

generalised form of social regulation. The law was an important compo-
nent of the new complex of government.

The central element of the transformation of criminal jurisdiction has
been identified as a movement towards the more intensive ordering of
public space. It is important to note that this is not just a question of more
order – following the expansion in policing – but the production of a
different kind of order. This is seen primarily in the movement from the
control of political order to the government of population within territory.
But if this was a change in the style of government it was at the same time a
shift in the locus and the quality of government, corresponding to the
emergence of summary jurisdiction. If the locus of government was
diffused, in a movement away from the central institutions into the
network of police, courts and other criminal justice agencies, this meant
also that decisions about the nature of the order that was being produced
were being taken in a very different way. Criminal justice policy emerged
for the first time, to ensure consistency and the more even distribution of
powers and responsibilities. Institutions produced order through the
substantive rules specifying norms of behaviour, regulating public space
and conduct. Criminal justice became a question of administration and
security, not of sovereign power.

This brought about a subtle change in the way that the criminal law was
conceived in relation to social order. Crimes were no longer regarded as
actions that offended the community viewed through the mirror of
political order. Instead they came to be seen as actions that breached the
public peace or offended a community or social interest viewed simply as
the aggregate of individual interests. This redefinition of the interest of the
state can be seen in the changing definitions of the nature of crime.[121] By
the end of the period, a crime was defined as, 'the violation of a public law
when considered with reference to the evil tendency of such violation as
regards the general community. . . A crime is a violation of the [civil rights
which belong to individuals] considered with reference to the community
in its aggregate capacity'.[122] That this could in turn only be defined as 'an
act forbidden by law under the pain of punishment',[123] according to the
positive criterion of whether it was tried by the criminal courts, merely
reflects the diversity of functions of the criminal law in the interventionist
state. There is no simple moral purpose that holds it together, and if we fall
back onto the definition of a crime as an act that harms the community or
social body we are merely reflecting the same tautology (though dressed
up as moral theory). The difficulty that must be faced, and this is
particularly true for the Scottish legal tradition, is that the law has lost any

[121] For a full discussion of this point, see Farmer 1996.
[122] A. M. Anderson 1904, p. 1.   [123] *Ibid.*

connection that it might once have had with community. Criminal justice is not the expression of community values. The informality of the rules is institutional. Guilt, punishment and harm are both legal and administrative categories.

Ordering the law 1750–1908

The order of the common law

As we have already had cause to note, Hume's *Commentaries* occupy an ambiguous position in the development of the law, between old and new. The professed aim was to provide a complete account of all the ordinary laws that applied to the inhabitants of the land, what he termed at one point a 'universal code'.[124] This comprised all those laws of a national application, excluding the offences contained in local laws, and so is readily seen as the counterpart of the establishment of the sovereign jurisdiction of the central courts. It is in this drive for completeness and order, rather than any theoretical flair or innovation, that the principal virtue of the *Commentaries* is to be found.[125] It is a crude, but not altogether inaccurate, understanding of Hume to depict him dealing with the disorderly nature of the law and its sources rather than with the more minute principles of its internal governance or regulation. In presenting the traditional categories of political order and authority, he is at the same time contributing to the establishment of that order, dealing with a number of vivid doctrinal challenges and problems. Notwithstanding, this is a powerful vision of the nature of common law jurisdiction which can account for much of the enduring influence of the work. This comes out very clearly in the discussion of substantive jurisdiction, centred as it is around questions of sovereign authority and community – the twin sources of justice.

For Hume the authority of the law depended on uniformity and consistency in its application: no one should be above the law and the criminality of actions should not be allowed to vary with the circumstances. The point was made by comparing the current state of political order with the disorder that was said to have prevailed in the past. Then, 'some parts of Scotland had not yet been reduced to a due state of discipline . . . [and] the condition of those quarters of the country was truly little different from a state of war'.[126] The inhabitants were often compelled to commit crimes by others, or to take the law into their own hands to defend themselves against attack. The criminal law could not apply uniformly

---

[124] Hume 1844 II, p. 43. This was also the national law that was discussed in ch. 2 above, pp. 34–9.   [125] Above, ch. 2, pp. 30 and 40–1.   [126] Hume 1844 I, p. 52.

because these situations would always have to be taken into account in assessing culpability. Thus, the conditions of individual liability, particularly in the application of pleas such as compulsion or self-defence, clearly depended on the strength of political authority. Where this was weak, in remote parts of Scotland or in situations of 'great commotion or extreme danger', individuals could not be blamed or punished. On the other hand, in the current 'well-regulated society where every man is under the shield of the law',[127] such pleas would be difficult to establish. Their possible scope should be restricted to an absolute minimum and the royal prerogative of mercy should operate in those cases where harsh results might result from the strict application of law.[128] The necessitous offender should,

supplicate his relief from his Majesty, who is the source of mercy . . . Thus the rigid and salutary precept of the law is maintained entire; and humanity is at the same time consulted; without the risk of any of those manifold evils and disorders, which would follow on a more enlarged scheme of indulgence. And herein, according to the judicious observation of Judge Blackstone, appears the benefit of that monarchical form of government, which so naturally admits of this gracious prerogative.[129]

The sovereign was not above the law. It is important to note that this was not a defence of arbitrariness, which was much criticised by the English penal reformers, but of discretion under the common law. Formality was not required as a restraint on power, but as an expression of the authority of the law. The prerogative of mercy could mitigate undue harshness rather than justify extreme severity.[130] Mercy could be exercised on the recommendation of the court or the assize, in such a way that the authority (or majesty) of the law was reinforced in the process. Universal rules, uniformly applied, were both the product and end of good government.[131]

I do not wish to dwell further on this. The defence of the constitutional monarchy and of the universal, national jurisdiction of the laws are by now familiar. It is merely necessary to underline the strong substantive concern with political authority. Instead, we shall turn to the other central theme of his account of substantive jurisdiction, that of community. The main body of the work begins with a statement on the nature of crimes. He stated that:

---

[127] *Ibid.*, pp. 51–3.
[128] Although by the early nineteenth century it appears to have played a fairly residual role in practice – possibly because the death penalty was so little used. Return of Number of Persons Committed for Trial in Scotland 1805–1810 PP.1812.X.217.
[129] Hume 1844 I, pp. 55–6. See also II, p. 495.   [130] Cf. Hay 1975.
[131] Cf. Adam Smith 1978, p. 106 characterising weak governments as those in early stages of development that were unable to intervene and punish crimes.

In determining the extent of that part of the Law of Scotland which has relation to CRIMES, I shall take that term in its ordinary acceptation; and shall consider every act as a crime for which our practice has appointed the offender to make satisfaction to the public . . .[132]

In exacting such atonement, he went on, 'the law always supposes that the delinquent has infringed, in some respect, those duties which he owes to the community'.[133] This obviously reinforced the anti-formalism of this 'code', in which the content of the criminal law need not be regarded as either fixed or complete (in the sense of being expressed in advance). All actions that offended the community were within the jurisdiction of the High Court, whether or not they had previously been recognised by the law. If this was the basis of the universal jurisdiction, it was elaborated by reference to the natural resentment of the victim or their relatives at the injury that had been suffered, and the need to satisfy this resentment as something that is social rather than individual.[134] However, the catalogue of crimes was also built up through the experience of legal practice and the legal institution, and it was this authority that gave final shape to the community experience. At times, though, this appeared to create a certain tension. In his account of political authority, Hume defended the value and authority of law as sovereign power. At other times he seemed to be defending the position that practice was more important than law. Yet this ambiguity played a productive role in Hume's work, not only in the justification of the stateless political order and the autonomy of Scottish institutions, but also permitting limited legal innovation on the basis of community and reason.[135]

Two examples can show the innovative aspects of this tension. The first concerns the law of provocation in homicide. The status of the rule mitigating punishment in the case of killing following provocation was uncertain in eighteenth-century Scotland. Some writers considered that it should always be capitally punishable.[136] Hume, however, defended the rule that it should not be regarded as wilful murder.[137] The main obstacle to the acceptance of this rule was a statute of 1661 that had exempted casual homicide from the death penalty, but without specifically referring to provocation as a species of casual homicide. Hume argued that the terminology of the statute was obscure in that it made no mention of a historical right to 'sanctuary' in the cases of killing in hot blood or on a

---

[132] Hume 1844 I, p. 22 (emphasis in original).   [133] *Ibid.*
[134] See, for example, Hume 1844 I, pp. 234; II, pp. 52.
[135] And sometimes both together as in the sedition trials of the 1790s! The theoretical bases for this tension are discussed in, ch. 2 above, pp. 44–7.
[136] W. Forbes 1730, pp. 102–3; Bayne 1748, p. 34: 'All homicide with us is punished capitally'; cf. Adam Smith 1978, p. 113. Cf the English position discussed in Horder 1992, ch. 1.   [137] Hume 1844 I, pp. 239–54.

sudden quarrel ('chaud melle' or 'in rixa'). He produced two arguments for disregarding the Act. The first was the argument from the current practice of the community: common usage of the term 'casual' would include acting under provocation. It was in part true that community practice probably favoured the recognition of provocation – there were a number of eighteenth-century murder trials in which juries had acquitted offenders in the face of specific directions to convict.[138] This, however, was mediated by legal experience. Initially, the legal reaction had been to attempt to restrict the powers of the jury, but by the late eighteenth century the courts had begun to permit the plea of provocation, although this was far from being a settled rule.[139] This was certainly a response to community sentiments, but the effect was to close the loophole that these had opened up in the legal definition of homicide, thereby ensuring that more offenders received some measure of punishment. The second argument was that the terms of the statute would have to have been more explicit in order to abolish something grounded in the ancient law and in reason and humanity. He argued that the offender ought to be punished for social reasons, but it would not be right that this should be capital.[140] He then continued, 'And our Judges, as long as they have it in their power, will properly refuse to believe, that the Legislature could intend to pass so barbarous a law'.[141] The natural rule grounded in both judicial practice and reason prevailed over the statute. The law must give way to practice and the reason that is inherent in that practice.[142]

The second example, though not coming specifically from the *Commentaries*, uses arguments that would have been familiar to Hume. In the early nineteenth century the state had begun to pass legislation relating to the conduct of vehicles and other machinery to ensure the greater security of the public. In a case arising from a railway accident the defence argued unsuccessfully that the prosecution at common law was incompetent, since the statutes which had been provided for railway safety in England had assumed that the offences were beyond the reach of the common law.[143] It was held that there was an established principle that the

---

[138] For a notorious example, see *Carnegie of Findhaven* (1728) in Hume 1844 I, p. 244; see also Alison 1832, pp. 13–14; Steele 1833, p. 80: 'It is sufficient to state that juries have no right to act in this manner'.

[139] Burnett 1811 dates the change from a case in 1771. The powers of the jury were restricted by the use of special verdicts (see Forsyth 1858, pp. 372–5).

[140] Hume 1844 I, p. 240.

[141] *Ibid.*, p. 244. Note that Burnett 1811, pp. 11–18 and App. I disagrees with Hume's interpretation of the medieval law; on the medieval law, see Sellar 1991.

[142] Cf. Postema 1986, chs. 3, 4.

[143] *Wm. Gray* (1836) 1 Swin. 328. The prosecution replied that, 'it is well known that the power of the English common law is not so great as the acknowledged power of the common law in Scotland' (p. 336).

provision of penalties by a statute could not abrogate the common law, and that actions penalised by statute might always be competently tried at common law in the High Court.[144] A final twist was given to this formulation when Hume's editor, Benjamin Bell, argued that the statutory provisions, far from superseding the common law, might actually be evidence of the dangerousness of certain activities and hence of the common law – to which end he even provided a list of the most relevant statutes![145]

I want to conclude this section by considering briefly the question of the significance of individual responsibility to the law in this period. Certain writers have argued that the doctrine of *mens rea* has existed in Scotland from medieval times.[146] They have pointed to the distinctions between premeditated and other murders and the existence of excusing conditions such as insanity and compulsion to claim that intention has always been central to the attribution of responsibility. But we must treat such claims with a certain degree of scepticism since such a broad approach misses important changes in the formulation of responsibility. The eighteenth-century writers, including Hume, share a common approach to the question of responsibility. Showing the strong influence of Roman law, they repeatedly state that 'dole' or intention was a necessary requirement for the commission of a crime and the infliction of punishment. Mackenzie argued, 'That seeing man can only offend in what is voluntar [sic] to him, it must follow, that the will is the only fountain of wickedness'.[147] Dole did not have to be proved in every case:

[I]t will be perceived on the smallest attention that all dole must be presumptive; for it is an act of the mind which can only be discovered by the outward circumstances from which it is presumed.[148]

It was considered that to seek to prove that there was an intention to do the particular act that had been done 'would screen many great offenders from the due punishment of their transgressions'.[149] Dole was to be presumed according to the wrongfulness of the act, and needed only to be

---

[144] *Trotter* (1842) in Bell's Notes, p. 74.   [145] *Ibid.*, pp. 74–5.

[146] See in particular Smith and Macdonald 1958, pp. 292–6; cf. Stephen 1883 II, p. 94, declining to give a historical account of the development of responsibility – 'The result in this case is more interesting and important than the process by which it was arrived at.'

[147] Mackenzie 1678, p. 8.

[148] Erskine 1871 IV, iv, 8. See also Steele 1833, p. 81; Mackenzie 1678, pp. 8–9; von Bar 1916, ch. 10 and Hume 1844 I, 25: 'The Judge cannot search into the heart of the prisoner; and even if he could, still the cause be what it may, which impels a man to do such things as are subversive of society, his will is not on that account the less inordinate, or his nature the less depraved.' Note that although Hume's treatment (I, pp. 21–6) collapses the civilian one in Mackenzie etc. its content is substantially the same.

[149] Hume 1844 I, p. 21.

specifically proved when there was an express requirement in a statute.[150] The requirements of liability could not therefore be expressed in a general form, applicable to all crimes, but depended on the particular definitions. In practice, the primary concern was with the action and its wrongfulness rather than the actor. Legal guilt was equivalent to moral wrong and, as a result, the degree of intention of the actor did not have to be explicitly proved as a condition of liability.[151] The finding of guilt was simply a judgement of the wrongful nature of the act defined by reference to the duty that the individual owed to the community.[152]

Responsibility was, thus, a judgement that established the relationship between political order and community. This law was not concerned with the conditions of subjective responsibility, but with the definition of legal subjects – those over whom jurisdiction was exercised. Provision was made for the excuses of compulsion, self-defence, insanity, accident and so on, but not in order to allow the wrongfulness of the act to be denied by proving the state of mind of the actor. These were strictly ways of limiting the punishment.[153] Even after the restrictions on the use of defences by the accused had been relaxed, the emphasis remained on the wrongfulness of the act.[154] Defences must instead be seen as disqualifying conditions related to the capacity of legal subjects.[155] In the case of insanity this was something that removed persons from the state of 'subjecthood' – like infants, they were not subject to the law or subjects of the law. In the case of compulsion, as we have seen, the absence of laws removed the

---

[150] Mackenzie 1678, pp. 8–9.

[151] In general, this meant that different degrees of culpability were irrelevant. See also ch. 5 below. This, in a certain sense, is more akin to the modern requirement of the *actus reus*, that the act should be voluntary. See G. H. Gordon 1978, pp. 64–7.

[152] Hume 1797 I, p. 11. It was often, of course, a literal constitution of the community because all the actors were brought together to confront each other. There were crimes of neglect in the law, such as neglect of duty by a judge, but these were not crimes of negligence. See the discussion in Mackenzie 1678, p. 19, and Alison 1832, ch. 34.

[153] See Fletcher 1978, pp. 235–42, 274–85. See also W. Forbes 1730, p. 111 where he argues that the presumption of innocence lies in favour of the deceased if the killing is acknowledged, in cases of self-defence; but also, curiously, excessive force in self-defence was not punished for the homicide but for the excess.

[154] The old theory was that the accused's guilt was inferred by the proof by the prosecutor of the facts in the indictment, and that to allow a contrary probation would encourage him or his witnesses to commit perjury. This was relaxed in the early eighteenth century. By the Act 1747 (20 Geo. II c. 43) defences were required to be lodged in advance. J. I. Smith 1958, pp. 439–40; Hume 1844 II, pp. 297–301; McLaurin 1774, pp. xviii–xxvii, 'On the Interlocutor on the Relevancy'.

[155] See e.g. Mackenzie 1678, p. 13; in Erskine's words they are 'those against whom an accusation can or cannot be brought' (1871 IV, iv, 82). This is also explicit in W. Forbes 1730. Cf. Hawkins 1739, p. 2: 'That those who are under a natural Disability of distinguishing between Good and Evil . . . are not punishable by any criminal Prosecution whatsoever.' For a modern account of capacity, see Lacey 1988, chs. 3, 5; Tur 1993, p. 233.

obligation to obey or be a legal subject. In more general terms, it can be
seen that legal subjects were recognised in their membership of the
national community, with the historical and moral understanding which
that entails. To the common law, the individual was not sovereign but
subject.

Towards the well-governed community 1830–1908

If, in the early part of the century, the criminal law was dominated by the
figure of Baron Hume, as it drew to a close the influence of J. H. A.
Macdonald, Lord Kingsburgh, was increasingly felt. There was no
monumental achievement of the order of the *Commentaries*, the lasting
impression being made through his manual on criminal law, the reform of
criminal procedure and, finally, as a senior judge. This in itself reveals
something of the changing nature of the law. While the *Commentaries* are
lengthy and complex, Macdonald's *Practical Treatise on the Criminal Law
of Scotland* is terse and absorbed with practical and technical questions.[156]
In substance it is largely derived from Hume, updated where necessary,
and its surprising influence must be attributed to a combination of
simplicity and the subsequent status of its author. A measure of its
acceptance can be seen in the fact that when the official criminal statistics
were re-classified in 1898, the reader was referred to the *Practical Treatise*
for the accepted common law definition of crimes.[157] We can note the
most important consequence of this immediately. The question of
political authority, which ran through the *Commentaries*, is replaced by the
narrower question of legal authority. To put this differently, questions
about the mode of government and the role of the criminal law in the
political order are regarded as settled by the unchallengeable authority of
Hume. The *Commentaries* are reduced to a set of increasingly flexible
rules, and questions of order are treated as purely technical questions of
interpretation, implementation and organisation.

This is nowhere more apparent than in relation to the crime of breach of
the peace. There was a singular absence of reflection on the question of the
meaning of the public peace. This is apparent, for example, in the leading
decision of *Ferguson v. Carnochan*.[158] Lord McLaren stated that, 'The
term peace is not used as the antithesis of war. Breach of the peace means a
breach of public order and decorum, causing disturbance and alarm to
members of the public'.[159] It was simply assumed that the value of 'public

[156] The *Practical Treatise* is discussed in ch. 2 above. Macdonald recorded in his memoirs
(1915) that the book was written to keep himself busy while a young advocate waiting for
work.   [157] Judicial Statistics 1898 in PP.1900.CIII.447.
[158] (1889) 2 White 278. See also the discussion in Christie 1990, pp. 24–7.
[159] (1889) 2 White 278 at pp. 281–2.

order and decorum' was obvious and uncontroversial. Judicial decisions and legal treatises noted the increasingly diverse situations in which the court had held that a breach might occur, without attempting to establish any general qualities or rules that might have fixed or limited the boundaries of the offence. The test was simply whether the conduct had excited 'reasonable apprehension' that the peace was being disturbed, or the belief that the behaviour might cause real disturbance of, or annoyance to, the community. The circularity of this was unwittingly revealed by Anderson, writing that if conduct 'is of such a nature as tends to produce a breach of the peace, then a breach of the peace has been committed'.[160] The question is technical, and its meaning can derive only from its implementation. Although this, as we have already noted, privileged middle-class values of order against the 'nomadic tribes' of the common people,[161] this was increasingly based on police assessment of the limits of public opinion. Indeed, it has been suggested that the very success of the police in minimising breaches of the peace created problems for the formation or measurement of that opinion.[162] This further underlines the significance and potential instability of the connection between legal flexibility and institutional closure. Breaches of the peace did not threaten political authority but an unspoken ordering of the community.

If this was how the law was increasingly tending to operate, contemporaries saw only the continuities with the past, with the values of community and the universal jurisdiction of the common law. Macdonald, discussing the development of the criminal law since Hume, stated that, 'the amendments have all been in the direction of development and adaptation, in no case of fundamental alteration'.[163] The question of criminal law reform that dominated English legal thought of the period failed to penetrate a Scottish legal mind wary of foreign incursions and confident in the belief that a flexible common law was competent to deal with problems of criminal legal order. Where legislation did threaten assimilation and the loss of a distinctive Scottish identity, in the growth of statutory offences for example, there was no attempt to analyse, 'the effect of this continued process on the national system of jurisprudence, with its diminishing half consisting of more or less elastic general principles, and its growing other half consisting of anything but elastic statutory statements'.[164] In crimes such as breach of the peace which could be prosecuted under either

---

[160] A. M. Anderson 1904, p. 72. It is difficult in these terms to see breach of the peace as a 'result-crime' (Christie 1990, p. 29) since the concern is with the conduct of the accused and its likely effects. Actual disturbance or annoyance need not be caused. In practice it would seem to depend on the conduct of the accused.

[161] *Durrin and Stewart v. Mackay* (1859) 3 Irv. 341 at p. 351.

[162] See Townsend 1993, p. 40.   [163] Macdonald 1891, p. 6.   [164] Anon 1905, p. 7.

statute or common law, judges increasingly drew attention to the common law origins to point out that the statutes did not create any new crimes but merely allowed the more efficient prosecution of existing ones, a process that was said to be sanctioned by the community.[165] There existed a sophisticated jurisprudence for distinguishing between common law and statutory crimes. A wonderful example is the case of *Martin v. Boyd*[166] – the leading judgement being given by none other than Lord Justice-Clerk Macdonald. Martin was charged with the statutory offence of being a known criminal suspected of being about to commit a crime. This depended on the proof of previous convictions of theft punishable by penal servitude – that is to say, of more serious thefts. The accused claimed that the charge was not relevant, since he had only previously been convicted for minor offences in the sheriff court, which could not impose a sentence of penal servitude. This objection was swept aside:

In this country every person accused of theft may be brought before a jury in the High Court of Justiciary . . . It is equally competent for the High Court to pronounce a sentence of penal servitude, if it thinks that the circumstances warrant that course, and therefore *every such case* is a case in which a sentence of penal servitude may be pronounced.[167]

Theft was a 'real' crime, irrespective of the value of the things stolen, and so the complications of particular statutory provisions could be overridden. The interpretation of penal statutes was not necessarily harsh – though Martin could testify to its occasional harshness – but it was normally strict.

Although many of these newly created offences were only cognisable under the statutorily created summary jurisdiction, even this did not place them beyond the common law. If they were not proper crimes, their administration was still within the general jurisdiction of the High Court. This was formalised in the procedural reforms introduced by Macdonald. Section 62 of the 1887 Act provided that where the facts proved under a statutory indictment 'do not amount to a contravention of the Statute, but do amount to a crime at common law, it shall be lawful to convict of the common law crime'.[168] Common law jurisdiction remained intact. Statutorily created offences were regarded as merely technical rules that the courts had a duty to enforce. This normally produced a strictly formalist reading of statutes, excluding the application of the ordinary rules of the criminal law (relating to actings in concert etc.), unless specific

[165] *Galbraith v. Muirhead* (1856) 2 Irv. 520; *Dougall v. Dykes* (1861) 4 Irv. 101; see also Lord Justice-Clerk Moncrieff in *Colquhoun v. Liddell and anr.* 1876 4R (J.) 3.
[166] 1908 S.C. (J.) 52 a prosecution under the Prevention of Crime Act 1871 (34 and 35 Vict. c. 112) s. 7.   [167] *Ibid.*, at p. 53 (my emphasis). Cf. the discussion above, pp. 118–20.
[168] 50 and 51 Vict. c. 35. See also *Markland v. HM Adv.* (1891) 3 White 21.

statutory provision had been made.[169] The statutory rules could only apply to the specific situation provided for and gave rise to no rules of general application. Thus, 'In the case of a breach of a statutory regulation, it is not a universal rule that intention to contravene the statute must be established. That may depend on the policy of the statute, and also on the language of the statute'.[170] Statutes might create absolute obligations,[171] or provide defences,[172] or impose a requirement of specific intent.[173] They were enforced by the courts, 'in the interests of the public' with an identical vigour and lack of concern. A strict boundary had been drawn and was rigidly observed – broad and flexible definitions on the one side, and on the other an unsparing attention to detail.

All this, of course, was directed towards the reinforcement of a certain understanding of the nature of crime and legal order. Statutes were regarded as 'cramping and limiting the efficiency of the law' by creating technical difficulties of interpretation, while the common law was 'direct, efficient and satisfactory'[174]. But this distinction was not analysed; it was already known through the practice of the law. There was no need to define positively the substantive jurisdiction of the criminal law, for the judiciary already knew what it was and what it was not. This is clear from the Introduction to Macdonald's *Practical Treatise*[175] where the scope of the work, and hence the boundaries of the criminal law, was very briefly discussed. He stated that the book would deal only with those offences punishable in the first instance by sentence of death or immediate deprivation of liberty without the option of paying a fine. He went on: 'To attempt an enumeration of, and commentary on, the offences which are punishable in the first instance by fine only . . . would be going beyond the legitimate bounds of a work on criminal law'.[176] Such offences, being for the enforcement of sanitary rules or the general comfort of the community, did not involve 'guilt' in their commission. Although he immediately pointed out that this division was unsatisfactory because it excluded certain 'real' crimes while including other actions that are not truly criminal, the distinction is left to stand.[177] The value of Macdonald's definition, and also no doubt the source of its attraction, was that practically all statutory offences were, at a stroke, excluded. Most

[169] *Colquhoun v. Liddell* 1876 4R (J.) 3 at pp. 7–8.
[170] Lord McLaren in *Gordon v. Shaw* 1908 S.C. (J.) 17 at p. 21.
[171] e.g. *Don v. Johnston* (1897) 2 Adam 416.
[172] e.g. *O'Brien v. Macgregor* 1903 5F (J.) 74.
[173] e.g. *HM Adv. v. Kinnison* (1870) 1 Coup. 457.   [174] Macdonald 1891, pp. 10–12.
[175] Macdonald 1867, pp. 1–2.   [176] *Ibid.*
[177] The distinction between *mala in se* and *mala prohibita* was said to have been introduced into Scots law by Lord Ivory in the case of *Campbell v. Young* (1835) 13S 535. In general, see Anon 1858. For criticism of Macdonald, see Fenton 1928; T. B. Smith 1962, ch. 5; G. H. Gordon 1978, pp. 13–23.

statutory offences provided the judge with the option of either imprisonment or a fine, while all common law offences were punishable by
imprisonment alone in the first instance (unless a specific statutory
limitation had been introduced). Macdonald thus implicitly glossed the
provisions of the Summary Procedure (S.) Act 1864[178] which had defined
criminal jurisdiction in terms of the procedural powers of disposal. He
accepted that the scope of the criminal law was to be defined in procedural
terms, but used this to restrict 'true' criminal jurisdiction to common law
offences.[179] The remainder, an increasingly important part of criminal
practice, were dismissed. The result was a 'practical treatise' on the law,
that excluded the major part of that practice.

The criminal law was, therefore, still legitimated by its relation to the
community. Even if the individual and subjective standards of responsibility were increasingly being recognised in particular legal rules, this did
not yet provide a basis for the conceptual organisation of the law. For Sir
James Fitzjames Stephen, for example, individual responsibility was one
way of attributing liability for actions regarded as criminal by the
community, but was not fundamental to the operation of the law.[180]
Reflecting the spirit of the age, however, there was a change in the way that
the community was regarded as legitimating the law. In this it is
instructive to compare the position in Scotland with the arguments in
favour of the codification of the law in England. There was a shared sense
of the progress of the law, the clarification of its principles, the integration
of substance and procedure,[181] and its importance as a tool in the
construction of social order. To advocates of codification, such as
Stephen, this would reach its highest form in the legislation of a criminal
code. This would bring together the community and the law through
legislative expression.[182] For him, 'the time has now unquestionably come
at which it is possible to express the criminal law of this country without
resorting to any technicalities whatever, and in a compact and systematic

---

[178] 27 and 28 Vict. c. 53 s. 28 defining criminal jurisdiction as those situations where the
judge had the power to imprison, with the option of a fine. For a discussion of this see ch.
3 above.

[179] See also Lord Justice-Clerk Inglis in *Eliz. Edmiston* (1866) 5 Irv. 219 at pp. 222–3: 'Every
crime is wicked and felonious, and the moment that you arrive at the conclusion that the
act charged against the prisoner is a crime, that of itself is sufficient proof of wicked and
felonious intent. The words mean no more than the act is criminal'. See also Lord
McLaren in *Gordon v. Shaw* 1908 S.C. (J.) 17.

[180] Stephen 1883 II p. 96. See also Lacey (forthcoming).

[181] Stephen 1883 III p. 365.

[182] *Ibid.* II ch. 17, esp. at p. 77: 'In these islands, where the legislature tends to represent
directly the will of a large proportion of the community, it is unnecessary to distinguish
between the morality of the legislature and that of the persons legislated for . . .'

form'.[183] The law would thus be freed from technicalities and infelicities, allowing the more perfect expression of principles which had emerged from 'the labours of the most powerful legislature and the most authoritative body of judges known to history'.[184] In Scotland, by contrast, the approval of the community or of 'public opinion' was not linked to any legislative activity or expression. It was not measured by the positive manifestation of assent, but the absence of adverse public criticism. Thus, a testimony to the justice of the law was seen in the fact that, '[I]n an age in which all organisations and officials are brought to the bar of a strongly active public opinion . . . [the law] should stand almost alone among the great institutions of Scotland in freedom from philosophical criticism or the adverse clamour of popular sentiment'.[185] This was attributed to the success of the judiciary in adapting the law to modern circumstances – unsurprising perhaps in the continuing absence of legislation dedicated to Scotland. With the progress of civilisation, it was said that 'an unfettered, unwritten law grows with the nation's growth and refines itself with the national refinement', reflecting the national character and temper.[186] This was contrasted unfavourably with the possibility of a code, which would freeze the life of the law, sundering it from the progress of the nation. Such an approach was regarded as profoundly anti-historical and anti-Scottish – though perhaps necessary in England where the common law was said to lack system and elegance.[187] The judges shared in and regulated this sentiment, presiding over the organic growth of the system, with the *Commentaries* providing a fertile source of principles. The argument was clinched with an appeal to progress. Although many of the laws it referred to had become obsolete or seemed unduly harsh, their underlying value lay in their expression of the principles of liberty. Society had reached a level of perfection at which these values, the national spirit, could be expressed.

Conclusions

The last two chapters have built up a picture of how the jurisdiction of the

---

[183] *Ibid.* II, pp. 348–9. Note that it was intended to close the principles of crime but leave open possibilities of new defences (pp. 358–61). On the principles and politics of the codifiers, see remarks in Hostettler 1992, chs. 11, 12.

[184] Stephen 1883 II, p. 355. The Scottish resistance to codification was perhaps unsurprising!

[185] Macdonald 1891, p. 8. This was in part due to the technical virtuosity of lawyers, see Anon 1893.

[186] Dixon 1874, pp. 313–14 citing von Savigny; on the influence of von Savigny in Scotland, see Harvie 1987. See generally Stein 1980, chs. 3–5.

[187] Craig 1882. Cf. Stephen 1883 III, p. 353 arguing that a code would not limit judicial discretion, but change the form of the rules by which the judges were bound.

criminal law was transformed, procedurally and substantively, during the nineteenth century, and it is important to draw together some of the main conclusions. We have challenged the idea that the Victorian criminal law was formal, individualistic and concerned primarily with the protection of property, by tracing an overriding preoccupation with order and the creation of legal instruments that would facilitate its production both inside and outside the legal system. The reconstructing of the criminal that is said to have occurred in this period, that is to say the growing concern with criminals rather than crimes, was accompanied by a reconstruction of the criminal law. But the shift in the content and the conceptual ordering of the law owes more to organisational and institutional change. The production of legal authority was separated from questions of political authority; there was a dramatic expansion in the scope of the law, as a range of different activities was criminalised; and, as new fields of law and types of regulation developed, the focus of the law was increasingly on the regulation of conduct rather than the adjudication of right and wrong.

With the diversification of the functions of the law, substantive jurisdiction was increasingly governed by the linkage of procedural and substantive concerns. This was most obvious in the downgrading of the seriousness of crimes so that they could be tried under the new forms of summary procedure, and in the flexibility of definition that facilitated prosecution by the agencies of criminal justice through a *de facto* shifting of the burden of proof. At a more fundamental level, however, the substantive jurisdiction of the law, its boundaries, came to be defined in terms of what fell procedurally within the jurisdiction of the criminal courts. This is not to say, as we have seen, that the law was not also concerned with right and wrong, or with individual responsibility, but that the dramatic shift came with the entry of 'society' and social concerns into the law. There was not so much a displacement of a system of individualised justice as a re-ordering. Individual justice remained important, but only within an overall concern with the management and production of social and legal order. It is this that is characteristic of the modern criminal law. The true origins of the modern law must be sought in the system that emerged in the late nineteenth century.

This account thus challenges many of the traditional assumptions about the nature and history of the criminal law, and in particular of the modernising transformation that was said to have been carried out by Hume. In doing so, we have seen that his description of the law and procedure was intimately connected to a form of political organisation and authority that was superseded in the course of the nineteenth century. Hume did not modernise the law, for the modern law only developed later in the century. However, we have also found that the strength of his work lies in the fact that he provides a conceptual terminology about the nature of common law jurisdiction, drawing on wider fears and concerns about Scottish identity, that was able to be exploited by later judges and writers concerned to preserve their authority in the face of the transformation of the legal order. We should understand Hume's significance to the modern law only in this more limited sense.

This, of course, must lead us to question the limits of the common law vision of legal order. We have traced the emergence of a new form of legality, that has changed the form of law and its position in relation to the social and political order. The Scottish common law tradition presents a picture of political autonomy and community that our analysis suggests has been limited or compromised. Statutory rules limit the adjudicative competence of the judiciary, and the vision of order and community is constructed by state agencies. Although this has been compensated for by a substantive flexibility and procedural openness that has allowed the law to continue to function, the problem is that, as the law has to produce community and order, the moral basis of the legal order – the judgement of right and wrong – on which the common law is founded has increasingly been cut away. This leads us to an important question, which has lain behind much of the discussion up to this point, and which must be addressed if we are to further our critical understanding of the nature of modern criminal law theory: why is modern legal theory apparently so preoccupied with individual responsibility? The individualism of the modern criminal law theory is one of its most remarked upon features, and an increasing amount of space is given over to the analysis and specification of the conditions of individual liability. Indeed, it must seem especially strange to us that the conceptual basis of the law should be narrowing so dramatically into a concern with individual liability at precisely the moment that the practice of the law and the means of attributing liability are expanding. An increasing preoccupation with individualism, an alternative moral basis for the law, must be traced from this period. It will be argued in the next chapter that this preoccupation relies on a thematisation of the moral basis of 'real' crime, which derives in particular from the treatment of the crime of homicide as paradigmatic for the modern law. The peculiarities of the modern law lie in the relationship between public order and homicide.

5   The perfect crime: homicide and the criminal law

Introduction: the 'murder mystery'

A staple feature of crime fiction, especially familiar no doubt to readers of Agatha Christie novels, is the quest for the 'perfect crime'. Usually, though not necessarily, it involves the murder of an unwanted spouse. The motive may be sexual jealousy, the desire for a more precipitate inheritance of the family fortune, or perhaps an unusually lavish insurance policy.[1] The murderer surrounds the crime with false clues to conceal the motive, to cast the blame on another and, crucially, to outwit the master-detective called in as a foil to the methodical but inevitably plodding police detectives. The real criminal is, of course, discovered because of some chance inconsistency in the evidence or some overlooked detail. They confess, remorsefully or cheerfully, and are carried off by the waiting police. The sword of justice inexorably, unerringly, falls on the transgressor. The moral of the story is that crime does not pay. There is no such thing as the perfect crime.

This chapter is also a kind of murder story, for it will be argued that the law of homicide has been fundamental to the development of modern criminal law theory. It has been the 'perfect crime', providing the central point around which the modern theory of the criminal law has been constructed.[2] The conventional history of the criminal law sees the origins of the individualism of the modern law in the great projects of codification in the period of the Enlightenment. These, it is argued, sought to systematise the law around a philosophical conception of the individual as rights bearer and property owner. Retributive philosophies limited the infliction of punishment to those cases where the crime was committed intentionally and voluntarily, and the criminal law was re-written to reflect these philosophical ideals. Here it will be argued that

---

[1] 'The means chosen should, of course, be poison . . .' (Orwell 1984, p. 352).

[2] Cf. Wells 1988; Lacey et al. 1990 where there is an attempt to 'demystify' the criminal process by comparing the perceptions of the 'typical' crime and of the 'normal' process of criminal detection and trial, as represented by the 'perfect crime', with the 'reality' of crime statistics etc.

such accounts grossly overstate the impact of such liberal philosophies on the law by paying insufficient attention to developments in legal practice. I shall argue that the 'general part' of the criminal law, comprising the definitions of responsibility, causation, excuse, justification and so on, derives almost exclusively from the law of homicide. The understanding of seriousness in terms of the mental state, and hence the blameworthiness, of the actor has its origins and its principal application in the definition of homicide. The mystery is the question of why these so-called general rules should be based on a crime that is, in most respects, atypical. An understanding of these 'homicidal tendencies' of criminal law theory is necessary to answer the question with which the last chapter concluded – that of the origins and significance of the individualism that runs through modern criminal law theory. The individualism of the modern law has a very different genealogy, and this must lead us to reassess its significance.

From a Scottish point of view the singling out of homicide might appear to be somewhat misguided. It is part of the conventional wisdom of the Scottish legal tradition that the law of homicide in general, and of murder in particular, stands apart from the rest of the law because of the special nature of the *mens rea* of murder.[3] If it is admitted to be atypical, how can it also be argued that it is paradigmatic? And if it is accepted that it is paradigmatic in the way that I shall argue, how can this also found the critical claim that homicide is atypical and should not provide a foundation for general rules of liability? To deal with these questions we must introduce some of the main features of the Scots law of homicide.

Although there are complex rules applying only to the law of homicide, in practice the distinctions that these draw between voluntary and involuntary homicide, or lawful and unlawful act homicide, are largely irrelevant as a result of a combination of the flexible definition of murder and prosecutorial and judicial discretion. The standard modern definition of murder was set out by Macdonald, in his *Practical Treatise*, in 1867:

Murder is constituted by any wilful act causing the destruction of human life, whether plainly intended to kill, or displaying such utter and wicked recklessness, as to imply a disposition depraved enough to be wholly regardless of the consequences'.[4]

---

[3] G. H. Gordon 1978, p. 237 '. . . but the reported cases [on recklessness] deal mainly with homicide where the rules regarding *mens rea* are very special and complicated' and p. 252: 'The *mens rea* of murder is a very special one'. See also Scottish Law Commission 1983, para. 2.4; cf. Turner 1945, p. 205.

[4] Macdonald 1867, pp. 140–3, citing Hume 1844 I, pp. 254, 256; by the fifth edition (1948), p. 89 this had been compressed still further by omitting the words 'utter' and 'wholly'.

Its primary feature is the reference to 'wicked recklessness'. This is not the same as intention, but is considered, by means of the epithet 'wicked', to cover those cases where, although the accused may not have intended to kill the victim, they showed a 'criminal' indifference or lack of care in the judgement of the jury. Yet although this definition is unquestionably concise and considered unlikely to confuse juries, it is also expressed in such general terms that it is hard to see what is being defined. The necessary standard of 'wickedness' can be determined only by reference to that class of cases that are sufficiently wicked to fall within the category of murder. It may be claimed in defence of this that it is for the community in the form of the jury to determine this question, but it is not clear that the pivotal decision is in fact always or mainly left to the jury. This vagueness has been encouraged by criminal procedure. The Criminal Procedure (S.) Act 1887 did away with the requirement that the prosecutor specify words of intent in every indictment.[5] In addition, the prosecution have traditionally been able to use their powers to reduce a charge of murder to one of culpable homicide at any stage of the proceedings.[6] This is not only more likely to produce a guilty plea, thereby saving time and money for the Crown Office, but can also when used in borderline cases lead to a sentence as severe as that for murder without the need to engage in time-consuming debate over the precise degree of intention required.[7] The combination of this and judicial control of sentencing has meant that, despite the establishment of the Court of Criminal Appeal in 1926,[8] there has been little modern judicial discussion of the definitions of murder or culpable homicide. We thus find the Scottish law of murder being referred to as the most pragmatic area of the law. There is agreement that the principles of the law of homicide are 'vague and flexible', or 'common-sense and non-technical' and that they are applied in an unprincipled and *ad hoc* manner.[9] The wide definition has developed hand in hand with administrative discretion, and the whole process has been hidden behind the supposed willingness of the jury – in reality the judiciary – to make 'moral judgements'.[10]

[5] 50 and 51 Vict. c. 35 s. 8. See G. H. Gordon 1978, pp. 233–6 on the effects of the 1887 Act on definitions of intention.   [6] G. H. Gordon 1978, Introduction.

[7] The English law of homicide is similar, but perhaps because of stricter procedural rules there have been repeated attempts to define the necessary mental element for murder in the most precise terms. On the debate over the definition of murder, see Goff 1988; see also the Report of the House of Lords Select Committee on Murder and Life Imprisonment (House of Lords Select Committee) 1989. Ashworth 1995, pp. 256–8 on the 'procedural context'.   [8] Criminal Appeal (S.) Act (16 and 17 Geo. V, c. 15).

[9] G. H. Gordon 1978, p. 732; see also Goff 1988, pp. 52–5; Scottish Law Commission 1983, para. 2.34.

[10] G. H. Gordon 1978, pp. 214, 737–8; House of Lords Select Committee 1989, III, p. 470 (Lord Emslie).

Yet rather than confirming to us that the law of homicide is atypical, these characteristics play on a familiar set of themes. Once more it is hard to avoid the impression that statements suggesting otherwise are 'red herrings', clues that lead us away from an understanding of the true nature of the crime. The flexibility of the definition reveals an essential continuity with other parts of the law – for have we not seen that the principal characteristic of the modern common law is that it is expressed through broad and flexible principles, the implementation of which are facilitated by a body of more precise procedural rules. But even without this we find that this crime exerts a strange fascination: though homicide is no ordinary crime, it is not so far removed from the ordinary concerns of lawyers. Discussions of homicide law, however atypical they are supposed to be, crop up with remarkable regularity. Analyses of the concepts of intention, recklessness, causation and so on, seem to be based largely on principles of law drawn from homicide cases.[11] It may, of course, be argued that murder has traditionally fascinated because in the modern law it is regarded as the supreme, the most serious, of crimes. Until recently it gave rise to the 'ultimate' punishment of death; even now, the mandatory life sentence is of a singular gravity. Perhaps it should not surprise us, therefore, that a discussion of the principles of homicide law should lie at the core of the law, for it protects values that are said to be of central importance to our society. However, the relationship between homicide and these core social values is assumed and left unexplored, and, as we shall see, this has gone further at times. The law of homicide has been depicted as the realisation of the genius of Scots law. At this point, where it is taken to represent the synthesis of practical reason, community and national character, it gathers an extra symbolic and moral value. Scots lawyers want to have it both ways – to treat the law as both atypical and a symbol of the whole. Homicide can indeed be the perfect crime.

But this is where the mystery deepens. The law of homicide can be regarded as both pragmatic and technical,[12] both typical and atypical. Although it is apparently that part of the law where individualism is strongest, we have seen that it is prosecuted in such a way as to make these distinctions between different degrees of intention irrelevant. The supposedly 'moral' test of blameworthiness or wickedness continually returns to a series of institutional decisions. Moreover, though it is empirically insignificant to the practice of the law, it casts a long shadow over criminal

[11] See e.g. G. H. Gordon 1978, p. 252: 'The typical picture of recklessness in Scots law is of a murder situation'; T. B. Smith 1962, pp. 133–7. Cf. Lord Bridge in *Moloney* [1985] 1 All E.R. 1025, analysed in Lacey 1993 esp. at p. 632.

[12] See House of Lords Select Committee 1989 III, p. 553 (evidence of Sheriff Gordon); Scottish Law Commission 1983 para. 2.34; for an example of the types of criticisms that could be made, see Williams 1989.

law theory. If this is the 'murder mystery' of the law, then how has it come about? Where is the legal detective to look for clues? To begin, it will help us to undertake a brief historical analysis of the formation of the modern law of homicide. The reconstruction of the development of the law in the last two chapters has demonstrated that the modern law is dominated by social rather than individual values, and that both individualism and the law of homicide have been marginal to these modern values and institutions. It is thus necessary to seek out the origins of this modern preoccupation with the law of homicide and the changing form of criminal law theory. This is additionally necessary because there exists a certain degree of confusion. For some, the existence of broad similarities between the law as described by Hume and the modern law, is treated as evidence that the law has changed little in substance over the last 200 years.[13] For others, this is the area in which the law has changed most.[14] There is some truth in both of these positions. With the transformation of the criminal law, the law of homicide was itself transformed – yet at the same time there has been a high level of procedural continuity with the past. A clarification of this issue will not only help us to situate the development of the law within the contours of our wider history, but will also provide us with a more precise account of the form of the modern legal doctrine. This history demonstrates, above all, that the modern law is a creation of the nineteenth century, within which we also find the origins of and explanations for the particular individualism of the modern law.

Looking for clues (1): the emergence of culpable homicide

'The different degrees of Homicide, considered as to their legal effect, are more the result of an improved system of law, than of any general and acknowledged rule, subsisting at all times, and founded on a just notion of the true nature of this crime'.[15]

The characteristic feature of the modern law of homicide is said to be that, unlike any other crime, the degree of seriousness is not based on the act committed, but on the intention of the actor. The act of homicide can only be punished according to the level of intention or foresight on the part of the accused person. The normal explanation for this is that it was a crime that until very recently could be capitally punished, which was sufficient to give rise to particular rules enlarging the categories of non-capital homicide and enabling the scope of the 'ultimate punishment' to be

[13] For example, Sellar 1991, p. 55 arguing that the modern law of homicide begins with Hume; House of Lords Select Committee 1989 para. 39.
[14] See e.g. T. B. Smith 1962, p. 181.   [15] Burnett 1811, p. 1 (note).

gradually restricted for reasons of humanity.[16] In crimes such as theft or criminal damage to property, the story goes, a similar process could occur through a narrowing of the factual circumstances in which the death penalty could apply – for example, only to thefts of property over a certain value, or damage to a particular type of property. In homicide, where the end result was always the same and all human lives were of equal value, this process could only be achieved by differentiating on the grounds of the state of mind of the assailant.[17] This is said to have required a greater formality in definition as the categories of murder and culpable homicide, or capital and non-capital homicide, were defined, or distinguished, on the basis of intention to kill. Thus, the emergence of modern concepts of intention and recklessness has traditionally been linked to reform of the old law and the humanitarian rejection of capital punishment.

Although there is some truth in this account of the development of the law, the recognition of individual responsibility in these terms was a much more complex process which cannot be explained by the humanitarian impulses of law reformers alone. Moreover, the development of the modern form of criminal intention was closely connected to the process of modernisation described in the previous chapter. We can trace the origins of this modern concept of intention by tracing the emergence of the crime of culpable homicide. To do this we must go back to the eighteenth-century law, the foundations of which were laid by an Act of Parliament of 1661, passed to clarify 'all doubts that may arise hereafter in criminal pursuits for slaughter'.[18]

This statute, which formed the basis of the law until the early nineteenth century, stated that certain types of homicide, principally 'casual' or accidental homicide and homicide in self-defence, would not be capitally punishable. It recognised two classes of homicide, distinguished in terms of the consequences following from their proof. The main class was murder, which was charged in every case of criminal homicide and was always to be capitally punishable. This was defined as 'forethocht felony' or killing with malice aforethought.[19] The formal requirements of the law were strict. Although there was no felony–murder rule in Scots law, in practice the doctrine of implied malice operated in a very similar manner.

[16] G. H. Gordon 1978, pp. 746–8. See Radzinowicz and Hood 1986, ch. 20 and Wiener 1990, pp. 266–79 on Victorian discontent with the rigidities of the definition of murder.

[17] This is also, in a certain sense, a narrowing of the factual situations in which the death penalty could apply. The old law recognised the identity of the victim in certain situations, as well as the circumstances of the death in the felony–murder rule. That this could be achieved only by treating a person's state of mind as a fact capable of proof before the court was a development of major importance in theories of evidence.

[18] Acts of the Parliament of Scotland c. 22, re-enacting 1649 c. 19. For an account of the not dissimilar development of the English law, see Horder 1992, chs. 1, 2.

[19] Hume 1844 I, pp. 254–64; Sellar 1991; cf. English law, Stephen 1883 III, ch. 26.

Intent, or dole, was to be presumed from the fact of violent killing, and the burden was always on the accused to bring evidence that the killing was the result of accident or self-defence. If successful, it would then fall into the second category, that of casual homicide. Although this was not capital, neither was it regarded as completely justifiable in all cases for, as Burnett argued, 'Our law presumes some fault or want of care on the part of the slayer, even in the case of casual homicide'.[20] The procedure in these cases would be that the accused would be charged with murder, but on the relevancy of the plea being challenged the libel would be restricted, concluding only for arbitrary pains and not the full pains of the law.[21] The offender might then be punished in proportion to their perceived fault. This happened, for example, in cases where excessive force had been used in self-defence or where a lawful act had been performed in a dangerous manner. Assythment (compensation) was still to be payable to the relatives of the victim in cases of casual homicide or where the offender escaped the death penalty by means of a royal pardon.[22]

Initially the Act seems to have been strictly interpreted with the courts recognising only these two classes of homicide, but towards the end of the eighteenth century a third category began to emerge: that of culpable homicide. This was a complex development, related to the increasing involvement of the state in the process of prosecution and the assertion of the priority of the royal jurisdiction. The growing temporal power of the state was manifested in the assumption of the power to control the life and death of its subjects, and hence the law of homicide took on an increasing importance.[23] In the course of the eighteenth century it would appear that the numbers of prosecutions for homicide increased, possibly motivated by a concern about levels of social violence, frequently for types of activities that would not previously have been regarded as criminal.[24] In the old system a certain degree of flexibility had been provided for by the selective

[20] Burnett 1811, p. 35 following Mackenzie 1678, pp. 118–19; see also Bayne 1748, p. 33. Unusually, the Act made provision for imprisonment but this should probably be regarded primarily as a means of enforcing assythment, particularly since imprisonment was not a common penalty at this time – and especially not for homicide. Cf. Black 1975, p. 56.

[21] That is, it would not conclude for capital punishment. See, for example, Hume 1844 I, 245.

[22] See Young forthcoming, ch. 3; Smith and Macdonald 1958, pp. 299–301; Gane 1980.

[23] The classic conceptual account is Kames 1792. See also K. M. Brown 1986, ch. 9.

[24] Beattie 1986, ch. 3 is a detailed study of the prosecution rates of certain crimes in England in this period. He argues that the state increasingly intervened in situations of interpersonal violence. See also J. S. Cockburn 1991. The Scottish courts seem to have begun to treat homicides arising from quarrels without weapons as giving rise to some degree of criminal liability. Compare Hume 1844 I, pp. 234–9 with the cases cited in Burnett 1811, pp. 32–3.

use of mercy and the payment of compensation in place of punishment, but as the state became more involved, it sought to enforce the formal requirements of the law more strictly, to establish a uniformity in jurisdiction. The law, however, proved to be simply too rigid in its categorisation and severe in its consequences and appears to have produced situations where juries would acquit a person charged with murder rather than expose them to the possible risk of capital punishment. The solution to this situation was found in the category of culpable homicide. Originally deriving from the Roman law, the term covered various types of homicide, such as killing without malice aforethought, killing where there was no violent design or killing in a sudden quarrel – thereby partially overlapping with the existing class of casual homicide (killing without violent design). Its most important application, though, was in the development of a partial defence of provocation.[25] A path was opened between the stark alternatives of execution or acquittal because the courts were flexible enough to allow a finding of culpable homicide in cases of homicides arising from provocation.[26] The entire process was facilitated, as Beattie points out, by the growing use of punishments such as imprisonment and transportation that allowed for the gradation of punishment according to the perceived degree of culpability of the offender.[27] By this means more offenders were opened up to some measure of punishment. Hence the extension of state activity into prosecution and punishment was achieved by means of a flexibility towards the formal categories of the law rather than an increasing formalism.

In the course of the eighteenth century the courts moved towards the position that, in general terms, the purpose of the Act of 1661 was to allow them to punish homicides arbitrarily (i.e. not by the mandatory death penalty) 'where the agent is in some degree blameable'.[28] In the law of murder it meant that some of the more rigid presumptions about malice were relaxed. Hume rejected the 'strained and artificial' principles of English law to argue that 'the intention must be gathered from the whole

---

[25] See above, ch. 4, pp. 130–1, for further discussion of this point.

[26] Cf. Stephen 1883 III, pp. 62–3, 87 arguing that in England the law of provocation was widened to escape the rigid presumptions about malice in English law. 'The whole law of provocation rests, as I have shown, upon an avowed fiction – the fiction of implied malice. Malice is implied when a man suddenly kills another without provocation' (p. 87). Probably, though, the motivation was not entirely humanitarian.

[27] Beattie 1986, pp. 88–9, 608–9. It should also be noted that the penalties for manslaughter were increased by a statute in 1822 (3 Geo. IV c. 38). This is discussed in Stephen 1883, III, pp. 78–9; Hume 1844 I, p. 254: 'For our Judges have a discretion in this matter, to condemn the offender to a punishment proportioned to the measure of his fault, and such as may truly serve for a correction to him, and a warning to others.'

[28] Erskine 1871 IV, iv, 41. Cf. Hume 1844 I, p. 233 'according to the quality of the fault'.

circumstances of the case'.[29] The cases presented by Hume suggest that
the use of certain weapons or the fact that death occurred in the course of
another unlawful act, which had previously founded the presumption of
malice, were beginning to be treated as evidence of the intention of the
accused.[30] Culpable homicide, however, was still closely tied to the old
law. It was a residual category, formed negatively by grouping those
situations that fell short of wilful murder together with a class that had
previously been regarded as casual homicides.[31] It was open to the jury to
find a person guilty of culpable homicide on any charge of murder, or for
the court to restrict a libel to only arbitrary pains, but it was only from the
late 1780s onward that the practice of libelling alternate charges of murder
or culpable homicide became established.[32] Even then, a charge of
culpable homicide on its own was rare before 1800 and did not become
common for another twenty years.[33]

It is not difficult to see why this should be the case. A charge of culpable
homicide would have required the prosecutor to establish positively the
degree of fault or state of mind of the accused as an element of the charge –
a practice which was antithetical to the old law for two principal reasons.
First, the requirement of malice or intention was largely formal, corresponding exactly to the general terms in which dole (or responsibility) was
discussed. The evil intent or dole did not have to be positively established,
but was 'presumed merely from the act of killing, otherwise no person
could be convicted of murder'.[34] It was inferred negatively, from the fact
that an event had occurred that was manifestly wrong, on the basis of the
assumption that persons having the use of reason would not perform such
acts. Second, the concept of dole did not admit different degrees of
intention – at most, only different degrees of 'wickedness' in the case of
less serious crimes. It was connected to the seriousness of the crime rather

---

[29] Hume 1844 I, pp. 238, 252. See also I, pp. 24–5 where the English felony-murder rule is
discussed and he seeks to avoid the formal criteria that killing in the course of an unlawful
act must be murder, arguing that there is no authority in Scots practice for such a rule.
Note also that Hume's criticism of English formalities was quoted with approval by the
English Law Commissioners Seventh Report 1843 PP.XIX.1.

[30] Cf. the shift in the English law of provocation described by Horder (1992, pp. 30–9, 87–9)
from regarding certain categories of affront as founding a claim of provocation to seeing
them merely as evidence of a certain state of mind.

[31] See Hume 1844 I, pp. 233–54.

[32] The earliest case is probably *Crichton* 1781 (Burnett 1811, p. 26); the most important
cases are *Geo. White* 1788 and *Jas. McGhie* 1791 (Hume 1844 I, 246).

[33] Cf. the unusual case of *Henry Inglis* 1784 (Burnett 1811, p. 27).

[34] Erskine 1871 IV, iv, 42 going on to say that this presumption may be 'excluded by special
circumstances'; Hume 1844 I, p. 255 'If the libel bear the crime of murder in the *major*
proposition, and affirm in the *minor*, that at such a time and place, the pannel did murder,
or did cruelly kill and slay the deceased, by such and such acts of great violence, these
terms are themselves an implied charge of the sort of malice which the law requires.' See
also above, ch. 4.

than to the state of mind of the actor. Thus, when writers such as Forbes and Bayne referred to homicide arising from negligence being equivalent to dole, they were not referring to a lesser degree of intention, but to the fact that the evil or wickedness of the outcome was less serious.[35] Since culpable homicide was not punished capitally it was technically not a 'serious' crime. The crucial point, if it needs to be stressed, was that although lip-service was paid to the importance of the requirement of intent this was still very much of secondary importance, even for Hume, in the definition and proof of homicide.

This point can be underlined by the fact that the classifications of the old law were based on the penal consequences that followed from certain acts, rather than the intention of the actor.[36] Certain types of killing were regarded as giving rise to certain types of consequences: execution, imprisonment, fining or acquittal. The category of culpable homicide, which was just beginning to separate itself from that of casual homicide, included acts that were punished for very different reasons (the excess in self-defence, provocation, death arising from lawful acts and so on). That these were grouped together because of the consequences is clear even in Hume, who introduces each class in terms of the punishment that follows on proof and retains, somewhat surprisingly, the category of aggravated murder (where additional punishment could be inflicted according to the character or social position of the victim).[37]

The decisive shift towards the modern law came in the early years of the nineteenth century when, as the result of the increasing use of the charge of culpable homicide, culpability began to be formulated in terms of the state of mind of the individual offender. We can best illustrate this by examining one of the leading nineteenth-century cases. In the case of *Paton and McNab*,[38] two railway employees, a superintendent and a train driver, were charged with culpable homicide. A passenger had died as the result of a collision between two trains, alleged to have been caused by a series of negligent acts on the part of employees of the railway company. Prosecutions such as this, for negligently caused culpable homicide, enjoyed a brief prominence in the middle years of the century before falling away altogether, and they are normally regarded as an aberrant (and short-lived) episode in the history of the law.[39] Their importance,

---

[35] W. Forbes 1730, p. 3; Bayne 1748, p. 3. Otherwise it would involve the apparent illogicality of saying that 'evil intent' was essential to all crimes, but then accepting in some cases that a lesser degree of intent such as gross fault or inexcusable negligence would amount to the same thing. The same point applies to Hume for whom 'negligent' actions were punishable where the 'wickedness' was palpable. See 1844 I, pp. 192, 233.

[36] On this point, see Stephen 1883 III, ch. 26.

[37] Hume 1844 I, 191. See also above, ch. 4 at p. 105.   [38] (1845) 2 Broun 525.

[39] See G. H. Gordon 1978, p. 115: 'They can probably now be regarded as little more than historical curiosities', and ch. 26.

however, has been underrated, for they provide us with a vital clue as to the character of the modern law. In these decisions we find the clearest formulations of the new conception of liability, which allows us to trace the 'reverberations' of this change through the criminal law as a whole.[40]

In his direction to the jury, Lord Justice-Clerk Hope made what was considered to be the classic statement of the contemporary law. He began by stating that for a finding of guilt the neglect of duty must be brought home to each pannel. This would be established 'if there is one material circumstance in the conduct of the pannels, which, by direct neglect of duty on their part, contributed towards the death libelled',[41] regardless of the conduct of others in the circumstances. He went on:

It is not necessary, in order to substantiate a charge of Culpable Homicide, either that there should be any intention to do another the injury which has occurred, or that the party should even know that another is actually exposed to risk . . . The general rule is that every person, placed in a situation in which his acts may affect the safety of others, must take all precautions to guard against the risk to them arising from what he is doing. Preservation of the lives of others is the first duty of all men in the pursuit of their own business and calling . . . Railway servants are not entitled to neglect any precaution necessary for the safety of others, whether laid down in the rules of the company or not . . . and if that has been omitted, which common sense and ordinary reflection as to the situation of others required, which their duty to the law required for the safety of others, the guilt is clear.[42]

The legal duties of railwaymen were thus considered to go beyond the normal duty not to harm others, and even beyond the specific duties laid down in company regulations, because of the special risks that their activity gave rise to. It was accepted that, although certain accidents were wholly unavoidable, there were none the less certain types of risk, such as those arising from 'defective and insufficient machinery',[43] that could be eradicated. If necessary, this would be done, 'by a stern and vigorous enforcement of the criminal responsibility of one and all concerned, by whom, in whatever situation, anything is neglected or omitted by which the safety of others is endangered'.[44] Employees were to take note that it was incumbent upon them to defend the safety of the passengers, even in the face of opposition from profit-hungry directors. The jury, recommending them to the mercy of the court, found both men guilty. Paton, the supervisor, was sentenced to twelve months' and McNab to nine months' imprisonment.

This is a typical small drama of mid-Victorian life: rapacious railway entrepreneurs enjoy the protection of the law, while the underpaid and

---

[40] Fletcher 1978, p. 239.   [41] *Paton and McNab* (1845) 2 Broun 525, p. 532.
[42] *Ibid.*, pp. 533–4.   [43] *Ibid.*, p. 535.   [44] *Ibid.*

overworked employees are sent to prison. The case, however, reveals a number of important legal developments. By the 1840s the practice of charging culpable homicide was firmly established. It was used, as the result of the increased organisation and interventionism of the prosecutorial system, in a range of situations that had not previously been prosecuted, particularly where (as in this case) accidental death was caused by the mishandling of machinery or vehicles.[45] Although these prosecutions later died out following the more systematic statutory regulation of these fields, the offence of culpable homicide continued to grow in importance. By the end of the century, in fact, culpable homicide, and not murder, had come to be regarded both in practice and doctrinally as the central category in the law of homicide. The point was made most graphically by Lord Young who, charging the jury in a murder case, stated that, 'All unlawful killing or destroying the life of a human being is culpable homicide; but the term murder is technically applied to that culpable homicide which is done maliciously'.[46] The primary appeal of culpable homicide was undoubtedly the flexibility that it offered, not only in sentencing, but also in the prosecution of the crime. The irresistible rise of culpable homicide, always widening the potential application of the law, can be read at one level as a series of pragmatic solutions to some of the difficulties posed by the formalism of the old law.

This first became apparent in the late eighteenth century with the recognition of the plea of provocation and the rejection of the limits placed on the law by the statute of 1661. It found further expression in the development of the concept of diminished responsibility.[47] From the early years of the century, weakness of intellect or mental disorder not amounting to insanity had been considered as factors that might mitigate

[45] On the expansion of criminal liability for accidents in this period, see Beattie 1986, ch. 3; J. S. Cockburn 1991, pp. 90–3. Both argue that, whether or not the actual number of accidents increased, there was undoubtedly an increased level of concern about accidental (and hence preventable) deaths. Cf. Alison 1832, p. 113 who expresses a concern that cases of this type 'have of late years received a great increase from the common use of steam vessels on friths (sic) of the sea and navigable rivers; and it is probable they will be still further increased by the application of the power of steam to land-carriages'. For a more complete list of the areas in which actions were prosecuted, see G. H. Gordon 1978, pp. 789–93. Cf. Fletcher 1978, p. 240 where it is argued that liability for negligence *limits* the general grounds of liability.

[46] *HM Adv. v. Marshall* (1897) 4 S.L.T. 217; cf. A. M. Anderson 1904, p. 149: 'The degree of recklessness which may bring a crime up to murder is always a question of circumstance'. Cf. *Macadam* 1960 J.C. 1 at pp. 4–5 where Lord Justice-General Clyde went even further in describing non-capital murder as a species of aggravated assault. Sellar 1991, p. 55 points out that in the early law the term manslaughter was sometimes used to denote the entire law of homicide.

[47] See generally G. H. Gordon 1978, ch. 11. An analogous development was the recognition in nineteenth century law that intoxication might reduce the culpability of the accused because of the absence of full intent. See *Kane* (1892) 3 White 386.

the sentence of the accused, or lead to a recommendation of mercy in capital cases.[48] In a series of murder cases in the late nineteenth century, the High Court, apparently on the initiative of a single judge, Lord Deas, accepted the principle that a successful plea of diminished responsibility could reduce a charge of murder to culpable homicide.[49] This was to accept that the mental state of the accused was not only relevant to sentencing, but could also affect the degree of culpability – in order to avoid the mandatory death sentence.[50] Moreover, the justification for this development was sought within the law of homicide rather than in any more fashionable scientific theory of alienation. Lord Deas argued that, 'The undoubted fact that under an indictment for murder a verdict might be returned of culpable homicide, although not alternatively libelled, of itself sufficiently proved that we had in our law the principle [of natural justice]'.[51] Undue severity was certainly avoided, but the judicial willingness to widen the principles of the law is striking.

However, to see developments simply in these pragmatic terms would be to overlook the way in which the new practice of culpable homicide was transforming the legal definition of homicide. As the category of culpable homicide grew in importance it came to be defined positively, on the basis of the degree of blame of each of the accused as this could be determined from the circumstances of the case. The prosecutor accordingly had to establish two things that had formerly been regarded as inseparable: first, it had to be proved that the death had been caused by the actions of the accused and, second, that the accused had acted wilfully or negligently. This second factor clearly required the formulation of a test by which the state of mind of the accused could be judged. The crucial difference from the old law lies in this separation between act and will – between the harm caused and the degree of blame – and we must examine this in more detail.

Obviously, the need to prove that the death was caused by the actions of the accused was not something that was new to the law. For Hume and earlier writers it had always been stated that, to found a charge of murder, death must have followed even the most serious injury, and that there had to be a direct connection between the injury inflicted and the death of the

[48] Hume 1844 I, pp. 37–47; Alison 1832, pp. 652–4; Bell's Notes, p. 5; cf. Mackenzie 1678, p. 16.
[49] The principal cases are: *Dingwall* (1867) 5 Irv. 466; *Miller* (1874) 3 Coup. 16; *Tierney* (1875) 3 Coup. 152; *McLean* (1876) 3 Coup. 334 (theft by housebreaking); *Granger* (1878) 4 Coup. 86; *Ferguson* (1881) 4 Coup. 552; *Brown* (1882) 4 Coup. 596; *Gove* (1882) 4 Coup. 598.
[50] See G. H. Gordon 1978, pp. 382–3: 'The reduction of category is only a device to avoid a fixed penalty, and is unnecessary where the crime charged does not have a fixed penalty or where, as in a number of crimes prior to the Criminal Procedure (S.) Act 1887, it is capital in name but is not in fact capitally punished'; cf. Keith 1959; T. B. Smith 1962, pp. 153–63.   [51] *Ferguson* (1881) 4 Coup. 552 at p. 558.

accused.[52] The rule was clear: if a person inflicted an injury on another then in law they would have to accept the 'natural consequences' of that injury.[53] However, the development of culpable homicide undermined this rule by opening up the possibility of the imposition of criminal liability for both 'acts' and 'omissions'. Prosecutions were frequently brought in situations where the accused had failed to act to prevent the occurrence of danger or had acted negligently or carelessly. In the case of *Wm. Gray*,[54] for example, the accused was an engine driver charged with culpable homicide for allowing a passenger to ride on the front of a train, as a result of which he was killed in an accident. The relevancy of the charge was challenged on the grounds that there had been no negligent action on the part of the accused, merely that he had not prevented someone else from putting themselves in a dangerous situation. This, it was claimed, could not be a crime at common law because there had been no act.[55] The prosecution, by contrast, argued that liability would arise wherever there had been fault leading to death, whether caused by act or omission, even though it was conceded that most of the existing cases had turned on positive acts of the accused. The outcome of this case was inconclusive, the charge eventually being abandoned by the prosecution for unspecified reasons, but it is interesting as an illustration of the extent to which the prosecution wished to push the law. The eventual solution for these types of cases was compromise. The wording of the indictment was changed so that it could always be alleged that, whether the death was caused by commission or omission, the accused was *acting* in a culpable manner.[56] This was to open the way for an emphasis on the conduct rather than the result. The concept of committing by omission was thus accepted, upholding the principle of the common law as stated by the defence, but at the same time expanding the conception of an act.[57]

This brought further problems, centring on the question of how a failure to act could be said to have directly caused death – something that

[52] See e.g. Hume 1844 I, pp. 179–91. See also Tur 1993, pp. 230–2.
[53] Hume 1844 I, p. 184.
[54] (1836) 1 Swin. 328; see also the discussion of this case in Bell's Notes, pp. 72–3.
[55] Hume 1844 I, p. 189: 'This obvious limitation must be acknowledged, that the manner of death must be such, wherein the act of the pannel plainly and palpably appears, and not by suspicion and conjecture only.'
[56] 1887 Act Schedule A has a specimen indictment in the following form: 'You did, when acting as a railway signalman, lower a danger signal and allow a train to enter on a part of the line protected by the signals under your charge, and did cause a collision, and did kill . . .' See also A. M. Anderson 1904, p. 154.
[57] *Henderson and Lawson* (1842) 1 Broun 262 chemist who failed to instruct assistant in the dispensing of dangerous drugs; *John and Mary Craw* (1839) 2 Swin. 449 cruel and unnatural treatment and wilful neglect of a child. As statutory duties increased these common law prosecutions also went into decline. Neglect of a statutory duty was a much easier charge to prove – see pp. 124–6, below.

we would now treat as an issue of causation. The natural consequences of a 'wicked' act could be specified relatively easily, but to talk about the 'natural' consequences of a failure to act seemed to cut any direct connection that would justify criminal liability. It implied that a sequence of events was already in motion that had not been initiated by the accused. It also raised the possibility that the death might have been caused by a combination of factors, some outwith the control of the accused, that taken separately might not have produced any harmful consequences at all. In practice, these questions of cause and effect were treated, as we have already seen from *Paton and McNab*, as questions of the failure of a duty that had to be brought home to each of the accused in the case. The factual question was therefore collapsed into the issue of whether or not the accused had a legal duty to perform, and whether they had acted in such a way as to neglect that duty – a question of legal fact. The negligence of each of the accused would have to be assessed on the basis of their position, skills and ability to influence the eventual outcome.[58] This was again to place the emphasis on the conduct obviating the need to prove that they had caused the result. In fact, the Crown later developed the practice of laying charges of both culpable homicide and culpable neglect of duty. Since the latter could be punished in the same way as culpable homicide, the result was that the question of whether the negligence had actually caused the death was increasingly irrelevant to liability.[59]

We must finally turn our attention to the question of wilfulness and blame. Fault or culpability was not only a question of the failure to carry out a legally recognised duty – although the extent of this duty had to be established as the first step in cases of negligence. It was also a question of degree, with the crime being regarded as more serious if it was committed deliberately or if the result was clearly foreseeable. This has been described as the move towards 'a theory of excessive risk-taking'.[60] Fletcher argues that this has three elements. The first is the likelihood that the activity might have caused death. This was a factual question concerning the probability or the gravity of the risk, and was to be calculated by balancing the degree of danger against the necessary precautions. This was made explicit in the case of *Kirkpatrick and Stewart*,

---

[58] *Paton and McNab*; *Macdonald and ors* (1853) 1 Irv. 164; *Baillie and McCurrach* (1870) 1 Coup. 442.

[59] Discussed in G. H. Gordon 1978, pp. 791–3. For the effect of the charges, see e.g. Lord Justice-Clerk Hope in *HM Adv. v. Stenhouse and McKay* (1852) 1 Irv. 94 at p. 111: 'You may lay aside the first part of the charge . . . for there would really be no difference in the punishment, whether it is regarded as a case of Culpable Homicide, or one of culpable neglect of duty, which caused the death of any of the lieges. A charge of Culpable Homicide sounds harsh, but here, in reality, there is little difference.' See also Macdonald 1867, pp. 143ff.

[60] Fletcher 1978, pp. 259–74 as part of the move towards an act-oriented law of homicide.

where it was stated that if a contractor were to undertake an operation consisting of a series of actions and 'if there be palpable danger unless certain probabilities shall be obviated by certain known precautions, such contractor may be answerable'.[61] This should also be seen as a way of reproducing the distinction between those accidents that were regarded as avoidable, because foreseeable, and those that were not – a point that was also made very clearly in *Paton and McNab*. The second element was that the risk should not exceed the degree of social benefit to be gained from the activity. This is not dealt with explicitly in any decisions,[62] although the concerns with passenger safety and precautions clearly demonstrate that such social considerations were taken into account. We shall thus move quickly on to the third element, the awareness of the actor of the risk that they were undertaking, for that is our major concern. The degree of culpability was measured in terms of the foreseeability of the risk and the perception by the actor of that risk. This standard of foresight was expressed by the courts in the terms of a general formulation of reasonable foreseeability, or by assessing the precautions 'which ordinary common sense and reflection'[63] would reveal to be necessary to prevent accidents. Certain other circumstantial factors could then be taken as evidence of this lack of care and attention. Compliance with their employers' instructions or company regulations was not of itself regarded as sufficient to fulfil the duty of care, but was regarded as evidence of the degree of blame along with other factors such as the following of normal trade practices.[64] The test was therefore based on a combination of objective factors (probability and acceptability of risk) and subjective conceptions (foreseeability of risk). The actor's state of mind had come to be regarded as something that could be proved as a question of fact. This, to use a phrase coined by Fletcher, marks the movement towards a pattern of 'subjective criminality', taking the actor's intention to violate a protected interest as the core of criminal liability.[65]

This transformation depended on a key inversion of the traditional definition. Prior to this the presumption of wilfulness had been made on the basis of the evil consequences and the 'social disregard' or malignant spirit that this was said to display. The important element of wilfulness

[61] (1840) Bell's Notes, p. 71.
[62] Though, see Lord Gillies in *Jas. Craw* 1827 Syme 188 at p. 211: 'Manufactures, expeditious modes of travelling, proving guns, are not intended to injure. Perhaps they cannot be carried on without some contingent risk to human life. At the same time everyone is aware, that in conducting the most necessary and useful operations attended with risk, all possible precautions are required.'   [63] *Paton and McNab* above, note 38.
[64] See *Stenhouse and Mackay* (1852) 1 Irv. 94 at 112; *Trotter* 1842 in Bell's Notes, p. 74; *Houston and Ewing* (1847) Ark. 252; *Auld* (1856) 2 Irv. 459.
[65] Fletcher 1976, chs. 4, 5.

was inferred from the general lack of humane feeling. It came to be argued, by contrast, that to approach the question of intent in this way was to put the test back to front. Rather than presuming the existence of malice, it was argued that if the wilful exposure of human life to danger was the true test of guilt, then the law ought to be based on this and not imply it from the want of humane feeling. This argument was summarised by the English Commissioners on the Criminal Law in 1839:

No facts or symptoms evidencing brutality or malignity of mind could possibly be material to the inquiry, except so far as they tended to show the wilful intention to occasion the risk; and when that was proved, the offence would be complete.[66]

Wilfulness, and hence responsibility, was a matter of degree. It was independent of the particular consequences (evil) and was legally quantifiable. The principal concern thus moved towards an examination of what the acts themselves revealed about the state of mind of the actor.[67] In practice this has never been a purely 'subjective' test based simply on intention or the actual foreseeability of consequences. The Scottish courts have consistently preferred, as we have already seen, to judge conduct rather than consequences, or the duty of care rather than the actual foreseeability of the harm. The legal test has always been treated as the more objective question of whether the actor should have foreseen harm as a likely result of neglecting their duty, or in murder whether there was 'wicked recklessness'. None the less, the crucial point is that there was a move towards regarding action as evidence of a state of mind and this led to a new focus on the mind and the individual subject of the law.

The greater concern with the state of mind and responsibilities of the individual reflected in these theories of subjective liability must, paradoxically, be seen as developing in the context of a greater degree of social intervention on the part of the courts. The responsible individual of the modern criminal law was emerging, but not, as is often assumed, as a representative of *laissez-faire* government and rampant individualism. The criminal law sought to build character and teach social behaviour by laying down duties and responsibilities in the control and regulation of risky activities and behaviour.[68] If the old law was connected to the establishment of temporal power over the subjects of a territory, this new

[66] Fourth Report PP.1839.XIX.235 at p. xxiv. See also Seventh Report PP.1843.XIX. 1. Although the idea of implied or constructive malice survived longer in the law of murder, this is linked to the foundation of the presumption of innocence since it does away with the idea of implied malice. See e.g. *D.P.P. v. Woolmington* 1935 A.C. 462.

[67] Fletcher 1978, pp. 238–40: 'The history of homicide is characterised by a gradual shift from the harm-oriented to the act-oriented mode of analysis.' See also, pp. 115–22. See also Horder 1992, pp. 96–100 on the development of the 'modern' theory of provocation.

[68] See Wiener 1990, pp. 52–6. For the view that nineteenth-century criminal law sought to impose a form of abstract individualism, see Norrie 1993, chs. 1, 2.

power increasingly sought to understand and allocate risks and maximise security.[69] The legal subject was built in response to these social concerns through the expansion of liability for homicide in the nineteenth century. While this could be unjust, criminalising employees who were as much victims as perpetrators, it is important to underline that the transformation of liability for homicide was part of a more general transformation in the nature of legal liability.

This can be illustrated through the changes in the way that criminal liability was conceived. The old form of liability was based on the presumption that 'all persons are bound to take due care that no injury is done to any of the lieges'.[70] The moral duties not to cause harm owed by each person to their neighbour were the basis of the legal duties. An act was thus culpable because it was immoral. Under this new conception the legal duty was a social duty that had to be established by the court for each type of activity. In Alison's words, 'Universally the law measures the degree of care which it requires of those who are intrusted with instruments of power, by the degree of risk which attends their mismanagement'.[71] This was reflected in the new legal conception of culpability which was highly complex, entailing a balancing of probabilities, duties, foresight and the contributory actions of several parties. The ascription of responsibility was reformulated as a technical–legal question, a matter of positive law, which may enforce moral values or have moral foundations. This bifurcation between law and morals is expressed very clearly by Gordon: 'The moral nature of the common law of crimes is not a matter of logical necessity or of the definition of crime, but is a matter of fact, and of social policy'.[72] The new conception of responsibility can therefore be seen to be linked to the more social conception of crime that was described in the last chapter.

The rise of negligent homicide thus illustrates a fundamental transformation in the definition and prosecution of the crime of homicide. While the use of this charge was superseded by new forms of state regulation and control of certain activities which reduced the practical importance of the common law of homicide in this area, the new understanding of the legal subject that this gave rise to was to provide the

---

[69] It was common in this period to see the crime of homicide promoted in importance in the categorisation of crimes because of the desire to recognise the sanctity of human life above the values of state, religion and so on (Cairns 1988). Although, ironically, we have to recognise that Hume only acknowledged its practical importance to the criminal law when reordering the categories.   [70] Alison 1832, p. 113.

[71] *Ibid*, p. 123 following the English commentator Russell. See also, p. 114.

[72] G. H. Gordon 1978, p. 47. He also, for example, argues at pp. 46–7 that the ascription of responsibility is essentially amoral i.e. legal, while arguing at p. 213 that the ascription of *mens rea* in the common law is a moral judgement.

basis for the new theories of criminal law. From Alison onwards the degrees of homicide were defined principally by reference to the intention of the person who had committed the injury rather than the consequences of conviction.[73] The distinction between murder and culpable homicide was based on the degree of intention, measured in terms of the probability and foreseeability of certain outcomes and risks. The elements of act and will had been separated. The former could provide evidence of the latter, but in theory both would have to be proved independently. These were not merely abstract questions of classification, but had come about as a direct result of the increasing use of the charge of culpable homicide in the courts. The rise of culpable homicide by negligence had completely transformed the law of homicide. It is now necessary to look at how the law of homicide, and the conception of individual responsibility that had developed, has been used to form the basis for more general theories of criminal law.

Looking for clues (2): the values of the modern law

Macdonald's 1867 definition of murder, quoted at the beginning of the chapter, can now be seen to have established a balance between the old and the new.[74] The impression of continuity is reinforced by the formulaic language of homicide which, in indictments and legal treatises, changes very little. The seeming interchangeability of terms such as 'wickedly', 'feloniously', 'maliciously' and so on, often seems to have blocked the path of conceptual clarification or development.[75] Further, the definition is formulated in terms of a wicked disposition or character, echoing the traditional conception of dole and inviting the equation of the wrongfulness of the act with the intention of the accused. In a similar manner, Hume's description of murder, expressed in a language that refers to the malicious purpose of the accused and their indifference to the consequences of their actions, can be read out of context as expressing a crude standard of foresight and as prefiguring the new law.[76] Some formal criteria remain; for instance, wicked recklessness may be implied where death results from any serious and dangerous crime, even where there was

[73] Alison 1832, p. 1.
[74] Macdonald 1867, pp. 140–3: 'Murder is constituted by any wilful act causing the destruction of human life, whether plainly intended to kill, or displaying such utter and wicked recklessness, as to imply a disposition depraved enough to be wholly regardless of the consequences.'
[75] See G. H. Gordon 1978, pp. 233–6 on the forms of indictment. This was exacerbated by the procedural reforms introduced by the Criminal Procedure Act 1887 (see above, p. 144). Cf. the survival of 'malice aforethought' in the English law of murder. See Lord Hailsham in *Hyam* [1974] 2 All E.R. 41.
[76] See e.g. Hume 1844 I, p. 257. See also G. H. Gordon 1978, pp. 731–48.

no positive intention to cause personal injury.[77] On the whole, though, these formal criteria have come to be treated as being of only evidential status. The categories may be the same but their content has altered quite substantially. The break with the old law and the acceptance of the new subjective form of liability is clear. The term 'malice aforethought' passed out of use in favour of a more general reference to intention.[78] Macdonald clearly distinguishes between the act – the destruction of human life – and the state of mind with which this was performed. It is murder if the act is performed either with intent to kill or with its equivalent – gross and wicked recklessness. Proof of recklessness depends on the circumstances and is established if the 'probable and foreseen result' of an action was the death of an individual.[79] This is no longer equivalent to dole for, in the words of a modern commentator, recklessness must 'involve indifference to the risk foreseen, and this indifference is regarded as evidence of the accused's wickedness'.[80] That this is, in modern terms, an 'objective' test of the mental state of the accused, should not be allowed to obscure the wider shift in the law towards basing liability on subjective mental states.[81]

The survival of this tension in the law between, on the one hand, the moralistic language that seems to revert to the old law, and, on the other, the continuing influence of the subjective pattern of liability, can none the less help us towards an understanding of the greater significance of the law of homicide to the modern criminal law. Its significance to the self-image of the Scottish legal tradition can be gauged from the memoranda and evidence presented by Lord Justice-General Cooper to the Royal Commission on Capital Punishment.[82] We have already had cause to note the immense influence of Lord Cooper, as both judge and scholar, in the 'revival' of the Scottish legal tradition, and his statement of the law would be of value on this basis alone.[83] However, owing to the paucity of judicial decisions, this was to be, until comparatively recently, the only sustained and authoritative discussion by a member of the judiciary of the principles underlying the law of homicide. This exercise was echoed more recently

[77] Macdonald 1867, p. 143; cf. A. M. Anderson 1904, p. 150. This whole question was to resurface in the controversy following the case of *Cawthorne* 1968 J.C. 32 where Lord Guthrie, drawing on a passage in Macdonald, argued that murder could be committed when a person acted with intent to cause another bodily harm. See discussion in Jones and Griffin 1990.   [78] *Chas. Macdonald* (1867) 5 Irv. 525.
[79] Macdonald 1867; see also *McCallum and Corner* (1853) 1 Irv. 259.
[80] G. H. Gordon 1978, p. 241.
[81] Cf. Holdsworth cited in Turner 1945, p. 200: 'We must adopt an external standard in adjudicating on the weight of evidence adduced to prove or disprove *mens rea*. That, of course, does not mean that the law bases criminal liability upon non-compliance with an external standard. So to argue is to confuse the evidence for a proposition with the proposition proved by the evidence.'
[82] Cooper 1950. Eleven of the thirteen judges consulted concurred in the statement (p. 427).   [83] Above ch. 2.

by a House of Lords Select Committee on Murder and Life Imprisonment which collected evidence from the Scottish judiciary on the advisability of bringing the English and Scottish laws of murder into line with each other,[84] and this provides us with a second valuable source of comment on the law.

The Royal Commission was appointed with the remit of making recommendations on whether the liability to capital punishment for murder should be limited or modified. Given that it was accepted that there was no possibility of complete abolition, this was regarded from the outset as a question relating to the scope of the definition of murder.[85] As a result of this, Lord Cooper was obviously concerned to prevent the possibility of legislative intervention in the Scottish legal process and, in a supplementary memorandum, presented an ardent defence of the Scottish law of homicide and, by extension, the system of criminal law. The argument was based on two principal claims: first, the leniency of the system and, second, the flexibility provided by the common law.

The leniency of the punishment of homicide in general was pointed to as evidence that the category of murder was already sufficiently restricted by the feelings of the Scottish public. Lord Cooper argued that Scots law had reached the position where in practice only intentional killings were prosecuted as murder, and therefore that the law was not harsh.[86] He claimed, for example, that cases that were charged as murder in England would be treated as culpable homicide in Scotland.[87] Indeed, he expressed some perplexity at the difficulties which were experienced by English lawyers over these questions.[88] Moreover, Cooper argued that since culpable homicide was the normal verdict in murder trials, the death penalty was used very little in Scotland.[89] To further confine the use of the death penalty in Scotland, then, would be in practical terms to abolish it – which would not be desirable. The death penalty, on the contrary, was

---

[84] See Report of the Select Committee on Murder and Life Imprisonment 1989.

[85] For the long history of attempts to deal with the question of capital punishment in this way, see Radzinowicz and Hood 1986, ch. 20.

[86] Cooper 1950 (Royal Commission on Capital Punishment) at qn 5417, with wicked recklessness, of course being evidence of intention.

[87] See e.g. *ibid.*, qn 5452. Cf. House of Lords Select Committee 1989 qn 1714 (Crown Office): 'Of course, Scotland has a wider definition than England at the moment and . . . probably always has had.'

[88] This echoes Hume's perplexity towards the formalities in which the English law of murder had contrived to entangle itself. See 1844 I, pp. 24–5, 254. It is interesting to note that Hume was quoted with approval on this point by the English Law Commissioners Fourth Report and Seventh Rept. 1840; most recently, see Goff 1988 where a senior English judge expressed admiration for the Scots law of murder.

[89] See the statistics in Cooper 1950 at p. 427: of 589 cases indicted for murder between 1900 and 1948, there were 242 verdicts of culpable homicide, 120 verdicts of not guilty or not proven, and 59 verdicts of murder, which led to 23 executions.

defended as an ultimately humane deterrent uniquely suited to the Scottish people, just as the mandatory life sentence was defended before the later Committee on the grounds that public confidence in Scotland would be severely dented if it were removed.[90] It is noteworthy that the leniency or otherwise of the sentencing of non-capital homicides, that is all culpable homicides and those cases where the Secretary of State exercised the royal prerogative of mercy, was not discussed, save to point out that they were subject to judicial or administrative discretion on the question of sentencing. Leniency, it seems, entailed the movement of cases into the wide category of culpable homicide – where the prosecutor and judge exercised discretion.[91] Lord Cooper's remarks underline our earlier argument that culpable homicide had become the most important category of the law.

The defence of Scots law was presented in its strongest terms when describing the flexibility of the common law. The supplementary memorandum begins with a declaration of intent:

I earnestly deprecate any attempt to prescribe for Scotland in a new and necessarily rigid statutory formula the essentials of murder, or of different degrees or classes of murder, or the dividing line between murder and culpable homicide . . . In Scotland it would be highly dangerous and undesirable'.[92]

This was, he argued, because the law could only be stated in relation to the circumstances of particular cases. He refused all invitations to comment on what the courts or law officers would do in certain hypothetical situations on the grounds that the distinctions between the different situations, and hence the rules, were so complex and subtle as to resist any verbal expression. This sort of expression would run the risk of fixing flexible rules and restricting their effectiveness. The position was defended by the marshalling of a familiar mixture of references to the community and the spirit of the law: that no valid criticism had been made of the Scottish system; that statutes were necessarily rigid; that they were always imposed from outside without regard to the organic life of the native system; and that rigid definitions would take discretion away from the jury and give the judges an unwarranted discretion to interpret ('a highly repugnant duty'[93]). It was asserted that the law had the capacity to

---

[90] Cooper 1950, qns 5380, 5390–1; 1989 at e.g. p. 469–74 (evidence of Lord Emslie), though cf., p. 471: 'the public perhaps does not understand'!

[91] Cf. Evidence to the House of Lords Select Committee 1989, qn 1407 (Faculty of Advocates) and qns 1514–27 (Scottish Law Commission) and at pp. 404–5 and qns 1695–1708 (Memorandum by the Crown Office) where the administrative aspects of the prosecution decision are recognised.

[92] Cooper 1950, p. 428. Cf. Lord Emslie's opening remark to the House of Lords Select Committee 1989 qn 2013: 'I would simply like to make the general point that we are of the opinion that our definition of murder should be left severely (sic) alone.'

[93] *Ibid.*, p. 428.

renew itself anyway, with the examples of diminished responsibility and automatism being pointed to as illustrations of the genius of the Scots law. The final, dramatic, twist of the argument came with the linkage between the national law and the national character. The common law was, of course, the accumulated wisdom of the Scottish people, and its development was therefore symbiotically linked to that of the Scottish people. Like those people it was said to be practical and pragmatic in character and not given to idle speculation.[94] This wisdom was given as a direct correlation of the legal and the moral sense. Written laws were unnecessary 'when dealing with the gravest of all crimes, which has been recognised as such by the moral sense of mankind since the days of Cain and Abel'.[95] Thus, the definition of murder, though complex and inexpressible even to a lawyer of Lord Cooper's experience, was something that was known to each member of the community not only in the form of a prohibition, but also in a way that allowed the judgement of their peers. That this was a characteristic that was peculiar to the Scottish people alone was emphasised in the following statement:

The Scottish community know that the ultimate sanction for murdering a fellow creature is death, and they take that fact to heart and do not test it out by committing a murder in order to see if they will be hanged. In England, on the other hand, more people take that risk, and in Ireland – it is a racial reaction . . . To put it in a pointed form, sane Scotsmen, or sane people in Scotland, do not commit murder so readily as sane people in England. That may be due to the fact that in many parts of England there is a very mixed population'.[96]

These are exaggerated and, at times, distasteful claims, but running through them there is a powerful conviction of the 'moral superiority' of the Scots law. This moral superiority is seen in the combination of two things. First, the fact that the Scottish system is practical. In one of the few discussions of the mental element in crime in Scotland, the Scottish Law Commission, the standing body appointed to review and recommend reform of the law, stated that 'We would not pretend that the Scottish test of murder is beyond criticism, but it does have this merit that in practice it causes very few problems'.[97] This is said to have occurred because, outside statutory crimes, the law has avoided the use of technical terms. Scots law is capable of reaching the same result as the English law without getting involved in 'conceptually difficult' considerations.[98] In the law of

---

[94] Cf. Lord Emslie, House of Lords Select Committee 1989, qn 2066: 'The deliberate or quasi-deliberate taking of life. That is something which the Calvinistic Scottish character seems to think is the worst thing that you can do.'   [95] Cooper 1950, p. 428.

[96] Cooper 1950 qns 5390–5391. Cf. the answer of Lord Emslie to the question of how to define the uniqueness of murder – 'The sanctity of human life as seen by the Scots' (House of Lords Select Committee 1989, qn 2063).

[97] Scottish Law Commission 1983, para. 2.34.   [98] *Ibid.*, para. 2.15.

murder this means that it is considered necessary that terms such as 'intention' and 'wicked recklessness' are given their ordinary and natural meaning.[99] The distinction between murder and culpable homicide is then said to turn on whether or not the quality of wickedness is attributed to the acts of the accused by the jury. This brings us to the second point, which is that the strength of the law is seen in just this willingness to allow juries, and hence the 'community', to make moral decisions.[100] It is thought impossible by Scots lawyers to have a concept of murder based only on intention, because it would be either too broad or too narrow, and this is used as an argument against change.[101] The concept of 'wickedness', on the other hand, cannot be reduced to a statutory formula both because it would be inappropriate to refer to wickedness in a modern statute and because in detracting from the jury's power of moral judgement it would be an attack on the character of Scots law. This is summed up by the Scottish Law Commission in the following terms:

It has been observed from time to time that the approach of Scots law to murder, and indeed in some instances of culpable homicide, lacks clarity and precision, and may rely inappropriately on what are essentially moral judgements. On the other hand, most Scots lawyers would, we believe, see this as no more than a sensible pragmatism . . .[102]

There is an attitude of suspicion towards formal definitions which, it is believed, would constrict the freedom to manoeuvre. This, paradoxically, has created its own 'formal' jurisprudence – the formulae of practical reason and community, intelligible only to lawyers, by which the flexibility of the law is preserved and the operation of the modern machinery of criminal justice smoothed. What is most interesting, though, is the way in which the argument is constructed. Its notable feature is that there is a continual slippage from arguing about the law of murder, which is said to have special features, to attributing the features of flexibility, practicality and the belief that it is supported by the moral judgement of the community, to the criminal law as a whole. The defence of the law of murder thus becomes a symbolic defence of the Scottish legal tradition. It

---

[99] *Ibid.*, para. 4.8.
[100] See e.g. G. H. Gordon to the House of Lords Select Committee 1989, p. 554: 'it offers to any particular jury a definition which allows its own views as to whether the circumstances do or do not deserve to be characterised as murder'; to the same Committee Lord Emslie said 'We have not, for centuries, found it difficult to invite juries to make what some people call a moral judgement' (qn 2028). Cf. the claim in Horder 1993, pp. 684–9.
[101] Goff 1988; cf. Burnett 1811, p. 11: 'The Law, however, cannot (such is the imperfection of human institutions) measure its punishments with a precision exactly proportioned to the nature of the offence, and its just rank in the scale of guilt . . .'
[102] House of Lords Select Committee 1989, p. 386.

is the 'perfect crime' for the Scottish legal tradition, embodying more than any other the individuality, or singular characteristics, of Scots law.

If this explains something of the attachment of Scots law to the values protected by the law of homicide, we have yet to see how that law is more deeply connected to the individualism of modern criminal law theory. In examining this question, we find that there are strong parallels between Scots law and the general trends of recent theorising in the Anglo-American world. Over the past one hundred years, criminal law theory in the common law world has been increasingly directed towards the attempt to specify general rules of individual criminal responsibility. Beginning from the maxim that there can be no legal guilt unless the state of mind of the actor was culpable (*actus non facit reum nisi mens sit rea*), the conditions of liability for individual crimes are then specified in the separate terms of the criminal act (*actus reus*) and the necessary mental state of the actor (*mens rea*).[103] In the common law world this exercise is normally preceded by the disclaimer that each crime is different and so there is no principle of *mens rea* that is common to all crimes and consequently no general state of *mens rea*.[104] Remarkably, although the impossibility of maintaining the distinction is increasingly acknowledged, successive theorists have continued to analyse the criminal law in terms of a general distinction between harmful or prohibited conduct and a blameworthy mental state on the grounds that the distinction is analytically useful.[105] This usefulness is thought to operate at two levels. The first is that of attempting to distinguish between those elements in the definition of particular crimes that relate to the forbidden situation[106] or conduct,[107] and those that relate to intention or the mental element of crime. The second is the elaboration of the general conditions of liability by defining the concepts of criminal conduct, the different degrees of criminal liability (intention, recklessness and negligence) and different conditions that either justify

---

[103] In fact, Stephen memorably describes this as less a maxim than a 'minim', 'for they give not a particularly great but a particularly small amount of information. As often as not the exceptions and qualifications to them are more important than the so-called rules' 1883 II, p. 94 (note); Sayre 1934, p. 402. For one of the most interesting and influential analyses, see Fletcher 1978.

[104] Stephen 1883 II, p. 95: 'The truth is that the maxim about *mens rea* means no more than that the definition of all or nearly all crimes contains not only an outward and visible element, but a mental element, varying according to the different nature of different crimes.'

[105] 'It is not always possible to separate *actus reus* from *mens rea*', Smith and Hogan 1992, p. 29. 'Dividing crime into its constituent elements in this way should be no more than a matter of convenience', Clarkson and Keating 1994, pp. 88–9. See also Lord Diplock in *R. v. Miller* [1983] 1 All E.R. 978. For criticisms of its analytical usefulness from within this tradition, see A. T. H. Smith 1978; Robinson 1993. For other criticisms, see Norrie 1993; Lacey *et al.* 1990, pp. 24–43.   [106] G. H. Gordon 1978, p. 61.

[107] Clarkson and Keating 1994, p. 90; Ashworth 1995, ch. 4.

the act or excuse the actor (insanity, necessity, duress/coercion and so on). These rules have been abstracted from the definitions of particular crimes to produce a set of general rules about the conditions under which an individual might be held responsible for a particular act or consequence.

The most striking feature of these general rules, however, is just how limited they are in both theory and practice. The rules of self-defence developed as a species of casual homicide, and even now have no application in offences against property. The defence of insanity is, in practice, almost never pleaded outside cases of homicide, for the consequence of its success (indeterminate confinement in a special prison) is too severe.[108] Rules of provocation and diminished responsibility provide certain conditions under which a charge of murder might be reduced to one of culpable homicide. Defences such as necessity or coercion are normally only discussed in relation to homicide, since in Scots law the defence of theft by reason of necessity fell into desuetude even before Hume wrote, in order to protect private property.[109] Negligence is attacked or defended as a form of *mens rea*, although its only common law application is in the law of homicide and so on.[110] The most vivid illustration of this is provided by recent textbooks on criminal law. One omitted the crime of theft from its first edition, because it was considered that it could offer little or nothing to the elaboration of a general theory of criminal liability.[111] Another, just entering its second edition, contains no discussion of offences against public order – presumably for similar reasons.[112] This is clearly a curious situation. Theorists of criminal liability attempt to escape the paradox by producing more, increasingly sophisticated theories, but at the cost of completely ignoring certain areas of the law. This leads to a very obvious and awkward conclusion, namely that many of the rules that are supposed by theory to be rules of general application have no general application at all. A 'general' theory that is based on the law of homicide alone is surely subject to limitations.

The most sustained and highly regarded attempt to produce a general theory of Scots criminal law along these lines is G. H. Gordon's *The Criminal Law of Scotland*, first published in 1967.[113] Although in certain respects this marks a break from the traditional approach, in the

---

[108] See now Criminal Procedure (Insanity and Unfitness to Plead) Act 1991, although this does not extend to murder.

[109] See Hume 1844 I, p. 55 on the law of *Burthensack*. Though it is now thought to be established in England that duress does not apply to murder, *Howe* 1987 AC 417.

[110] See e.g. Hall 1960.

[111] Clarkson and Keating 1984, p. v. This was amended in the second edition (1990).

[112] Ashworth 1995. Discussions of other crimes, such as criminal damage seem only to have been included for what they can contribute to the general principles.

[113] Though, see now also Gane and Stoddart 1988; Jones and Christie 1992.

willingness to attempt to specify the definitions of crimes and the general conditions of liability, overall it remains firmly within that tradition. The discussion is always drawn back to actual decisions and the authoritative doctrinal writings, and the justification of the theory is ultimately sought in the relationship between common law and the community. We shall return to this point shortly, but for the present I want to look at the way that this general theory is constructed. It is possible to see very clearly the practical reliance on the law of homicide as foundation of many of the supposedly general rules and as the unacknowledged source of the authoritative case law.

Gordon discusses the questions of omissions as part of the *actus reus* of the crime. The treatment of omissions begins by making a distinction between what are termed 'crimes of omission' and 'crimes of commission committed by means of omission'.[114] The former are regarded as 'conduct crimes' for they are defined so that the crime is completed if a person acted in such a way as to breach a legal duty to act that had been imposed on them. The latter would be 'result-crimes', comprising those situations where certain criminal consequences occur as the result of a person's failure to act. The category of 'result-crimes' is comprised of common law crimes, the prime example being that of homicide. This type of distinction is standard,[115] but it bears further consideration for a number of reasons. The first is that it reproduces, at a level of some theoretical abstraction, the distinction between common law and statute law that we have seen to be fundamental to the self-definition of the tradition. Thus, although Gordon had at the outset of his work disavowed the validity of this distinction,[116] we find that it is smuggled back in again when we are then told that only the latter category is relevant to the discussion. The former, it is said, are really crimes of commission – the action being the breach – and in any case are almost entirely statutory crimes. But we can go further. When we look at the discussion of the rules on omission we find that they are based, when they refer to Scottish authority at all, on a series of nineteenth-century homicide cases. In these cases the courts had either inferred a legal duty to take care on the part of the accused or were concerned with reckless actions of the accused. As we have already seen, and as Gordon himself subsequently concedes, negligent homicides stopped being prosecuted in the late nineteenth century following the creation and enforcement of statutory duties.[117] As

---

[114] G. H. Gordon 1978, p. 82.
[115] See e.g. Smith and Hogan 1992, pp. 45–8 referring to 'offences of omission causing a result'; Clarkson and Keating 1984, pp. 111–12; Fletcher 1978, p. 422.
[116] G. H. Gordon 1978, p. 3: 'Statutory and common law offences have been treated . . . as parts of one system . . .'   [117] *Ibid.*, pp. 259–63, 789–93.

a consequence this concept of an omission is of rather limited application even within the law of homicide.

It may be objected, of course, that the discussion is intended also to be of prospective or normative force, which would also explain the relevance of citing cases from other jurisdictions. This, however, cannot make the rules of any more general application. They would still only apply to 'result-crimes', certain of which, such as theft, are practically impossible to commit by means of omission anyway. The same is true in relation to causation. The Scottish examples discussed by Gordon are, once again, drawn entirely from the law of homicide. This should not surprise us for, in the absence of homicide, there are few 'result-crimes' that can conceivably give rise to issues of causation. Unfortunately, as we noted above, the Scottish courts have historically solved the issue of causation either by ignoring it altogether or by eliding the question of the foreseeability of certain outcomes with the question of foreseeability in recklessness.[118] Most importantly, this approach has fostered a fundamental misunderstanding of the process of the development of the criminal law. The picture that is commonly presented is that liability for omissions has traditionally been limited. It is said that '[l]egal duties to act are few in number and narrow in scope'[119] because the law is wary of imposing obligations where there have been no positive actions because that might unfairly restrict individual freedom. This runs directly contrary to the development of the law in the nineteenth century. As we have seen, the common law was frequently ready either to impose social duties or to reformulate omissions as continuing actions in order to facilitate the imposition of liability.[120] Many more duties were imposed by statute as a means of facilitating the control of certain activities. These are of enormous importance to the modern criminal law, but it is precisely these statutory duties that have been written out of consideration by being defined as 'conduct crimes'.

None of this, of course, should be read as suggesting that problems of omissions or causation might not arise. However, such problems can only arise in relation to a limited number of mainly common law crimes, that are not numerically of the greatest significance to the operation of the criminal law and which do not characterise the sort of issues of liability that are dealt with in practice by the courts.[121] What is striking about such analyses, though, is the determined attempt to present the

---

[118] For a particularly scandalous recent example, see *Lord Advocate's Reference (no. 1 of 1994)* 1995 S.C.C.R. 177.   [119] Robinson 1993, p. 195.

[120] See also the discussion in Lacey *et al.* 1990, p. 28. Note also that the English Law Commission's draft criminal code has moved towards the formulation of 'causing death' rather than 'killing' because it avoids the issue of omissions. See Ashworth 1995, p. 108.

[121] Described by Lacey 1993 as descriptive scepticism.

moral individual as the centre of the law.[122] Although we have concentrated up to this point on the supposedly 'factual' element of the general part, the element of conduct, we have already had cause to note the stress that is placed on voluntary actions or the 'fault' element in conduct. It is not considered enough that conduct simply be defined as criminal, for theorists have sought to introduce the additional condition that action be intended, in order to attempt to restrict liability for omissions while leaving open the possibility of penalising violent conduct that 'causes' harm.[123] This does more than merely underline the impossibility of separating conduct and mental state or reveal the many contradictions that underlie the philosophical project, for these can be seen as ways of allocating responsibility in the criminal law. It points towards the insight that the questions of responsibility and culpability in general theories of criminal liability are actually mainly concerned with questions of mental state anyway.[124] Here we come to a crucial point in the argument. This particular model of individualism is based on a yet more fundamental connection with the law of homicide, for the structure of responsibility stands in a close conceptual relationship to the structure of culpability in homicide law.

It was pointed out at the beginning of the chapter that in homicide the degree of seriousness is not based on the act committed, but on the intention or awareness of risk of the actor.[125] The most serious crime is said to be murder – homicide committed with intention or a great degree of recklessness. Leaving aside the special rules on provocation or diminished responsibility, culpable homicide or manslaughter comprises, generally speaking, criminal homicides carried out either recklessly or with gross negligence. The general discussions of *mens rea* are based on just such a model of seriousness. The states of *mens rea* are conceived of in a descending order of seriousness from intention or knowledge, to recklessness, to negligence,[126] reflecting, it is said, the requirement that liability should only be imposed on individuals to the extent that they are aware of what they are doing. Intentional harm is taken as the paradigm case of blameworthy conduct. It may very well be the case that we should only blame and punish those who are in some sense responsible for their actions, but it does not follow that there is a necessary link with a structure of culpability in this form. Indeed, the failures of this structure to capture

---

[122] See e.g. G. H. Gordon 1967, ch. 1 and p. 257.   [123] See Norrie 1993, chs. 6, 7.
[124] Lacey forthcoming.
[125] The offence of criminal damage is also defined in these terms (see Criminal Damage Act 1971 s. 1), but this is a comparatively recent development. The Malicious Damage Act 1861 (24 and 25 Vict. c. 97) classified offences according to the means by which property was damaged, the classes of persons committing the damage, and the type of property.
[126] G. H. Gordon 1978, p. 218.

successfully what are considered to be the most culpable or even the most harmful actions is notorious. It is hardly necessary to repeat the point that the attempt in English law to restrict the category of murder to the most serious intentional killings has been riven with conflict and contradiction,[127] or that the forms of subjective intention in the definition of other crimes are somehow rarely included in the general part,[128] or to reiterate that this does not fit with the account of criminal liability in the modern criminal justice system described in the last chapter. The connection is plain. The question is not so much that of the 'practical, moral and political issues' that are supposedly excluded by this narrow concept of intention,[129] but that of the issues that are included. The question that we must address is how this remarkable coincidence should have come about.

One response to this is very obvious. It is to reply that the criminal law, particularly in modern times, is concerned above all with the protection of the autonomy of the person and that the principle of the sanctity of human life should have a special position within this, because of what Ashworth calls the 'principle of finality'.[130] Our understanding of 'wrong' and our understanding of blame should have a common basis in the individual personality. It seems to me that there are good reasons for regarding the taking of life as the most serious of crimes, but it does not necessarily follow that the law of homicide should form the basis of a general theory of criminal liability. Indeed there may be good reasons for seeing it as a special case – as Fletcher does in his remarkable analysis of the development of homicide.[131] But this reply normally goes further, to argue that wrongs against personality occupy a special foundational position in the law, as opposed to those actions which merely harm defined social interests.[132] These wrongs are said to be of the sort that 'one may commit in a pre-political state of nature and that are of common-law origin, [these are] wrongs against the life, bodily integrity and property of the person'.[133] This illustrates a remarkable and highly revealing elision of the supposedly

---

[127] *D.P.P. v. Smith* [1960] 3 All E.R. 161; *Hyam* [1974] 2 All E.R. 41; *Moloney* [1985] 1 All E.R. 1025; *Nedrick* [1986] 1 W.L.R. 1025; *Hancock and Shankland* [1986] 2 W.L.R. 357. Discussed in Lacey 1993; Horder 1995.

[128] Ironically in crimes such as theft where subjective intent is required this has been expanded in such a way as to break down any meaningful distinction between act and intention. See Theft Act 1968 ss. 3, 6. See e.g. *Gomez* [1993] 1 All E.R. 1.

[129] Lacey 1995, p. 626.

[130] Ashworth 1995, p. 254: 'This finality makes it proper to regard death as the most serious harm that may be inflicted on another, and to regard the person who chooses to inflict that harm without justification or excuse as the most culpable of offenders'; Fletcher 1978, pp. 235–42.   [131] Fletcher 1978, chs. 4, 5.

[132] See Brudner 1993, pp. 21–4.

[133] *Ibid.*, 1993, pp. 24–5. Horder 1995, pp. 681–4 where it is difficult to see the distinction between the role of intention in constituting a wrong and in protecting autonomy. The former is simply a special case of the latter. Cf. Simmonds 1984.

abstract foundations of criminal law theory and their presumed origins in the common law. The common law, it is being argued, offers a moral foundation for the protection of fundamental values of autonomy and so on. Other penal laws relate only to the lesser considerations of welfare, defined solely in terms of social harm rather than the wrongfulness of the actions. It is not only that these values are fundamental, but that historically they precede the creation of statutory laws. We are returned to the idea that the criminal law has an essential core, protecting fundamental values, that was discussed and dismissed at the beginning of chapter 4. But at this point we have to ask whether it is the common law that protects the fundamental value of human life, or whether the law of homicide is being used to protect the territory of the common law.

We are now in a position to answer the question of why homicide has been privileged by these attempts to develop a general theory of criminal liability. The primacy of homicide establishes a certain form of theoretical understanding about the nature of the criminal law. On this view the core – and the unity – of the criminal law is to be found in common law crimes. These are individualistic, protecting individual liberty by resisting state intrusion. Homicide is the perfect crime, not only because it can be taken to represent these values, but because it stands furthest from the type of policy concerns which dictate practice in the modern criminal justice system.[134] It can be represented as the fundamental crime, the common law origin of the criminal law, the standpoint from which other parts of the criminal justice system can be attacked for being severe, arbitrary or unprincipled.[135] It allows the boundaries of the criminal law to be drawn in a way that removes it from the everyday practices of criminal justice. The claim as to the autonomy of the person is used to establish and defend the autonomy of the field of criminal law.

Conclusion: solving the murder mystery

Murder, for instance, may be laid hold of by its moral handle (as it generally is in the pulpit and at the Old Bailey), and *that*, I confess, is its weak side . . .[136]

The mystery has in a sense been solved without it being necessary to gather the protagonists together in the drawing room of a country house for a grand denouement. This is entirely appropriate. The English detective story has been criticised for taking murder off the streets into the middle-class drawing room, turning the messy business of crime into a sterile intellectual exercise. The obsession with the conventions of the murder mystery – the search for the perfect crime – is said to have led to

[134] A point made by Lord Hailsham in *Hyam* [1974] 2 All E.R. 41 at p. 54.
[135] See Lacey forthcoming.   [136] de Quincey 1965, p. 86 (emphasis in original).

an increasing alienation from 'real' crime. This, in a sense, is precisely what the over-concentration on the law of homicide has done for criminal law theory. The discussion of the conceptual bases of culpability has led to the criminal law becoming an introverted, dry and overly academic exercise.

Homicide is the perfect crime for modern criminal law theory. It is the 'metaphysical' centre of the modern law. It is the point around which the rules applying to all other crimes are distributed in terms of seriousness. More importantly, it is also the lens through which other legal practices and rules are interpreted, persistently marginalising some and privileging others through the appeal to the 'moral side' of the crime. The combinations of responsibility and moral evaluation, of individualism and moral wickedness, have drawn the boundaries of modern criminal law theory, defining what are and are not permissible theoretical understandings. However, discussions of responsibility are abstract and bland, the search for theoretical consistency leading always away from the practice of the law. This is not to argue that there is, or should be, no philosophical basis for the modern law, but that the importance of individual responsibility has been overstated. Individual responsibility may offer some sort of spurious unity for criminal law theory, but it does not offer an adequate account of the modern law for a number of reasons.[137]

Such theories rarely deliver the theoretical consistency that they promise. Norrie has analysed at length the contradictions in the modern English criminal law from a critical perspective, and in fact these inconsistencies are regularly acknowledged by other commentators.[138] The point that I want to make is not simply that the pre-eminence of individual responsibility is ideological, though there is an important sense in which it is, but that the analysis in these terms does not attempt to understand the historical development of the law. The analysis of responsibility for homicide in this chapter has offered a means of understanding both how the paradigmatic form of responsibility that emerged derived from changes in the organisation of the law, and the significance of the appeals to the moral basis of the crime. The emergence of culpable homicide as an attempt to regulate violence and other risky activities gave rise to certain problems in the ascription of responsibility. The concept of individual blame and the separation of action and mental state that were developed in response to these problems were subsequently generalised to form the basis of a general theory of liability. While this has provided us with an analysis of why homicide has been of such importance, at the same time it has made us aware of the inadequacies of contemporary theory. The narrow focus on individualism in legal theory is

---

[137] Cf. Horder 1995.   [138] Norrie 1993; Shute *et al* 1993.

continually clashing with the function of the criminal law as an instrument of modern government. This is historically inaccurate for, as we have seen, the common law of crime was never so libertarian, this form of individualism developing only as homicide law was modernised in the middle of the nineteenth century. Nor is the prosecution of homicide typical of the whole for in practice it is conduct that falls below certain standards that is the target of prosecution. There is no attempt to see the criminal law as a specific instrument of the regulation of social security and the control of risk – although that is the type of analysis that our examination of the law of homicide suggests would be appropriate. This is neither explained, nor adequately theorised by the concentration on the common law as the moral foundation of legal order.

These criticisms can also apply to the more diffuse and symbolic sense in which the law of murder is represented as the core of the Scottish legal tradition. Laying aside some of the more exaggerated claims made by Lord Cooper, it still cannot be said that the law of murder is typical of the whole. Even if a jury does always decide in murder cases, this is highly unrepresentative of normal criminal law practice. More importantly the jury certainly cannot be used, as Cooper would have it, to support a general claim about the nature of the relationship between law and the community. If the law of homicide is representative of the Scottish criminal law, it is in the process whereby the flexible definition passes administrative discretion to the prosecution and enforcement agencies – which is then by a legal sleight of hand presented to us as the enforcement of community values. Community values are always reconstructed within the legal system. The 'community' and the 'moral' values that are contained in the law are, in all but a very few cases, those of the institutions that enforce the law.

6   Conclusion: crime and the genius of Scots law

> I learn that some beginners find Chapter 1, in its attempt to define the nature of Crime, exceptionally difficult. Those who do so, I advise to postpone its perusal until after they have read the rest of the volume. Definitions belong, indeed, rather to the end of our knowledge than to the beginning of it.[1]

The definition of crime

The perceived need to produce a definition of crime has been one of the most extraordinary preoccupations of modern criminal lawyers. The debates on this question are difficult and impenetrable for beginners and more experienced criminal lawyers alike. The definitions that have been produced are not only uniformly technical in character but also seem ultimately to be trite and uninformative in their conclusions. Although viewed by many as a 'sterile and useless' exercise[2] the question has none the less exerted a strange fascination over criminal lawyers. Between the beginning of this century and the late 1950s it was the subject of much debate. Even now the standard books on the criminal law almost invariably begin by attempting to define crime, and hence the scope of the criminal law. The most immediate feature of these scholarly definitions of crime and the criminal law is their circularity: a crime is that which is proceeded against in the criminal courts, and the criminal law deals with those acts that are crimes. However, this apparently unpromising insight reveals much about nature of the modern criminal law and its relationship with legal theory. It defines the object of criminal law in such a way as to mark out the space within which the theory of the criminal law can be constructed. It establishes the disciplinary boundaries of the subject. As this study draws to a conclusion, it is appropriate that the question of definition should be addressed. Indeed, it belongs properly to the end of our account for it draws together some of the main themes of the book and

---

[1] Kenny 1918, Preface.   [2] Fitzgerald 1960, p. 257.

175

raises a number of important further questions about legal tradition and national identity in the criminal law.

The classic formulation of the definition of crime is contained in Kenny's *Outlines of Criminal Law*. First published in 1902, this book went through nineteen editions, of which nine were under the supervision of the original author. The first chapter, entitled 'The Nature of a Crime', survived with small modifications, and the addition of an accompanying warning from the author, until the sixteenth edition. At this point it was relegated to an appendix, where it was printed along with certain key criticisms. The final editions of the book dropped it altogether. Even then, though it was no longer valued for its conclusions, it was still regarded as 'a splendid model of legal presentation, clear, eloquent, and in the highest degree instructive'.[3] It is a remarkable analysis, differentiating between no less than eight potential definitions of crime.

The first definition was based on Blackstone's statement that a 'crime or misdemeanour is an act committed, or omitted, in violation of a public law, either forbidding or commanding it' and accordingly looked at whether there is something about the act itself which rendered it distinctive.[4] The second was also drawn from Blackstone, defining a crime as a public wrong, a 'violation of the public rights and duties, due to the whole community, considered as a community'.[5] These were both considered to be adequate as rough general descriptions, but insufficient to constitute a precise formal definition holding true for all crimes. Kenny accordingly moved on to the third, that crimes were those legal wrongs which violently offended our moral feelings.[6] This was also considered to break down in practice, for not all legal wrongs were moral wrongs and vice versa. At this point the quest for a quality that was intrinsic to the act was abandoned in favour of extrinsic features. Fourth, then, was a consideration of the respective degrees of activity manifested by the state in criminal and civil proceedings, and fifth that the proceedings took place in different tribunals. Both of these failed to produce a watertight definition because of the existence of certain proceedings on the border-line between the civil and criminal law, where the function of the state could be carried out by private parties for their own benefit. Sixth was the possibility that punishment is always the aim of criminal proceedings and never of civil ones. This was felt to be getting nearer to the target, but was still inconclusive because civil proceedings could at times be brought with a punitive aim. The seventh possibility, barely considered, was that of a difference in the nature of the sanctions themselves. The crucial difference was then sought in the respective degrees of control exercised over

---

[3] Kenny 1952, p. 547.   [4] Blackstone 1765, IV, p. 5   [5] *Ibid*; cf. Hall 1960.
[6] Cf. Allen 1931, pp. 233–6.

the proceedings by the sovereign, and particularly in the matter of their termination and the exercise of the royal prerogative.[7] Thus the eighth and final definition was that: '[A] crime is a wrong whose sanction is remissible by the Crown, *if remissible at all*'.[8]

It is not difficult to find fault with this as a definition. Winfield has pointed out that its main substantive weakness stemmed from the fact that the scope of pardon could only be determined by asking which sentences were of a punitive character, thereby throwing the enquirer back onto one of the previously rejected definitions.[9] The alternative was plainly circular, an outcome which Kenny had clearly wished to avoid: a pardon only applies to crime, therefore crimes are those actions that can be pardoned. In another sense the definition is plainly absurd: if the royal prerogative were to be abolished, this would logically entail the abolition of crime.[10] A solution to these apparently intractable problems was put forward by Glanville Williams in an article published in 1955. He proposed to rescue the question from 'the unwelcome attentions of certain criminologists and philosophers'[11] by framing a definition that would state the legal use of the word.[12] He rejected the possibility that there was a moral basis to the criminal act, to argue that the legal phenomenon of crime has no reality beyond that created by the working of criminal justice. The strength of his approach, he argued, was that it was supported by legal authority, since it reproduced the distinctions used by the courts in settling questions of jurisdiction, procedure and sanctions.[13] A crime was thus defined as,

an act capable of being followed by criminal proceedings having a criminal outcome, and a proceeding or its outcome is criminal if it has certain characteristics which mark it as criminal.[14]

Crime is defined by reference to the legal consequences of the act, and conversely the criminal law is, according to Sheriff Gordon, 'that branch of the law which deals with those acts, attempts and omissions of which the state may take cognisance by prosecution in the criminal courts'.[15] It is notable that the end result is similar to Kenny, although it is both wider, in the sense that it relies on the whole of criminal procedure rather than a

---

[7] For a comment on the extent that this is based on Austin's jurisprudence, see Kenny 1902, pp. 13–15 and Pollock 1959.   [8] Kenny 1902, p. 15, emphasis in original.
[9] The sixth one, Winfield 1931, p. 197; see also Kenny 1952, p. 547.
[10] Pollock 1959, p. 496.   [11] Williams 1955, p. 130.   [12] *Ibid*, p. 109.
[13] *Ibid*, p. 123. See also Fitzgerald 1960, pp. 260–1. We must not overlook the extent to which Williams could be said to be following the path taken earlier by Hart in his famous paper on 'Definition and Theory in Jurisprudence' (1983) first published in 1953. It is noteworthy that Williams is closer to the strand in Hart's thought that was based on the 'ordinary legal usage' rather than the 'ordinary usage' *per se*. For a discussion of these two strands, see Simmonds 1993.   [14] Williams 1955, p. 130.
[15] G. H. Gordon 1978, p. 15.

small and rather anomalous element, and narrower, in that by circumscri-
bing the task the ambition of providing a definition that will hold good for
all legal systems at all times is abandoned.

What is striking about this definition is the breathtaking movement
between the universal and the particular. It combines an ambitious
breadth with a simultaneous and constricting narrowness. It claims to
produce a universal, positivist definition of crime – but this is limited by
the terms of legal usage and authority within a particular legal system. The
claim of criminal law theory to define the law is undiminished but, and this
is the point which is normally overlooked, the boundaries of the criminal
law are conceded to be subject to the constraints of time and space. The
analysis in this book has sought to trace the tensions that arise on this
border between the universal claims of criminal law theory and particular
legal traditions. These concluding remarks will address the implications of
this analysis of the modern criminal law for legal theory in terms of the
theoretical constraints that have been imposed on our understanding of
the modern law by the ahistorical approach of criminal law theory.
Finally, we will look at the challenge that this analysis poses to the Scottish
legal tradition and the continuing belief in the genius of Scots law.

Criminal law and legal theory

In historical terms, it can be seen that the definition synthesises two of the
main characteristics of the modern law. The positivism, the narrow
procedural grounds on which crime is defined, reflects the general rise in
the importance of procedure as the means of defining the scope of criminal
jurisdiction. The contingency of the definition, the broad range of actions
that may consequently be regarded as falling within the scope of the
criminal law, reflects in its turn the diversity of functions of the criminal
law in the modern state. This underlines the point made at length earlier in
the book that the distinctively modern form of criminal jurisdiction is
founded in procedural law. The significance of this is that the positivism of
modern legal theory actually tells us something about the reality of the
law, reflecting an important change in the nature of legal practice. In the
course of the nineteenth century, as the summary courts expanded,
jurisdiction came to be defined primarily in terms of the type of procedure
under which the prosecution was conducted. In fact, as the law was being
used to implement an ever more diverse range of social policies and an
ever wider range of conduct was deemed to be socially harmful and
criminalised, it is striking that the criminal law should come to be defined
according to the positive criterion of whether an act is tried under criminal
proceedings. As crime was defined by the development of stricter

procedural rules, so the criminal law could no longer easily be defined in terms of the values it sought to protect. It can be seen that the interest in the question of definition was of more than purely theoretical significance, being a matter of intense practical concern to lawyers dealing with the problems that arose from the new forms of regulation. The theoretical transformation of the definition of crime, rejecting definition in terms of moral or political wrong, thus has its counterpart in institutional and social practice. To put this claim in its strongest form, it is to state that it is actually a condition of the operation or function of the modern law in the diverse forms that it takes.[16] The central importance of procedure in defining, regulating and administering within the modern legal system has been neglected – a point which further suggests that there is no easy distinction to be drawn between criminal law and criminal justice. The truth is that the positivism of the law reflects something of the awkward reality of the modern criminal justice system, and any theory of criminal law must come to terms with the full implications of this point.

By arguing that there is no object outwith the process that defines it, Williams's definition of crime makes it clear that the modern criminal law accepts, and indeed is predicated upon, the idea of contingency in its content and practice. In general terms it is acknowledged that the criminal law is connected to no single set of ethical or political values, or more precisely that the law may enforce a range of values. Hence, the key critical point is not simply to argue that the law might in fact enforce other values (for this much is conceded by modern criminal law theory), or that the values enforced by the law are arbitrary and unjust (which they frequently are). It has been argued here that a critical method also requires the analysis of the range of values that are acceptable to the criminal law. In other words, it is a question not only of the values that are excluded or repressed by the criminal law, but also of how certain values are promoted and fitted into a coherent theoretical framework. The theoretical distinctions that are produced by the practices, such as the idea that there is a core of more serious crimes, or that of the boundaries between law and context or criminal law and criminal justice, must be subjected to critical analysis. In its most simple formulation, critical method is the requirement that in tracing the boundaries of the criminal law we have also to take into account the way that the law itself draws those boundaries – turning the question back onto itself in order that we ask not only about the scope of criminal jurisdiction but also about its nature.

The understanding of the nature of criminal jurisdiction developed here has drawn us towards a new understanding of the peculiar nature of

[16] See Ewald 1987 and 1988 for a discussion of Kelsen and the positivism of the modern law.

contingency in the legal system. Although the content of the law (or its practices) may be contingent in a historical sense, this is not true in the same way of the defining process. Thus, while it is true to argue that things could be otherwise, this does not necessarily mean that things can be otherwise at a particular point in time. To put this in another way, it is to argue that there are limits to the openness of legal discourse. An important point about the definition of crime is not that it does away with diversity, but that it must be read as a powerful attempt to impose order on the unruly practices of the legal system. It is clear, for example, that there is a sense in which Williams does not 'solve' the problem of definition. The procedures and sanctions that are said to define crime are diverse and probably cannot of themselves impose unity on the criminal law without some further specification of what makes certain proceedings 'criminal'.[17] Yet the modernity of the law is the factor that may be said to have given rise to the circularity of the definition in the first place. It is precisely because of the recognition of diversity that it takes the form that it does. The historical study of the criminal law presented here has led to the conclusion that contingency has become the necessity of law. The definition thus solves the problem of criminal jurisdiction in a very particular way – its breadth providing the means of coping with diversity. What has been overlooked about the definition, however, is the fact that this is an answer produced from within the legal system, reinforced by legal authority, thereby placing limits on the acceptability of alternative definitions. The contingency of law is managed by the legal system as a means of sustaining its own autonomy. Hence, the question of the definition of crime stands both as a key to an understanding of the emergence and character of the modern law, and as a means by which the contingency of the modern law is managed at the level of theory. The critical question is therefore that of our orientation towards the way that the legal system selects between the various alternatives to produce authoritative or settled definitions.[18]

This raises two distinct questions. One is the question of the particular content and uses of the criminal law (or 'definitions' of the law) at any particular point in time. By focusing on the changing nature of legal practices, this study has sought to answer this question by tracing the historical development of the modern criminal law in terms of the crimes that were prosecuted, the procedures under which they were prosecuted and the terms in which culpability was defined. The other question is what might be termed the 'second order' question of how the problem of definition is solved by the legal system: the problem of criminal jurisdic-

---

[17] Lacey 1995, pp. 16–21.   [18] Luhmann 1988.

tion. The question of jurisdiction must be answered, more or less successfully, to stabilise the legal system against such competing definitions, instituting the distinctions that maintain or sustain a particular legal order. The emergence of summary jurisdiction, the transformation in the nature of criminal liability and the broadening of the scope of the criminal law in the course of the nineteenth century, all presented challenges to the existing common law version of legal order. However, the transformation in the scale and character of the criminal law was accompanied by a decisive shift in legal rationality, or the order of law, that made an understanding of the modern law possible. The legal order was, as I have shown, reconstructed in such a way as to attempt to minimise the impact of these changes and to stress the continuity and authority of the common law tradition. Theories of the universal and natural jurisdiction of the common law courts, or of the centrality of individual responsibility in the law, were developed in response to particular challenges to the jurisdiction, or legal order, of the common law. The historical analysis of the tradition is thus essential, for we cannot begin to challenge the particular definitions until we begin to understand how and why they are important to the law.

However, our analysis of the development of the modern criminal law has led to a number of critical conclusions. The character of the modern criminal law has been consistently misrepresented by criminal law theory because of the failure of historical understanding. Notwithstanding the theoretical acknowledgement in the definition of crime of the contingency of the modern law, criminal law theory has never fully acknowledged the consequences of the positivism of the modern law. The recognition of the contingency of the law has been misunderstood as placing the criminal law outside history, rather than within it. Theoretical explanation of the law is understood to preclude a historical or spatial understanding of criminal jurisdiction. One of the principal weaknesses of contemporary criminal law theory is that it cannot explain, or even denies, the modernity of the law because of this boundary drawn in time. In general terms, modern criminal law theory has either devoted itself to the elaboration of an abstract structure of responsibility, or it has sought to justify the authority of the law and the process of adjudication by an appeal to the community which the law is said to represent.[19] The first combines universal and ahistorical claims about culpability with an appeal to the need for conceptual clarity as a means of achieving certainty and predictability in the law, while the second represents elements of the conceptual structure of the common law as being representative of the structure of the whole

---

[19] Cf. the distinction drawn in Lacey 1993 between 'conceptual analysis' and 'ordinary usage' as the ways of understanding intention.

criminal law. Both have fundamental weaknesses that have been revealed by our historical analysis. To write the history of the modern criminal law, tracing the drawing of this boundary, is to offer a fundamental challenge to existing theories of the criminal law.

The weakness of theories of individual responsibility is their failure to acknowledge their own history, which is seen in particular in the connection to the crime of homicide. The emergence of this particular model of responsibility was related to organisational changes in the attribution of culpability. The subsequent elevation of this theory of individual responsibility to the level of principle for the system was, in its turn, a response to the perceived encroachment of new forms of liability on the jurisdiction of the common law. This has had important consequences. The concentration on individual responsibility has led to a blind eye being turned to those areas of legal practice where legal culpability is attributed without the finding of individual responsibility. In practice, of course, much of the law operates with a 'presumption of guilt', subordinating the moral question to that of organisation. This cannot be addressed except by denying that these are 'proper' crimes, because to do so would mean revealing the insularity of theory and addressing the limits of its claims about the nature of culpability. By treating certain historical categories, of responsibility and autonomy, as being of universal significance, the need for conceptual clarity has been elevated above a proper philosophical understanding, cutting criminal law adrift from an understanding of criminal justice. The growing scepticism about the general part of criminal law perhaps reflects an awareness of these problems, but until this is attached to a historical analysis it is merely groping around in the dark.[20] Philosophical analysis of the law is necessary, but it should be linked to a historical understanding of the contingency of the modern law.

Appeals to community values and the legal order of the common law deny the modernity of the criminal law in two further ways. The contingency of the law is acknowledged through the deference to the legal authority of the common law, the power of the law to define jurisdiction. The historical authority and continuity of the common law is stressed but without questioning that authority or attempting to understand its historical origins. The modern criminal justice system is a complex administrative system geared towards dealing with large numbers of people in a summary manner and controlling behaviour through small penalties for minor offences. And the crucial period for its formation was

---

[20] The essays in Shute *et al.* 1993 are representative of this discontent. Many of the contributors criticise general theories of criminal liability to argue in favour of multiplying the paradigms of criminal law, or producing 'unified' rather than 'general' theories of liability. See especially the Introduction and essays by Brudner, Robinson and Tur.

the nineteenth century. In a sense, it is not the growth of summary courts and procedure that should be regarded as anomalous, but rather the survival of the common law in the face of developments that have challenged its authority. Instead, the traditional assumptions about the nature of legal, political and social order are accepted at face value. The acknowledgement of the modernity of the law requires an analysis of the relationship between the legal order of the common law and these developments. In addition, the criminal law, and Scots law in particular, is frequently enforced in the name of the community to buttress the authority of the common law. Judges labour to connect the operation of the law to community feelings or community interests, connecting the law to the present through the assumed presence of the community in the law. The difficulty that legal theory must face is that just as crimes are no longer public wrongs, so too the modern criminal law has lost any connection that it might once have had with community. The consequences of this can be illustrated by a consideration of the 'reasonable man' as the emblem of the modern criminal law.[21] While often regarded as the ideal subject of the modern law, the means by which community values can be represented in the law, this could not be further from the case. He is not the legal subject but the means by which the object of legal regulation, the community, is conjured up. His importance is therefore not as a rational, calculating individual, but as the individual who can be known and calculated – subjectified – through reason. He is the 'representative' of the community, whose individual interests can be made to stand for the whole as the ideal representative of average interests. It is thus the means by which a governable community can be imagined by the modern law. Criminal law does not express community values through this device, but seeks to create them. Guilt, punishment and harm have become legal and administrative categories, and they cannot be appealed to in order to legitimate the modern law, for they come from within the law.

Both approaches fundamentally misrepresent the character of the modern criminal law, for neither has ever quite come to terms with the extent to which the modern criminal law is a peculiar amalgam of old procedures, half-forgotten fears and the accidental survivals of the common law. The continual attempts to build on these as though they represented some rational core model is doomed to failure. The history of the law cannot be written until we acknowledge this and come to terms with the present.

---

[21] Cf. Goodrich 1993, pp. 387–8 who argues that the reasonable man offers a version of subjectivity.

Crime and the genius of Scots law

Many of these general points have a special application within the Scottish legal tradition for, as has been noted throughout, Scots law has assiduously cultivated the belief in a special historical relationship with the community and the Scottish personality. The 'genius' of the law has provided a means of representing both the ageless spirit and resourcefulness of the tradition and the ideal community of Scotland administered by judges and the courts.

The Scottish legal tradition has managed the contingency of the law by constructing a particular relation with its past in which it has relentlessly privileged the demands of legal practice. The autonomy of the system has been preserved through the belief in the continuity and timelessness of legal concepts and more particularly in the reverence for authority. Past and present co-exist in a continuing relationship of authority and justification, reinforcing the presence of the law. The outcome is that the only questions it is competent to ask about legal practice must be asked from within this framework, and we have been denied the possibility of posing questions about the changing nature of legal practice because that would ultimately delegitimate the legal tradition. But this has been at the cost of fostering a particular breed of legal conservatism. The study of history has been limited to the study of antiquities or to endless celebration of the 'Golden Age' of Scots law.

As a result, the space which Scots law occupies has become increasingly isolated,[22] paying the price of an unthinking deference to the genius of the law. This argument might appall the Scottish lawyer for whom the beliefs in the cosmopolitan origins and principled basis of the law are, after all, axiomatic. None the less, I would argue that it is precisely because of the view that Scots law is rational and cosmopolitan that the history of the criminal law in the nineteenth century has not been written. This has consistently directed the attention of legal historians away from the nineteenth century and towards what is regarded as the 'last truly Scotch age'. By defining our identity in terms of the genius of the law, we have continually directed our attention backwards in time, to celebrations of the institutional writers, preferring the elusive belief in maturity to the encounter with modernity. The present identity of the legal system is defined by this version of the past, with the result that the nineteenth century can only be regarded as a period of degeneracy and decline. This is the period in which the rationality of the law was said to have been undermined by English influences and the institutional structure by administrative and legislative developments. The charge of isolation is

---

[22] See Maitland 1911, pp. 487–8 on the isolation of English law.

therefore justified on two counts. There is an isolation in time, a narrowing of the range of our concerns, that is also a refusal to acknowledge the modernity of the system. This has brought a geographical isolation, because a recognition of the characteristics of the modern system would compel the recognition that most Western European systems have undergone similar transformations. By its failure to recognise this, the Scottish legal identity suffers from a form of arrested development.

What are we to conclude about the state of Scots criminal law? The history of this tradition has revealed a relentless nostalgia. Legal practices have been fitted into a conservative vision of political and legal order that, ironically, owes a greater debt to the English common law than has ever been acknowledged. Many Scots lawyers are uncomfortable with questions of change or reform. The attitude we have uncovered is the belief that to meddle with the law is to invite disaster for, after all, there have been no complaints about the way that it works. This is one of the central pillars of the Scottish tradition, the repetition of which traps any discontent within the coils of traditional reasoning. To attempt to write the history of the law is something that is treated with equal alarm, bringing the accusation that those who wish to interfere are not proper Scots, and have therefore misunderstood the nature of the tradition in their desire to hasten the process of annihilation or assimilation of certain areas of the law with the English. This history has revealed a remarkable degree of complicity on the part of Scots lawyers with the myths of the tradition, coupled to a continuing failure to address the nature of the modern law. The fact that this is so is not warrant for our own complicity in the tradition's vision of criminal justice.

From this point of view, then, the state of Scots criminal law offers considerable cause for concern. But if a clearer vision of the modernity of the Scottish legal system is required this will not necessarily help us in a legal context. The strength of the common law tradition has lain in its procedural and substantive flexibility, and the vision of legal order is, therefore, incorporated into the interpretation and control of criminal jurisdiction. An important conclusion has been that, in spite of the diminishing practical importance of the common law, it is still the language in terms of which a reflective understanding of the criminal law and the criminal justice system is constructed. Critical understandings can none the less begin to develop through the construction of a better understanding of legal practice.

Finally, this is an argument for a vision of Scots criminal law that shows a greater respect for the present than that displayed by the tradition. It is possible to argue for the transformation of our understanding of the law without running the risk that that law may lose its identity. The fact that the modern law shares characteristics with the developments in other legal systems is not in itself reason for either congratulation or regret. The Scottish legal order has a distinctive character that does not have to be protected by taking refuge in the past – only a relentless nostalgia has prevented us from recognising this. In the development of our understanding of the modern state of Scots law, however, we no more need scarcely credible rhetoric about the law expressing the genius of the Scottish people, than we can be expected to swallow unthinkingly the implicit unionism of the Scottish legal tradition. We may, on the other hand, do well to recognise that Scottish institutions and culture are not the exclusive property of a patrician class of lawyers. It is in any case better to recognise the character of modern criminal jurisdiction than to hang on blindly to a nostalgic and romantic vision of our law.

Bibliography

Agnew, A. (1893). *The Hereditary Sheriffs of Galloway* (2 vols.). Edinburgh: David Douglas

Alison, A. (1825). *Remarks on the Administration of Criminal Justice in Scotland and the Changes Proposed to be Introduced into it (by a Member of the Faculty of Advocates)*. Edinburgh: W. Blackwood

(1832). *The Principles of the Criminal Law of Scotland.* Edinburgh: W. Blackwood (reprinted 1989 Law Society and Butterworths)

(1833). *The Practice of the Criminal Law of Scotland.* Edinburgh: W. Blackwood (reprinted 1989, Law Society and Butterworths)

(1883). *Some Account of My Life and Writings. An Autobiography.* (2 vols.). Edinburgh: Blackwood (ed. Lady Alison)

Allen, C. K. (1931). *Legal Duties.* Oxford: Clarendon Press

Anderson, A. M. (1904). *The Criminal Law of Scotland.* Edinburgh: Bell and Bradfute (2nd edn)

Anderson, B. (1983). *Imagined Communities. Reflections on the Origin and Spread of Nationalism.* London: Verso

Anon. (1858). 'Civil and Criminal Jurisdiction', *Journal of Jurisprudence* 2, pp. 276–84

Anon. (1865). 'The Summary Procedure (S.) Act 1864', *Journal of Jurisprudence* 9, pp. 51–9

Anon. (1867). 'Obituary: Sheriff Archibald Alison', *Journal of Jurisprudence* 11, pp. 311–14

Anon. (1893). 'A Word for Codification', *Scottish Law Review* 9, pp. 203–7

Anon. (1905). 'Review: the Criminal Law of Scotland by A. M. Anderson', *Scottish Law Review* 21, pp. 6–7

Ardmillan, (Lord) (James Crawfurd). (1846). 'Scottish Criminal Law. Review of Bell's Supplement to Hume's Commentaries', *North British Review* 4 (part viii), pp. 313–46

Ash, M. (1980). *The Strange Death of Scottish History.* Edinburgh: Ramsay Head Press

Ashworth, A. (1995). *Principles of Criminal Law.* Oxford: Clarendon Press (2nd edn)

Austin, J. (1885). *Lectures on Jurisprudence* (2 vols.). London: John Murray.

Baker, J. H. (1977). 'Criminal Courts and Procedure at Common Law 1550–1800' in J. S. Cockburn (ed.), *Crime in England 1550–1800.* London: Methuen

Baldwin, T. (1992). 'The Territorial State' in H. Gross and R. Harrison (eds.), *Jurisprudence: Cambridge Essays*. Oxford: Clarendon Press

von Bar, C. L. (1916). *A History of Continental Criminal Law*. New York: Augustus M. Kelley (reprinted 1968)

Bartrip, P. W. J. and Burman, S. B. (1983). *The Wounded Soldiers of Industry: Industrial Compensation Policy 1833–1897*. Oxford: Oxford University Press

Bayne, A. (1748). *Institutions of the Criminal Law of Scotland*. Edinburgh: Gideon Crawfurd

Beattie, J. M. (1986). *Crime and the Courts in England 1660–1800*. Oxford: Clarendon Press

Black, R. (1975). 'A Historical Survey of Delictual Liability in Scotland for Personal Injuries and Death', *Comparative and International Law Journal of South Africa*, 8, pp. 46–70, 189–211, 318–43; 9, pp. 57–80

Blackstone, W. (1765). *Commentaries on the Law of England* (4 vols.). Oxford: Clarendon Press (reprinted 1966, University of Chicago Press)

Blomley, N. (1994). *Law, Space and the Geographies of Power*. London: Guilford Press

Brown, B. (1993). 'Troubled Vision: Legal Understandings of Obscenity'. *New Formations* 19, pp. 29–44

Brown, H. H. (1895). *The Principles of Summary Jurisdiction According to the Law of Scotland*. Edinburgh: T. and T. Clark

Brown, K. M. (1986). *Bloodfeud in Scotland 1573–1625. Violence, Justice and Politics in an Early Modern Society*. Edinburgh: John Donald

Brudner, A. (1993). 'Agency and Welfare in the Penal Law' in S. Shute *et al.* (eds.), *Action and Value in Criminal Law*. Oxford: Clarendon Press

Burnett, J. (1811). *A Treatise on Various Branches of the Criminal Law of Scotland*. Edinburgh: Arch. Constable and Co

Cairns, J. W. (1983). 'Institutional Writings in Scotland Reconsidered', *Journal of Legal History* 4, pp. 76–117
   (1984). 'Blackstone, An English Institutist: Legal Literature and the Rise of the Nation State'. *Oxford Journal of Legal Studies* 4, pp. 318–60
   (1988). 'John Millar's Lectures on Scots Criminal Law', *Oxford Journal of Legal Studies* 8, pp. 364–400
   (1993). 'Hamesucken and the Major Premiss in the Libel, 1672–1770: Criminal Law in the Age of Enlightenment' in R. F. Hunter (ed.), *Justice and Crime: Essays in Honour of the Right Honourable Lord Emslie*. Edinburgh: T. and T. Clark

Cameron, J. (Lord) (1988). 'The High Court of Justiciary' in *Stair Memorial Encyclopedia*, vol. 6 (pp. 366–79). Edinburgh: Butterworths and Law Soc.

Carlen, P. (1976). *Magistrates' Justice*. Oxford: Martin Robertson

Carson, W. G. (1979). 'The Conventionalisation of Early Factory Crime', *International Journal of the Sociology of Law* 7, pp. 37–60
   (1984–5). 'Policing the Periphery: The Development of Scottish Policing 1795–1900', *Australia and New Zealand Journal of Criminology* 17 pp. 207–32; 18, pp. 3–16

Carson, W. G. and Idzikowska, H. (1989). 'The Social Production of Scottish Policing 1795–1900' in D. Hay and F. Snyder (eds.), *Policing and Prosecution in Britain 1750–1850*. Oxford: Oxford University Press

Christie, M. (1990). *Breach of the Peace*. Edinburgh: Butterworths

Clarkson, C. M. V. and Keating, H. M. (1994). *Criminal Law: Text and Materials*. London: Sweet and Maxwell (1st edn 1984; 2nd edn 1990)

Cockburn H. (Lord) (1824). 'Office of Lord Advocate in Scotland', *Edinburgh Review* 39, (January), pp. 363–92

(1825). 'Untitled Review of Alison's Remarks on Administration . . .', *Edinburgh Review*, 82, (January), pp. 450–64

(1846). '(Untitled) Review of Supplement to Hume's Commentaries by B. J. Bell 1844'. *Edinburgh Review* 168, pp. 196–223

(1888). *An Examination of the Trials for Sedition which have hitherto Occurred in Scotland* (2 vols.). Edinburgh: David Douglas

Cockburn, J. S. (1991). 'Patterns of Violence in English Society: Homicide in Kent 1560–1985', *Past and Present* 130, pp. 70–106

Cohen, S. (1989). 'The Critical Discourse on "Social Control": Notes on the Concept as a Hammer', *International Journal of the Sociology of Law* 17, pp. 347–57

Colley, L. (1992). *Britons: Forging the Nation 1707–1837*. New Haven: Yale University Press

Commission Of Inquiry (1819). *Commission of Inquiry into the Courts of Justice in Scotland. Fifth Report (Court of Justiciary)*. Parl. Papers.1819.XI.69

Connolly, S. J. (1980). 'Albion's Fatal Twigs: Justice and Law in the Eighteenth Century' in R. Mitchison and, P. Roebuck (eds.), *Economy and Society in Scotland and Ireland*. Edinburgh: John Donald

Cooper, T. (Lord) (1950). Evidence presented to the Royal Commission on Capital Punishment (18th day, 4 April 1950). London: HMSO

(1957). *Selected Papers 1922–1954*. Edinburgh: Oliver and Boyd.

(1991). *The Scottish Legal Tradition*. Edinburgh: The Saltire Society (with re-assessments by M. C. Meston and W. D. H. Sellar)

Cornish, W. R. and Clark, G. (1989). *Law and Society in England 1750–1950*. London: Sweet and Maxwell

Cotterrell, R. (1989). *The Politics of Jurisprudence. A Critical Introduction to Legal Philosophy*. London: Butterworths

Craig, A. (1882). 'The Codification of the Law', *Journal of Jurisprudence* 26, pp. 281–92, 337–48

Dalrymple, A. and Gibb, A. D. (1946). *Dictionary of Words and Phrases Judicially Defined*. Edinburgh: W. Green and Son

Davies, S. J. (1980). 'The Courts and the Scottish Legal System 1600–1747. The Case of Stirlingshire' in V. A. C. Gattrell, B. Lenman and G. Parker (eds.), *Crime and the Law. The Social History of Crime in Western Europe since 1500*. London: Europa

Davis, J. (1984). 'A Poor Man's System of Justice. The London Police Courts in the Second Half of the Nineteenth Century', *Historical Journal* 27, pp. 309–35

(1989). 'Prosecutions and their Context. The Use of the Criminal Law in Later

Nineteenth-Century London' in D. Hay and F. Snyder (eds.), *Policing and Prosecution in Britain 1750–1850*. Oxford: Clarendon Press

de Quincey, T. (1965). 'Murder Considered as One of the Fine Arts' in B. Dobrée (ed.), *Thomas de Quincey*. London: Batsford

Deleuze, G. (1988). *Foucault*. Minneapolis: University of Minnesota Press (tr. S. Hand)

Departmental Committee (1895). *Report of the Departmental Committee on Habitual Offenders, Vagrants, Beggars, Inebriates, and Juvenile Delinquents*. Parl. Papers.1895.XXXVII.1

Departmental Committee (1899). *Report of the Departmental Committee on Rules for Inebriate Reformatories*. Parl. Papers.1899.XII.775

Devine, T. M. (1990a) (ed.). *Conflict and Stability in Scottish Society 1700–1850*. Edinburgh: John Donald

(1990b). 'The Failure of Radical Reform in Scotland in the Late Eighteenth Century: the Social and Economic Context' in T. M. Devine (ed.), *Conflict and Stability in Scottish Society 1700–1850*. Edinburgh: John Donald

Devlin, P. (1965). *The Enforcement of Morals*. Oxford: Oxford University Press

Dickinson, W. C. (1958). 'The High Court of Justiciary' in *An Introduction to Scottish Legal History*. Edinburgh: Stair Society (vol. 20)

Dixon, J. A. (1874). 'The Codification of the Law', *Journal of Jurisprudence* 18, pp. 305–22

Dove Wilson, J. (1895). 'Appendix XXI' in *Report of the Departmental Committee on Habitual Offenders etc*. Parl. Papers.1895.XXXVII.1 (pp. 556–61)

Duff, A. (1987). 'Codifying Criminal Fault: Conceptual Problems and Presuppositions' in I. Dennis (ed.), *Criminal Law and Justice*. London: Sweet and Maxwell

Edwards, Ll. J. (1955). *Mens Rea in Statutory Offences*. London: Macmillan

Elliott, W. A. (1956). 'Nulla Poena Sine Lege', *Juridical Review*, pp. 22–44

Emsley, C. (1987). *Crime and Society in England 1730–1900*. London: Longman

Erskine, J. (1871). *An Institute of the Law of Scotland*. Edinburgh: Bell and Bradfute (7th edn, ed. J. B. Nicolson; 1st edn 1773)

Ewald, F. (1985). 'Droit et Histoire' in *Droit, Nature, Histoire: Etudes sur la Pensée de Michel Villey*. Marseille: Presses Universitaires d'Aix

(1986a). 'A Concept of Social Law' in G. Teubner (ed.), *Dilemmas of Law in the Welfare State*. Berlin: de Gruyter

(1986b). *L'Etat Providence*. Paris: Editions Grasset

(1986c). 'Pour un Positivisme Critique: Michel Foucault et la Philosophie du Droit', *Droits* 3, pp. 137–42

(1987). 'Justice, Equality and Judgement: On "Social Justice"' in G. Teubner (ed.), *Juridification of Social Spheres*. Berlin: de Gruyter

(1988). 'The Law of Law' in G. Teubner (ed.), *Autopoietic Law*. Berlin: de Gruyter

(1991). 'Norms, Discipline and the Law' in R. Post (ed.), *Law and the Order of Culture*. Oxford: University of California Press

Farmer, L. (1989a). 'The Boundaries of the Scottish Criminal Law', *SCOLAG Bulletin* 148, pp. 9–12

(1989b). 'Recognising Marital Rape', *SCOLAG Bulletin* 154, pp. 102–5

(1995). 'Bringing Cinderella to the Ball: Teaching Criminal Law in Context', *Modern Law Review* 58, pp. 756–66

(1996). 'The Obsession with Definition: the Nature of Crime and Critical Legal Theory', *Social and Legal Studies* 5, pp. 57–73

Farmer, L., Brown, P. and Lloyd, J. (1987). 'AIDS and the Scottish Criminal Law', *Scots Law Times (News)*, pp. 389–92

Feeley, M. and Simon, J. (1994). 'Actuarial Justice: the Emerging New Criminal Law' in D. Nelken (ed.), *Futures of Criminology*. London: Sage

Fenton, J. C. (1928). 'Crime – General', in the *Encyclopedia of the Law of Scotland* (vol. 5) Edinburgh: W. Green and Son

Fitzgerald, P. J. (1960) 'A Concept of Crime', *Criminal Law Review*, pp. 257–62

Fletcher, G. (1978). *Rethinking Criminal Law*. Boston: Little, Brown and Co.

Forbes, D. (1975). *Hume's Philosophical Politics*. Cambridge: Cambridge University Press

Forbes, W. (1730). *The Institutes of the Law of Scotland* (2 vols.). Edinburgh: Mossman and Co.

Forsyth, W. (1858). 'Scotland and England', *Edinburgh Review* 108, pp. 343–76

Foucault, M. (1977). *Discipline and Punish. The Birth of the Prison*. Harmondsworth: Penguin (trans. A. Sheridan)

(1979). *The History of Sexuality. Vol. I The Will to Knowledge*. Harmondsworth: Penguin

(1988). 'The Dangerous Individual' in L. Kritzmann (ed.), *Politics, Philosophy, Culture. Interviews and Other Writings 1977–1984*. London: Routledge

(1991a). 'Governmentality' in G. Burchell, C. Gordon and P. Miller (eds.), *The Foucault Effect. Studies in Governmentality*. Hemel Hempstead: Harvester Wheatsheaf

(1991b). 'Politics and the Study of Discourse' in G. Burchell, C. Gordon and P. Miller (eds.), *The Foucault Effect. Studies in Governmentality*. Hemel Hempstead: Harvester Wheatsheaf

(1991c). 'Questions of Method' in G. Burchell, C. Gordon and P. Miller (eds.), *The Foucault Effect. Studies in Governmentality*. Hemel Hempstead: Harvester Wheatsheaf

Fraser, W. H. (1988a). *Conflict and Class. Scottish Workers 1780–1838*. Edinburgh: John Donald

(1988b). 'Patterns of Protest' in T. Devine and R. Mitchison (eds.), *People and Society in Scotland 1760–1830* (vol. I). Edinburgh: John Donald

(1990). 'Developments in Leisure' in W. H. Fraser and R. J. Morris (eds.), *People and Society in Scotland 1830–1914* (vol. II). Edinburgh: John Donald

Freestone, D. and Richardson, J. C. (1980). 'The Making of the English Criminal Law (7). Sir John Jervis and His Acts', *Criminal Law Review*, pp. 5–16.

Fry, M. (1992). 'The Whig Interpretation of Scottish History' in I. Donnachie and C. Whatley (eds.), *The Manufacture of Scottish History*. Edinburgh: Polygon

Gane, C. (1980). 'The Effect of a Pardon in Scots Law', *Juridical Review* 25, pp. 18–46

Gane, C. and Stoddart, C. (1988). *A Casebook on Scottish Criminal Law*. Edinburgh: W. Green and Son

Garland, D. (1985). *Punishment and Welfare. A History of Penal Strategies.* Aldershot: Gower

Gattrell, V. A. C. (1980). 'The Decline of Theft and Violence in Victorian and Edwardian England' in V. A. C. Gattrell, B. Lenman and G. Parker (eds.), *Crime and the Law. The Social History of Crime in Western Europe since 1500.* London: Europa

(1990). 'Crime, Authority and the Policeman-State' in F. M. L. Thompson (ed.), *The Cambridge Social History of Britain 1750–1950.* Cambridge: Cambridge University Press

Gibb, A. D. (1950). *Law From Over the Border: a Short Account of a Strange Jurisdiction.* Edinburgh: W. Green and Son

Gillon, S. A. (1936). 'Criminal Law' in *An Introduction to the Sources and Literature of Scots Law.* Edinburgh: Stair Society (vol. 1)

Glaser, S. (1942). 'Nullum Crimen Sine Lege', *Comparative Legislation and International Law* 24, pp. 29–37

Glazebrook, P. (1978) (ed.). *Reshaping the Criminal Law.* London: Stevens

Goff, R. (Lord) (1988). 'The Mental Element in the Crime of Murder', *Law Quarterly Review* 104, pp. 30–59

Goodrich, P. (1986). *Reading the Law. A Critical Introduction to Legal Method and Techniques.* Oxford: Blackwell

(1990). *Languages of Law. From Logics of Memory to Nomadic Masks.* London: Weidenfeld and Nicolson

(1992). 'Poor Illiterate Reason: History, Nationalism and Common Law', *Social and Legal Studies*, 1, pp. 7–28

(1993) 'Oedipus Lex: Slips in Law and Interpretation', *Legal Studies* 13, 381–95

(1995). *Oedipus Lex. Psychoanalysis, History, Law.* Berkeley: University of California Press

Gordon, G. H. (Sheriff) (1978). *The Criminal Law of Scotland.* Edinburgh: W. Green and Son (1st edn 1967)

Gordon, R. W. (1981). 'Historicism in Legal Scholarship', *Yale Law Journal* 90, pp. 1017–56

(1984). 'Critical Legal Histories', *Stanford Law Review* 36, pp. 57–125

Gray, J. L. (1928). 'The Law of Combination in Scotland', *Economica* 8, pp. 332–50

Hall, J. (1960). *General Principles of Criminal Law.* Indianapolis: Bobbs-Merrill Co. (2nd edn)

Hallard. (1878). 'Public Prosecutors and Superintendents of Police', *Journal of Jurisprudence* 22, pp. 207–11

Hanham, H. J. (1965). 'The Creation of the Scottish Office 1881–7', *Juridical Review*, pp. 205–44

(1969). 'The Development of the Scottish Office' in J. Wolfe (ed.), *Government and Nationalism in Scotland.* Edinburgh: Edinburgh University Press

Hart, H. L. A. (1983). 'Definition and Theory in Jurisprudence' in H. L. A. Hart, *Essays in Jurisprudence and Philosophy.* Oxford: Clarendon Press

Harvie, C. (1987). 'Legalism, Myth and National Identity in Scotland in the Imperial Epoch', *Cencrastus* (Summer), pp. 35–41

Hawkins, W. (1739). *A Treatise of Pleas of the Crown*. London: Savoy (3rd edn; 1st edn 1716)

Hay, D. (1975). 'Property, Authority and the Criminal Law' in D. Hay, P. Linebaugh, J. G. Rule, E. P. Thompson and C. Winslow (eds.), *Albion's Fatal Tree. Crime and Society in Eighteenth-Century England*. London: Allen Lane
(1984). 'The Criminal Prosecution in England and Its Historians', *Modern Law Review* 47, pp. 1–29
(1989). 'Prosecution and Power. Malicious Prosecution in the English Courts, 1750–1850' in D. Hay and F. Snyder (eds.), *Policing and Prosecution in Britain 1750–1850*. Oxford: Clarendon Press

Hay, D., Linebaugh, P., Rule, J. G., Thompson, E. P. and Winslow, C. (1975) (eds.). *Albion's Fatal Tree: Crime and Society in Eighteenth-Century England*. London: Allen Lane

Hay, D. and Snyder, F. (1989). 'Using the Criminal Law, 1750–1850. Policing, Private Prosecution and the State' in D. Hay and F. Snyder (eds.), *Policing and Prosecution in Britain 1750–1850*. Oxford: Clarendon Press

H.M. Law Commissioners (Scotland) (Fourth Report) (1840). Parl. Papers. 1840.XX.115

Hobsbawm, E. J. (1983). 'Inventing Traditions' in E. J. Hobsbawm and T. Ranger (eds.), *The Invention of Tradition*. Cambridge: Cambridge University Press

Horder, J. (1992). *Provocation and Responsibility*. Oxford: Clarendon Press
(1995) 'Intention in Criminal Law – a Rejoinder' *Modern Law Review* 58, pp. 678–91

Hostettler, J. (1992). *The Politics of Criminal Law Reform in the Nineteenth Century*. Chichester: Barry Rose

Houston, R. A. (1994). *Social Change in the Age of Enlightenment: Edinburgh 1660–1760*. Oxford: Clarendon Press

Hume, D. (Baron) (1797). *Commentaries on the Law of Scotland Respecting the Description and Punishment of Crimes* (2 vols.) Edinburgh: Bell and Bradfute
(1800). *Commentaries on the Law of Scotland Respecting Trial for Crimes* (2 vols.) Edinburgh: Bell and Bradfute
(1844). *Commentaries on the Law of Scotland Respecting Crimes*. Edinburgh: Bell and Bradfute (4th edn. with supplement by B. J. Bell; 2nd edn 1819; 3rd edn 1829), (reprinted 1986 Law Society of Scotland)
(1939). *Lectures 1786–1822* (vol. 1). Edinburgh: Stair Society (vol. 5) (ed. G. C. H. Paton)

Ignatieff, M. (1978). *A Just Measure of Pain. The Penitentiary in the Industrial Revolution 1750–1850*. London: Macmillan
(1985). 'State, Civil Society and Total Institutions: a Critique of Recent Histories of Punishment' in S. Cohen and A. Scull (eds.), *Social Control and the State*. Oxford: Basil Blackwell

Inglis, J. (Lord) (1863). *The Historical Study of Law (Address to the Juridical Society 1863–4)*. Edinburgh: W. Blackwood and Sons (2nd edn)

Innes, J. and Styles, J. (1986). 'The Crime Wave: Recent Writing on Crime and Criminal Justice in Eighteenth Century England', *Journal of British Studies* 25

Jackson, R. M. (1936–8). 'Common Law Misdemeanors', *Cambridge Law Journal* 6, pp. 193–201

(1937). 'The Incidence of Jury Trial During the Past Century', *Modern Law Review* 1, pp. 132–44

Jamieson, G. (1994). 'The Trial for Treason of James Wilson', *Juridical Review*, pp. 50–9

Jones, T. H. (1990). 'Common Law and Criminal Law: The Scottish Example', *Criminal Law Review*, pp. 292–301

Jones, T. H. and Christie, M. G. A. (1992). *Scottish Criminal Law*. Edinburgh: W. Green and Son

Jones, T. H. and Griffin, S. (1990). 'Serious Bodily Harm and Murder', *Scots Law Times (News)*, pp. 305–8

Kames, (Lord) (Henry Home) (1792). *Historical Law Tracts*. Edinburgh: Bell and Bradfute (4th edn)

Keith (Lord). (1959). 'Some Observations on Diminished Responsibility', *Juridical Review*, p. 109

Kenny, C. S. (1902). *Outlines of Criminal Law*. Cambridge: Cambridge University Press

(1918) *Outlines of Criminal Law*. Cambridge: Cambridge University Press (9th edn)

(1952) *Outlines of Criminal Law*. Cambridge: Cambridge University Press (16th edn. ed. J. W. C. Turner)

Kidd, C. (1993). *Subverting Scotland's Past. Scottish Whig Histories and the Creation of an Anglo-British Identity 1689–c. 1830*. Cambridge: Cambridge University Press

Krygier, M. (1986). 'Law as Tradition', *Law and Philosophy* 5, pp. 237–62

Lacey, N. (1985). 'The Territory of the Criminal Law', *Oxford Journal of Legal Studies* 5, pp. 453–62

(1988). *State Punishment. Political Principles and Community Values*. London: Routledge

(1993) 'A Clear Concept of Intention: Elusive or Illusory?' *Modern Law Review* 56, pp. 621–42

(1995). 'Contingency and Criminalisation' in I. Loveland (ed.), *Frontiers of Criminality*. London: Sweet and Maxwell

(forthcoming). 'Contingency, Coherence and Conceptualism – Reflections on the Encounter Between "Critique" and "the Philosophy of the Criminal Law"' in R. A. Duff (ed.), *Philosophy and Criminal Law*. Cambridge: Cambridge University Press

Lacey, N., Wells, C. and Meure, D. (1990). *Reconstructing Criminal Law. Text and Materials*. London: Weidenfeld and Nicolson

Ladeur, K-H. (1994). 'Coping With Uncertainty: Ecological Risks and the Proceduralisation of Environmental Law' in G. Teubner, L. Farmer and D. Murphy (eds.), *Environmental Law and Ecological Responsibility. The Concept and Practice of Ecological Self-Organization*. Chichester: John Wiley and Sons

Landau, N. (1984). *Justices of the Peace 1679–1760*. Berkeley: University of California Press

Langbein, J. H. (1978). 'The Criminal Trial Before the Lawyers', *University of Chicago Law Review* 45, pp. 263–316

(1983a). 'Albion's Fatal Flaws', *Past and Present* 97, pp. 96–120

(1983b). 'Shaping the Eighteenth-Century Criminal Trial: a View from the Ryder Sources', *University of Chicago Law Review* 50, pp. 1–136

Larner, C. (1981). *Enemies of God. The Witch-Hunt in Scotland*. London: Chatto and Windus

Lenman, B. (1981). *Integration, Enlightenment and Industrialisation. Scotland 1746–1832*. London: Edward Arnold

(1984). *The Jacobite Risings in Britain 1689–1746*. London: Methuen

Lenman, B. and Parker, G. (1980a). 'The State, the Community and the Criminal Law in Early Modern Europe' in V. A. C. Gattrell, B. Lenman and G. Parker (eds.), *Crime and the Law. The Social History of Crime in Western Europe since 1500*. London: Europa

(1980b). 'Crime and Control in Scotland 1500–1800', *History Today* 30, (January), pp. 13–17

Levack, B. P. (1987). *The Formation of the British State. England, Scotland, and the Union, 1603–1707*. Oxford: Clarendon Press

Lieberman, D. (1983). 'The Legal Needs of a Commercial Society: the Jurisprudence of Lord Kames' in I. Hont and M. Ignatieff (eds.), *Wealth and Virtue. The Shaping of Political Economy in the Scottish Enlightenment*. Cambridge: Cambridge University Press

(1989). *The Province of Legislation Determined. Legal Theory in Eighteenth-Century Britain*. Cambridge: Cambridge University Press

Lobban, M. (1990). 'From Seditious Libel to Unlawful Assembly: Peterloo and the Changing Face of Political Crime *c.* 1770–1820', *Oxford Journal of Legal Studies* 10, pp. 307–52

(1991). *The Common Law and English Jurisprudence 1760–1850*. Oxford: Clarendon Press

Logue, K. J. (1979). *Popular Disturbances in Scotland 1780–1815*. Edinburgh: John Donald

Luhmann, N. (1988) 'The Third Question: the Creative Use of Paradoxes in Law and Legal History', *Journal of Law and Society* 15, pp. 153–65

McBarnet, D. (1981). *Conviction! Law, the State, and the Construction of Justice*. London: Macmillan

McConville, M., Sanders, A. and Leng, R. (1991). *The Case for the Prosecution*. London: Routledge

Macdonald, J. H. A. (Lord Kingsburgh) (1867). *A Practical Treatise on the Criminal Law of Scotland*. Edinburgh: Wm. Paterson (2nd edn 1877; 3rd edn W. Green and Son 1894; 4th edn (ed. R. Macgregor Mitchell), W. Green and Son, 1929; 5th edn (ed. J. Walker and D. J. Stevenson), W. Green and Son, 1948)

(1891). *The Scottish Criminal Law System. (Address to the Glasgow Juridical Society)*. Glasgow: W. Hodge

(1915). *Life Jottings of an Old Edinburgh Citizen*. Edinburgh: T. N. Foulis

Macintyre, A. (1977). 'Epistemological Crises, Dramatic Narrative and the Philosophy of Science', *The Monist* 60 (4), pp. 453–72

(1985). *After Virtue. A Study in Moral Theory*. London: Duckworth (2nd edn)

McKechnie, H. (1931). 'Reparation' in *Encyclopedia of the Law of Scotland* (vol. 12). Edinburgh: W. Green and Son

Mackenzie, G. (1678). *Laws and Customs of Scotland in Matters Criminal, Wherein it is to be seen how the Civil Law, and the Laws and Customs of Other Nations do agree with and Supply Ours*. Edinburgh: Jas. Glen

McLaurin, J. (Lord Dreghorn) (1774). *Arguments and Decisions in Remarkable Cases Before the High Court of Justiciary and other Supreme Courts in Scotland*. Edinburgh: J. Bell

(1798). *Collected Works* (2 vols.). Edinburgh: Bell and Bradfute

MacLean, A. J. (1985). 'The House of Lords and Appeals from the High Court of Justiciary 1707–1887', *Juridical Review* pp. 192–226

McNeill, P. G. B. (1984). 'Discours Particulier D'Escosse 1559–60' in W. D. H. Sellar, *Miscellany II*. Edinburgh: Stair Society (vol. 35)

MacQueen, H. (1986). Report on the Scottish Legal History Group Conference 1984. *Journal of Legal History* 7, pp. 88–9

Maitland, F. W. (1911). 'Why the History of the English Law is not Written' in *Collected Papers* (vol. I), pp. 480–97. Cambridge: Cambridge University Press

Manchester, A. H. (1980). *A Modern Legal History of England and Wales 1750–1950*. London: Butterworths

Moncrieff, H. (1877). *A Treatise on the Law of Review in Criminal Cases*. Edinburgh: W. Green

Montesquieu Baron De (1949). *The Spirit of the Laws*. New York: Hafner Pub. Co. (trans. T. Nugent)

Moran, R. (1981). *Knowing Right From Wrong. The Insanity Defence of Daniel McNaghten*. London: Macmillan

Murdoch, A. (1980). *'The People Above'. Politics and Administration in Mid-Eighteenth-Century Scotland*. Edinburgh: John Donald

Murphy, W. T. (1991). 'The Oldest Social Science? The Epistemic Properties of the Common Law Tradition', *Modern Law Review* 54, pp. 182–215

Nairn, T. (1981). *The Break-Up of Britain*. London: Verso (2nd edn)

(1988). *The Enchanted Glass. Britain and its Monarchy*. London: Radius

Nelken, D. (1987a). 'Criminal Law and Criminal Justice: Some Notes on their Irrelation' in I. Dennis (ed.), *Criminal Law and Justice*. London: Sweet and Maxwell

(1987b). 'Critical Criminal Law', *Journal of Law and Society* 14, pp. 105–17

Nietzsche, F. (1969). *On the Genealogy of Morals*. New York: Vintage, (trans. W. Kaufman and R. J. Hollingdale)

Normand, W. G. (Lord) (1938). 'The Public Prosecutor in Scotland', *Law Quarterly Review* 54, pp. 345–57

Norrie, A. W. (1991). *Law, Ideology and Punishment. Retrieval and Critique of the Liberal Ideal of Criminal Justice*. Dordrecht: Kluwer

(1993). *Crime, Reason and History. A Critical Introduction to Criminal Law*. London: Weidenfeld and Nicolson

Orwell, G. (1984). 'The Decline of the English Murder' in *The Penguin Essays of George Orwell*. Harmondsworth: Penguin

Pasquino, P. (1991). 'Criminology: the Birth of a Special Knowledge' in G. Burchell, C. Gordon and P. Miller (eds.), *The Foucault Effect. Studies in Governmentality*. Hemel Hempstead: Harvester Wheatsheaf

Paterson, L. (1994). *The Autonomy of Modern Scotland*. Edinburgh: Edinburgh University Press

Paton, G. C. H. (1958). 'Biography' in D. Hume, *Lectures 1786–1822* (vol. VI), pp. 327–410. Edinburgh: Stair Society

Paulus, I. (1974). *The Search for Pure Food. A Sociology of Legislation in Britain*. London: Martin Robertson

Petrow, S. (1994). *Policing Morals. The Metropolitan Police and the Home Office 1870–1914*. Oxford: Clarendon Press

Philips, D. (1977). *Crime and Authority in Victorian England 1835–60*. London: Croom Helm

(1985). ' "A Just Measure of Crime, Authority, Hunters and Blue Locusts": The "Revisionist" Social History of Crime and the Law in Britain 1780–1850' in S. Cohen and A. Scull (eds.), *Social Control and the State*. Oxford: Basil Blackwell

Phillipson, N. (1969). 'Nationalism and Ideology' in J. N. Wolfe (ed.), *Government and Nationalism in Scotland*. Edinburgh: Edinburgh University Press

(1981). 'The Scottish Enlightenment' in R. Porter and M. Teich (eds.), *The Enlightenment in National Context*. Cambridge: Cambridge University Press

(1989). *Hume*. London: Weidenfeld and Nicolson

(1990). *The Scottish Whigs and the Reform of the Court of Session 1785–1850*. Edinburgh: Stair Society (vol. 37)

Pocock, J. G. A. (1987). *The Ancient Constitution and the Feudal Law. A Study of English Historical Thought in the Seventeenth Century*. Cambridge: Cambridge University Press (reissue with retrospect)

Pollock S. (1959) 'The Distinguishing Mark of a Crime', *Modern Law Review* 22, pp. 495–9

Postema, G. (1986). *Bentham and the Common Law Tradition*. Oxford: Clarendon Press

Radzinowicz, L. (1948). *A History of English Criminal Law and its Administration from 1750. Vol. I: The Movement for Reform*. London: Stevens and Sons

(1968). *A History of English Criminal Law and its Administration from 1750. Vol. IV: Grappling For Control*. London: Stevens and Sons

Radzinowicz, L. and Hood, R. (1986). *A History of English Criminal Law and its Administration from 1750. Vol. V: The Emergence of Penal Policy*. London: Stevens and Sons

Ralston, A. G. (1980). 'The Tron Riot of 1812', *History Today* 30, pp. 41–5

(1988). 'The Development of Reformatory and Industrial Schools 1832–72', *Scottish Economic and Social History* 8, pp. 40–55

Reiner, R. (1985). *The Politics of the Police*. Hemel Hempstead: Harvester Wheatsheaf

Renton, R. W. (1908). 'The Summary Jurisdiction (Scotland) Bill', *Scottish Law Review* 24, pp. 219–22

Richardson, G. (1987). 'Strict Liability for Regulatory Crime: the Empirical Research', *Criminal Law Review*, pp. 295–306

Robertson, A. (1878). *A Course of Lectures on the Government, Constitution and Laws of Scotland, From the Earliest to the Present Time*. London: Stevens and Haynes

Robinson, P. H. (1993). 'Should the Criminal Law Abandon the *Actus Reus–Mens Rea* Distinction?' in S. Shute, J. Gardner and J. Horder (eds.), *Action and Value in the Criminal Law*. Oxford: Clarendon Press

Rose, G. (1995). ' "Would that they forsake Me but observe my Torah" – Midrash and Political Authority', *Modern Law Review* 58, pp. 471–85

Royal Commission (1870). *Royal Commission to Inquire into the Courts of Law in Scotland (Fourth Report)*. Parl. Papers.1870.XVIII.455

Royal Commission (1871). *Royal Commission to Inquire into the Courts of Law in Scotland (Fifth Report)*. Parl. Papers.1871.XX.257

Sayre, F. B. (1934). 'The Present Signification of *Mens Rea* in the Criminal Law' in R. Pound (ed.), *Harvard Legal Essays*. Cambridge, Mass.: Harvard University Press

Scottish Law Commission (1983). *The Mental Element in Crime*. Edinburgh: HMSO (Scottish Law Commission no.80)

Select Committee (1854–5). *Report of the Select Committee on Public Prosecutors*. Parl. Papers.1854–5.XII.1

Select Committee (1856). *Report of the Select Committee on Public Prosecutors*. Parl. Papers.1856.VII.347

Select Committee (1890). *Select Committee on the Police (S.) Bill*. Parl. Papers.1890.XVII.69

Select Committee (1989). *Report of the House of Lords Select Committee on Murder and Life Imprisonment*. London: HMSO (House of Lords Paper 78 I–III)

Select Committee on Police (1852–3). Parl. Papers.1952–3.XXXVI.107

Sellar, W. D. H. (1991). 'Forethocht Felony, Malice Aforethought and the Classification of Homicide' in W. M. Gordon and T. D. Fergus (eds.), *Legal History in the Making. (Proceeedings of the Ninth British Legal History Conference, Glasgow 1989)*. London: Hambledon Press

Shute, S., Gardner, J. and Horder, J. (1993). 'Introduction: the Logic of Criminal Law' in S. Shute, J. Gardner and J. Horder (eds.), *Action and Value in Criminal Law*. Oxford: Clarendon Press

Silver, A. (1967). 'The Demand for Order in Civil Society. A Review of Some Themes in the History of Urban Crime, Police and Riot' in D. Bordua (ed.), *The Police. Six Sociological Essays*. New York: John Wiley and Sons

Simmonds, N. (1984). *The Decline of Juridical Reason*. Manchester: Manchester University Press

(1993) 'Bringing the Outside In', *Oxford Journal of Legal Studies* 13, pp. 147–65

Simpson, A. W. B. (1973). 'The Common Law and Legal Theory' in A. W. B. Simpson (ed.), *Oxford Essays in Jurisprudence* (2nd Series). Oxford: Clarendon Press

Smith, A. (1978). *Lectures on Jurisprudence*. Oxford: Clarendon Press (eds. R. L. Meek, D. D. Raphael and P. Stein)

Smith, A. T. H. (1978). 'On *Actus Reus* and *Mens Rea*' in P. Glazebrook (ed.), *Reshaping the Criminal Law*. London: Stevens

(1984). 'Judicial Law-Making in the Criminal Law', *Modern Law Review* 47, pp. 46–76

Smith, D. B. (1978). ' "A Respectable Infusion of Dignified Crime" ', *Juridical Review* 23, pp. 1–11

Smith, J. I. (1958). 'Criminal Procedure' in *An Introduction to Scottish Legal History*. Edinburgh: Stair Society (vol. 20)

Smith, J. I. and Macdonald, I. (1958). 'Criminal Law' in *An Introduction to Scottish Legal History*. Edinburgh: Stair Society (vol. 20)

Smith, J. C. and Hogan, B. (1992). *Criminal Law*. London: Butterworths (7th edn; 5th edn 1983)

Smith, R. (1981). *Trial by Medicine: Insanity and Responsibility in Victorian Trials*. Edinburgh: Edinburgh University Press

Smith, T. B. (1961). *British Justice: The Scottish Contribution*. London: Stevens

(1962). *A Short Commentary on the Law of Scotland*. Edinburgh: W. Green and Son

(1970). 'Scottish Nationalism, Law, and Self-Government' in D. N. MacCormick (ed.), *The Scottish Debate. Essays on Scottish Nationalism*. Oxford: Oxford University Press

(1982). 'British Justice: a Jacobean Phantasma', *Scots Law Times (News)*, pp. 157–64

Smout, T. C. (1986). *A Century of the Scottish People 1830–1930*. London: Collins

Sousa Santos, B. (1987). 'Law: a Map of Misreading. Toward a Postmodern Conception of Law', *Journal of Law and Society* 14, pp. 279–302

Spens, W. C. (1875). *Jurisdiction and Punishments of Summary Criminal Courts (with special reference to the Lash)*. Edinburgh: T. and T. Clark

Stair (Viscount) (James Dalrymple) (1832). *The Institutions of the Law of Scotland*. Edinburgh: Bell and Bradfute (ed. J. S. More), (1st edn 1681)

Stallybrass, W. (1936). 'The Eclipse of Mens Rea', *Law Quarterly Review* 52, pp. 60–7

Steedman, C. (1984). *Policing the Victorian Community. The Formation of English Provincial Police Forces 1856–80*. London: Routledge

Steele, W. (1833). *Summary of the Duties and Powers of Juries in Criminal Cases*. Edinburgh: T. and T. Clark

Stein, P. (1980). *Legal Evolution. The Story of an Idea*. Cambridge: Cambridge University Press

(1988). *The Character and Influence of the Roman Civil Law. Historical Essays*. London and Ronceverte: Hambledon Press

Stephen, J. F. (1877). 'Suggestions as to the Reform of the Criminal Law', *Nineteenth Century* 2, pp. 735–59

(1883). *A History of the Criminal Law of England* (3 vols.). London: Macmillan and Co.

Storch, R. (1975). 'The Plague of Blue Locusts. Police Reform and Popular Resistance in Northern England 1840–57', *International Review of Social History* 20, pp. 61–90

Straka, W. W. (1985). 'The Law of Combination in Scotland Reconsidered' *Scottish History Review* 69, pp. 128–42

Styles, S. (1993). 'Something to Declare: a Defence of the Declaratory Power of the High Court of Justiciary' in R. F. Hunter (ed.), *Justice and Crime: Essays in Honour of the Right Honourable Lord Emslie*. Edinburgh: T. and T. Clark

Sugarman, D. and Rubin, G. (1984). 'Towards a New History of Law and Material Society in England 1750–1914' in G. Rubin and D. Sugarman (eds.), *Law, Economy and Society. Essays in the History of English Law 1730–1914*. Abingdon: Professional Books

Teubner, G. (1989a). ' "And God Laughed . . ." Indeterminacy, Self-Reference and Paradox in Legal Thought' in C. Joerges and D. Trubek (eds.), *Critical Legal Thought: an American–German Debate*. Baden Baden: Nomos Verlagsgesellschaft

(1989b). 'How the Law Thinks: Toward a Constructivist Epistemology of Law', *Law and Society Review* 23, pp. 727–57

Thompson, E. P. (1975). *Whigs and Hunters. The Origins of the Black Act*. London: Allen Lane

Thompson, F. M. L. (1988). *The Rise of Respectable Society. A Social History of Victorian Britain 1830–1900*. Cambridge, Mass.: Harvard University Press

Townsend, C. (1993). *Making the Peace. Public Order and Security in Modern Britain*. Oxford: Oxford University Press

Trotter, T. (1909). *The Summary Jurisdiction (Scotland) Act 1908*. Edinburgh: Wm. Hodge and Co

Tur, R. H. S. (1986). 'Criminal Law and Legal Theory' in W. Twining (ed.), *Legal Theory and the Common Law*. Oxford: Basil Blackwell

(1993). 'Subjectivism and Objectivism: Towards Synthesis' in S. Shute, J. Gardner and J. Horder (eds.), *Action and Value in Criminal Law*. Oxford: Oxford University Press

Turner, J. W. C. (1945). 'The Mental Element in Crime' in L. Radzinowicz and J. W. C. Turner (eds.), *The Modern Approach to Criminal Law*. London: Macmillan (English Studies in Criminal Science, vol. IV)

Vogler, R. (1991). *Reading the Riot Act. The Magistracy, the Police and the Army in Civil Disorder*. Milton Keynes: Open University Press

Walker, D. M. (1952). 'The Growth of Reparation', *Juridical Review* 64, pp. 101–34

(1985). *The Scottish Jurists*. Edinburgh: W. Green and Son

Walker, J. (Lord) (1958). 'The Growth of the Criminal Law', *Juridical Review* pp. 230–41

Walker, N. (1968). *Crime and Insanity in England* vol. I. Edinburgh: Edinburgh University Press

Weber, M. (1969). *Economy and Society*. London: Badminster Press (eds. G. Roth and C. Wittig)

Wells, C. (1988). 'The Decline and Rise of English Murder: Corporate Crime and Individual Responsibility', *Criminal Law Review*, pp. 788–801

Whatley, C. (1990). 'How Tame were the Scottish Lowlanders during the Eighteenth Century?' in T. M. Devine (ed.), *Conflict and Stability in Scottish Society 1700–1850*. Edinburgh: John Donald

(1992). 'An Uninflammable People?' in I. Donnachie and C. Whatley (eds.), *The Manufacture of Scottish History*. Edinburgh: Polygon

Whetstone, A. E. (1981). *Scottish County Government in the Eighteenth and Nineteenth Centuries*. Edinburgh: John Donald

White, J. Boyd (1985). 'Making Sense of What We Do. The Criminal Law as a System of Meaning' in his *Heracles' Bow. Essays on the Rhetoric and Poetics of the Law*. Madison: University of Wisconsin Press

Wiener, M. (1990). *Reconstructing the Criminal. Culture, Law and Policy in England 1830–1914.* Cambridge: Cambridge University Press

Williams, G. (1955). 'The Definition of Crime', *Current Legal Problems* 8, pp. 107–30

(1978). *Textbook of Criminal Law.* London: Stevens

(1989). 'The *Mens Rea* For Murder: Leave It Alone', *Law Quarterly Review* 105, pp. 387–97

Willock, I. D. (1966). *The Origins and Development of the Jury in Scotland.* Edinburgh: Stair Society (vol. 23)

(1976). 'The Scottish Legal Heritage Revisited' in J. P. Grant (ed.), *Independence and Devolution. The Legal Implications for Scotland.* Edinburgh: W. Green and Son

(1981). 'Scottish Criminal Law – Does It Exist ?', *SCOLAG Bulletin* 54, pp. 225–9

(1989). 'The Declaratory Power: an Untenable Position'. *SCOLAG Bulletin* 157, pp. 152–4

Winfield, P. (1931) *The Province of the Law of Tort.* Cambridge: Cambridge University Press

Withers, C. (1992). 'The Historical Creation of the Scottish Highlands' in I. Donnachie and C. Whatley (eds.), *The Manufacture of Scottish History.* Edinburgh: Polygon

Wormald, J. (1980). 'Bloodfeud, Kindred and Government in Early Modern Scotland', *Past and Present* 87, pp. 54–97

(1981). *Court, Kirk and Community. Scotland 1470–1625.* London: Edward Arnold

Young, P. (forthcoming). *Punishment, Money and Legal Order.* Edinburgh: Edinburgh University Press

Index